"… man shall not live by bread alone;

but man lives by every word

that proceeds from the mouth of the LORD."

Deuteronomy 8:3, Matthew 4:4, Luke 4:4

A sampling of comments received for the first and second editions of

Connected – Above & Below

"Thanks, Leith, for sending me a copy of your finished – and now published book – a personally written autobiography that turns a reader's attention to an understanding of God's love and the salvation available to us through the gift of His son Jesus. You have put it together as both a personal 'lived' account and an endorsement of the truth of the Biblical account and the Gospel message. Together with you, I am praying that God will use it to bring others to Christ." – Dwight

(Dr. Dwight Jessup is the former chief academic officer of Bethel, Biola, Indiana Wesleyan and Taylor universities, and the Nairobi Evangelical Graduate School of Theology. Dr. Jessup also chaired the student programs committee for the Council for Christian Colleges & Universities (CCCU) for several years and faithfully served for many years on the Board of Directors of Global Oceanic (GO), a non-profit ministry started by Leith.)

"Hi, Leith: Your book was a delight to read. I hardly put it down. I am sure that you feel God's generosity towards you in terms of an adventurous life. Each chapter could be a separate article! I sincerely appreciate how you advocate meeting Jesus, not a religious system called Christianity." – Rich

(Dr. Richard Gathro served as Executive Vice President and COO for the Council for Christian Colleges and Universities. He recently retired from his post as Director of Pepperdine University's Washington, D.C. Program and is a trustee of The Seattle School of Theology and Psychology.)

"Leith, thanks for forwarding your work. Your words are an inspiration and testimony to our glorious Father. As a fellow adventurer, I too am thankful for the grace and mercy of God who continues to save me from myself. Your legacy is your life. Thanks for sharing your story with me." – Dave

(For many years Dave Sander served as the National Director for Fund Development for the Campus Ministry of Cru, formerly Campus Crusade for Christ, before leaving to serve the Lord in the private sector.)

"Leith, I'm almost through the first version. So well done in every way! Your love for the oceans goes way back. Very interesting background and journey with the Lord. Thank you!" – Bob

(Dr. Robert Andringa served as the president of the Council for Christian Colleges & Universities (CCCU) for twelve years. The CCCU is a consortium of 184 Christ-centered colleges and universities around the world.)

"Leith, thanks so much for sharing your "Connected" autobiography with me. What a beautiful story of the Lord's faithfulness to you and your family! Wish I could discipline this activist to sit down and compile my memoirs as you have done so brilliantly!" – John

(John Robb is the Chairman of International Prayer Connect, a coalition of 4,000 Christian prayer networks and organizations who share a common vision to mobilize and equip worldwide prayer for the blessing, healing, and transformation of nations.)

"Leith, thank you for sending me a printed copy of your impactful book!! I love it and love the sub-title! Glory to God! I am thankful for you and your friendship and encouragement. Blessings." – Frank

(Frank Erb has served as the Pastor to the California State Capitol since 2008 and serves as the Founder and President of Illuminate California, and as the California State Minister for Capitol Commission, an international ministry committed to making disciples of Jesus Christ in the Capitol communities of the world, as well as following the Biblical mandate of praying for our elected officials nationwide.)

"Thank you for sharing your book. It was very clear to see the Potter's hands working on the lump of clay that eventually was formed into an honorable vessel. God has blessed you with the gift of writing and I pray that He will bless others (especially unbelievers) with the writing of this book." – Bob

(Bob Quintas is a retired physical therapist and twenty-five-year member of Leith's men's prayer group.)

"Leith, I have to tell you that I appreciate you allowing me to read Connected. All I can say is your writing of Connected was brilliant. I read page after page non-stop and just read the last words. God the Author and you the scribe wrote a book that I could not put down. The excitement of your experiences and the Word of God rocked me in ways that were profound. Questions I have had for many years are crystal clear. The eyes of my heart have been opened to a new and powerful understanding of God's word. This book would be a great read for anyone looking for God, believer or unbeliever." – Harvey

(Harvey recently retired after a 30-year career as a police officer for a high-crime, major metro police department. During his career he served as a patrolman, motorcycle cop, undercover narcotics officer, detective, and pilot of the police force Cessna 210.)

"Leith, thanks for sending your book. It is really well done and a total spiritual and life inspiring message. It must have been really rewarding just writing it. Truly amazing." – Tom

(Tom Sudberry is the founder and chairman of Sudberry Properties, a commercial real estate development company that has developed approximately 10 million square feet of retail, office, apartment and industrial projects. Earlier in life, Tom served as a naval aviator aboard the USS Constitution.)

TABLE OF CONTENTS

Connected – Above & Below

To God by whom are all things,

my wife Judy who led me to Him,

our daughter Alli and her husband Bobby,

and our grandchildren, Jude and Reese,

His answer to our prayers.

GLOSSARY

Throughout this book there are certain key Biblical terms that are familiar to many, but not all. In most cases, when first mentioned, I have explained the term and provided this glossary for additional reference.

ANGELS – pages 155, 202,232, and 249

APOSTLES – pages 16, 67, and 234

BELIEF and UNBELIEF – pages 10, 11, 31, 180, and 257

BIBLE – pages 13-14, and 15-19

BORN AGAIN – pages 13, 16, and 179-179

CHURCH – pages 8, 11-12, 16-17, 251-252, and 261-262

CHURCH AGE – pages 8, 235, 252, and 254-255

CONVERSION – pages 11-13, 66, 131, and 176-177

CRUCIFIXION OF JESUS – pages 103-104

FAITH – pages 10-12, 176, 178-179, 187-188, 211-212, 218, 232-233, and 259-260

FORGIVENESS – page 67

GOD – THE TRINITY: FATHER; SON; AND HOLY SPIRIT – Essentials and His Story

GOD'S: CREATION – page 133; **KINGDOM** – page 10; **LAW** – page 11; **LOVE** – pages 121-122; **WISDOM** – page 137

GOSPEL – pages 10, 13, 16-17, 65, and 195

GRACE – pages 10, 112, and 195

GREAT TRIBULATION – page 8 and Chapter 27

HEAVEN – pages 103, 235, and Chapter 26

HELL – pages 94-95 and Chapter 26

MILLENNIUM – Chapter 27

RAPTURE – page 8 and Chapter 27

RELIGION – pages 31 and 64-65

REPENTANCE – page 67

RIGHTEOUSNESS – pages 11, 19, 31, 57, 104, 171, 178-179, 251, 255, and 260

SALVATION – pages 10-12, 16, 65-66, 104, 170-171, 175-176, and 187-188

SANCTIFICATION – page 65

SATAN – pages 16, 58, 179, 202, 232-233, and Chapter 26

SECOND COMING OF JESUS – Chapter 27

SIN – pages 10-11, 171, and 187

WORKS – pages 10-11, 31, 57, 65, 178, and 180

PREFACE

The first edition of this book was printed in 2020, during the onset of the Covid pandemic and the run-up to the American presidential election. In 2021, following the inauguration, a global spiritual pandemic erupted necessitating this revision. Despite the fact God foreordained the events unfolding around us and prophetically revealed them in the Bible, unbelievers—and many professing belief—are blind to Scriptural truth. This was true in Noah's day and is true today. Noah built an ark and preached God's pending judgment to a wicked world for 120 years before God judged the world and destroyed mankind—except for Noah and seven members of his family. Over 2,300 years later, during the ministry of Jesus on earth, His disciples questioned Him regarding the signs of the times and the end of the age. Jesus answered:

"But as the days of Noah were, so also will the coming of the Son of Man be." – Matthew 24:37

Mankind is again on a collision course with God and God wins. Although the word of God unequivocally expresses the reality of heaven and hell, many live lives totally unaware of the raging spiritual battle for their eternal souls. Throughout the world we are witnessing the fruits of geopolitical insanity premised on the hatred and rejection of God. From the murder of millions of babies on the altar of abortion, to the indoctrination of young children and adults in the Satanically-inspired ideologies of evolution, gender neutrality, LGBTQ sexuality, CRT, and manmade climate change. From an American president spiraling out of control, to those who dictate his policies and the media conglomerates that parrot them. From the leadership of intragovernmental organizations like the UN and EU, to the globalist elites who pull their strings. All involved are unwittingly committing spiritual suicide and all will be judged, but their evil ways are tearing the world apart and blinding many—who will suffer, die, and experience eternal separation from God in the process. Nevertheless, until the end of the age, God's word clearly reveals His divine grace—even for those who hate and reject Him—as exemplified by the prayer of Jesus on the cross:

"Father, forgive them, for they do not know what they do." – Luke 23:34

God's chosen people, the Jews, are a miraculous testimony to the wonder of God's love and longsuffering. Despite God's divine covenants of promise—given to them over 4,000 years ago—the Jews have continuously rebelled against God and were instrumental in crucifying His Son. Yet, in Jerusalem, fifty days after the resurrection of Jesus on the day of Pentecost—the day the church was birthed—the Apostle Peter preached the gospel of God's grace and about 3,000 Jews believed, were baptized, and received the free gift of eternal life. At the end of the church age—prior to the second coming of Jesus to judge and rule the world, and restore and glorify the nation of Israel—all believers, dead and living, will leave earth for heaven in what is known as the rapture of the church and a seven-year tribulation period will begin on earth. Jesus refers to the latter half of this period as the "great tribulation", when everyone alive on earth will suffer horribly—those rejecting God destined for hell and those believing in God destined for heaven. Jesus' last words recorded in the Bible are a warning, a comfort, and a promise:

"Surely I am coming quickly." – Revelation 22:20

FOREWORD

Some stories just need to be told. Leith Swanson's life is one of these stories. Like a cat with nine lives, Leith has lived multiple lives, and each is told in these pages.

We all long for adventure but Leith was born into it. To read these chapters is to go on a spiritual, historical and personal travelogue into some of the most interesting and geopolitically sensitive parts of the world. His childhood was during a time in world history when everything was in flux. Leith experienced the turbulent shift from the secure *Leave it to Beaver* world of the 50's to the turbulent 60's and beyond. The uniqueness of his story is he lived much of it as a westerner in the Middle East.

Leith and I have been friends for a couple decades, but it wasn't until we traveled together to the Middle East on two occasions that I really got to know him. I awoke early one morning to greet the Alexandria sunrise only to find my traveling roommate was already up and gone. I grabbed a cup of Turkish coffee and headed toward the Mediterranean beach where I found Leith swimming laps in the Egyptian dawn.

This was the clue to the nature of Leith Swanson. Most of us rise and meet the morning but Leith reaches out and grabs the day. He seizes every moment to fully live.

On another trip Leith and his wife Judy joined me to explore what God was doing in the Arab world. As I watched him interact with my Arab friends as we explored the streets of Larnaca, Cyprus, I realized how comfortable he was in this part of the world. For Leith it was his childhood backyard. He is multi-cultural and sees every culture with God's loving eyes.

Leith is a spiritual man who loves Jesus. But he is aware of God's patience in his own journey to faith and allows his friends and readers the same privilege. Still, Leith is honest to share with us the spiritual insights he has learned along the way. To read this book is a pilgrimage of sorts.

Leith carries us through time to distant lands and takes us into a time of dignity, adventure and innocence. In a way, the pages before you are the diary of an Indiana Jones without the hype. Lives like Leith's don't happen often. Read his story bit by bit or all at once. But allow yourself the luxury of curiosity, discovery, and adventure. Then live your own life in the same way. You're in for a treat.

Mark Foreman
Lead Pastor
North Coast Calvary Chapel
Carlsbad, California

In addition to pastoring a large, thriving church, Mark Foreman is known internationally as a strategist, conference speaker, church planter, worship leader, published songwriter, counselor and seminary professor. He is the author of "Wholly Jesus: His Surprising Approach to Wholeness and Why It Matters Today" and "Never Say No: Raising Big-Picture Kids", which he co-wrote with his wife, Jan. Together they are parents to two grown sons, Jon and Tim, who are part of the band "Switchfoot".

ESSENTIALS

J. Paul Getty, a famous American industrialist and founder of Getty Oil Company, died at the age of 83 in 1976. He was married and divorced five times. His life was marked by both phenomenal material success and horrible tragedy. In 1957, Fortune magazine named him the richest living American. In 1973, his 16-year-old grandson was kidnapped in Rome and had his right ear sliced off by the kidnappers—because Getty refused to meet their ransom demand. Legend has it, when asked about his favorite memories, Getty reflected for a moment before sharing that his favorite memories were the day's he surfed Malibu as a kid.

Like each of us, the end of Getty's life on earth was the culmination of all the people he had met and everything he had experienced.

All of us have memories to share: some good, some bad. I've written this book to share how, in a special moment of time, God rescued me from certain death and eternal condemnation, to assured salvation and eternal life. He forgave and forgot the bad memories and connected me to the most important person I will ever meet, Jesus, God incarnate (God in human form). The good memories of a loving family growing up, several trips around the world, an amazing wife, daughter, son-in-law, grandson, granddaughter, and a passion for the ocean, are all precious memories, but none surpass my everlasting relationship with Jesus.

The forces at play that resulted in my transformation are, on the one hand, as unfathomable as those that result in the birth of a child, but on the other hand, are so simple even a young child can comprehend them. Connecting to God through Jesus, who is the express living image of God, is a spiritual rebirth with eternal consequences. It can occur at any age to anyone on earth; it is a miracle and the greatest gift known to mankind.

It cost Jesus everything to give; it cost me nothing to receive. I did nothing to deserve it and there is nothing I can do to improve upon it. It is the gift of God's grace, known in the Bible as the gospel of Christ—the good news of salvation by grace alone, through faith alone, in Christ alone.

Grace is unmerited favor. It is getting what we don't deserve, versus mercy, which is not getting what we deserve. Grace cannot be earned through self-righteous works or by practicing certain religious rituals. It encompasses forgiveness of sin, freedom from the power of sin, everlasting life, restoration of our relationship with God, and communion with God. Grace centers upon who Jesus is, what Jesus did, His kingdom, and the gift of salvation God offers to those who believe in His Son, who paid the price for all of their sins—past, present, and future. God's grace is the means by which we are saved from the power of sin and darkness—and translated, here and now, into His kingdom.

> *"I have come as a light into the world, that whoever believes in Me should not abide in darkness."*
> *John 12:46*

God's kingdom is the sphere of spiritual union and intimacy of all believers with God, who rules over all who belong to Him. Sin is lawlessness—it is not living up to God's divine standard of holiness by breaking His law and violating His commandments. Both believers and unbeliever's sin on a daily basis. As an example, other than Jesus, everyone has violated God's first commandment to love the Lord their God with all their heart, soul, and mind—every moment of every day. Only Jesus perfectly obeyed all of God's laws and commandments.

Heaven is exclusively for people who believe all of their sin was forgiven when Jesus died on the cross and rose again to save them—thus accrediting or imputing God's perfect righteousness to whoever believes in Him. Jesus is God's standard of sinlessness and righteousness. The question is not whether we can receive salvation unto eternal life because we are murderers, adulterers, thieves, liars, or some other type of sinner, but whether we will believe that Jesus paid the price for every sin ever committed by mankind, except the sin of unbelief—the rejection of Jesus. Without Jesus, all unbelievers will suffer eternally in hell.

We are all sinners and spiritually dead by nature, not because of some sinful act we have committed.

"For God so loved the world that He gave His only begotten Son, that whoever believes in Him should not perish but have everlasting life." – John 3:16

God is omnipotent (all-powerful), omniscient (all-knowing), and omni-present (everywhere all the time). He is three persons in one: God the Father, God the Son, and God the Holy Spirit. All are involved in the conversion experience. They are all co-equal and co-existent. As such, there are Scripture quotations and narratives in this book where all three are mentioned. They are all God expressing His profound heart of love for mankind through His word, the Bible.

God's law was given to the Israelites over three thousand years ago, through Moses, to demonstrate man's inability to obey God's law through unrighteous carnal works. God's gospel was given about two thousand years ago, through the Lord Jesus Christ, who freely sacrificed His perfectly righteous life to pay—in full—for all of the sins of all the people who would ever believe in Him. "Lord" is His title, which signifies a believer's relationship to Him, that of servant to Master. "Jesus" is His name, which is derived from the Hebrew word Jehovah and signifies God is our salvation. "Christ" is the Greek word for the Messiah, the Anointed One, who came in the flesh and fulfilled God's salvation promise to those who believe in Him.

Believing in Jesus occurs by faith, faith comes by hearing, and hearing by the word of God. Like a seed that brings forth life when it is planted in fertile soil and watered, God plants the seed of His living word in the hearts of those open to receiving Him. At the age of thirty-six, after numerous attempts to share His love for me through my faithful wife and other people, and in countless other ways, God lovingly prepared my heart to receive His word. Despite the blind eye I had turned to Him up to that moment in time, He led me to prayerfully invite Jesus into my heart as my personal Lord and Savior.

One of the ways God attempted to share His love for me was through His church. As the moon reflects the light of the sun, His church reflects the love and light of the Son of God, not flawlessly all the time, but in phases and often obscured by clouds of man-made rituals and traditions. The church is an imperfect body of believers being healed in the hospital of God's love. Some are in intensive care, some are bedridden, and some are ambulatory, but all are in the hospital until, in the twinkling of an eye, they pass from earth and are transformed into the perfected spiritual body reserved for them in heaven.

In the original Greek, the word *church* is spelled ekklesia (or its alternative spelling ecclesia) and is defined as a "called-out assembly or congregation." The ekklesia is made up of all believers in Jesus, living and dead, throughout the world. Local churches are smaller gatherings of the global church that often meet in buildings, but it is the believers, not the buildings, that comprise God's church.

Unfortunately, over the last two thousand years, the church has often created religious systems of man-dominated hierarchy, that have served to turn many from God to man and have left a dark stain on church history. The Crusades, during the 11th and 12th centuries, when Christians traveled to the Holy Lands to capture Jerusalem, and the Spanish Inquisition, from the 13th to 19th centuries, established to purify Roman Catholicism, are but two of the most commonly known examples.

Jesus is the Head of the church and it is only by His presence in our hearts, and by the indwelling power of the Holy Spirit, that a believer can grow in Him and be used by God to grow His kingdom. Connecting with Jesus is a conversion process that occurs within the heart. It can happen in a few minutes, as it did two thousand years ago to a criminal hanging on a cross next to Jesus, but it usually takes days, weeks, or years, often unbeknownst to others.

At some point in time, during this process, God the Father, through God the Holy Spirit, by the gift of faith implanted by the seed of His living word, draws unbelievers to confess with their mouth that Jesus is Lord and believe in their heart that God raised Him from the dead. In that moment:

- they are indwelt by the Holy Spirt;

- they become alive in Jesus spiritually;

- they are complete in Him eternally;

- and there is nothing they can do or not do to become more or less complete in Him.

One of the ways God uses to connect with us is through the universe He created. He has always touched my life through the oceans and seas of the world. He takes great pleasure in watching us enjoy His creation and each of us bonds to His creation in a special way. For some, it's as simple as experiencing a sunrise or a sunset. For others, it's as extreme as climbing Mount Everest or surfing an 80-foot wave. Each of us is unique and each of us relates to God's creation in a unique way.

"The heavens declare the glory of God; and the firmament shows His handiwork. Day unto day utters speech, and night unto night reveals knowledge. There is no speech nor language where their voice is not heard. Their line has gone out through all the earth, and their words to the end of the world." – Psalm 19:1-4

For those unfamiliar with ocean sports, such as surfing or freediving, I have tried to express these experiences in ways that will help the reader to better understand and appreciate them. All of us are gifted in different ways. Some have the ability to unravel the complexities of the human genome, plant a garden, fix a car, prepare a gourmet dinner, fly an airplane or ride a wave; and each of these pursuits has its own lexicon or vocabulary. To the best of my ability, I have attempted to straddle the language difference for those unfamiliar with ocean sports.

Sunset in Laguna Beach, California – Fall 2018 [1]

MY APPROACH IN SHARING MY journey to faith and my life thereafter is threefold: first, to provide insightful stories of how I was raised and how I lived my life before and after my conversion, with a focus on my passion for the ocean; second, to reflect on those stories from the vantage point of the present in sections titled, "In Retrospect"; and third, to share certain spiritual insights I have learned over the years.

My intent is to share the truth of the word of God, to encourage receiving and following the word of God, and to teach certain fundamental attributes of the word of God. I have prayerfully attempted to be totally transparent and true to the word of God in everything I have written. Nevertheless, Biblical truth is sometimes difficult to hear, particularly for an unbeliever.

The most important words in this book are the highlighted Scripture quotations. They are the inspired words of God that He prompted people to write by the power of the Holy Spirit in order to declare the gospel of His kingdom and transform lives. They are words so powerfully alive they grip our souls and turn us inside out, from self-absorption to eternal life in Him. They are words that deserve to be prayerfully read and reverently considered. They are words of love. The Bible is God's love letter to us and His word is the seed of life.

"...having been born again, not of corruptible seed but incorruptible, through the word of God which lives and abides forever..." – 1 Peter 1:23

The other words in this book are life experiences and lessons learned before and after I met Jesus. I have tried to frame them in the context of spiritual truth and to occasionally insert a verse from the Bible for amplification and clarification. As such, if Jesus should return to earth after I'm long gone (see Chapter 27) and this book should reach future generations, my spiritual insights might seem old-fashioned, but God's word will never be old-fashioned because Jesus is the same yesterday, today, and forever.

All the Scripture quotations found in this book are from the New King James Version (NKJV) of the Bible, first published in 1982 to update the vocabulary and grammar of the King James Version (KJV), which was first published in 1611. I have used the NKJV for several reasons:

- it is the version of the Bible I am most familiar with;

- I felt led by God to use one version of the Bible throughout the entire book;

- the NKJV has been proven to be a highly accurate translation of the KJV, which was translated "word-for-word" from the original Hebrew, Aramaic, and Greek texts;

- and when compared to the Dead Sea Scrolls by Biblical scholars such as Norman Geisler and William Nix, the KJV was found to be 98.33% accurate. (Norman Geisler and William Nix, A General Introduction to the Bible, 1974, p. 263). The Dead Sea Scrolls are ancient Jewish manuscripts discovered during the mid-twentieth century in the Qumran Caves near the Dead Sea in Israel. They date back to the centuries just before and after the birth of Christ.

That said, there are many other contemporary translations of the Bible that have proven useful to those who seek the truth of God's word. Over the centuries, the Bible has been updated by gifted Biblical scholars to help us better understand, remember, and research it. During the 14th century, the Bible was divided into chapters, and during the 17th century, the chapters were divided into verses. The 20th and 21st century translations were created to update older terminology for the contemporary reader.

I also want to mention that there are a variety of ways the Bible can be interpreted and my insights are not infallible. In most cases, I have only scratched the surface of Scriptural subjects that many excellent Bible commentaries have covered in depth. For anyone reading this book who does not agree with my spiritual insights, I would like to quote 17th-century German Lutheran theologian, Rupertus Meldenius, who once stated in a tract: "In essentials unity, in non-essentials liberty, in all things charity."

MY PRIMARY PURPOSE IN WRITING this book is to share how God can rescue anyone from themselves, including a wretch like me. Many of us are hard nuts to crack. It took God thirty-six years to open my eyes. He has taken another thirty-eight years, so far, to begin to improve my vision. My prayer is that the story of my faith journey will be instructive to those who know and follow Jesus, and life-changing to those who don't.

For every story of fun and adventure included in this book there is a story of self-will and sin I have excluded. All of my sins are forgiven and forgotten and I have chosen not to sensationalize my past sinful life.

Although I still sin and fall short daily, I don't practice the same sins over and over like I used to. I now know, that if I confess my sins and seek God's empowerment to turn from them, He blesses me with His peace that surpasses all understanding and draws me closer to Him. God's grace is infinitely greater than my sin.

When I die and depart this carnal body of flesh and corruption: I will receive a resurrected and glorified body in heaven; I will be conformed spiritually and eternally into the image of Jesus; and I will sin no more.

I can now look back on my life from birth to age 36 and consider it my old testament or my "old self," while viewing my life from age 36 to 74 (my age as I write this) as my new testament or my "new self."

I had a temporal, physical birthday in December of 1948, and I had an eternal, spiritual birthday in September of 1986. This book is the story of how God rescued me from myself. It is just one story among immeasurable millions that demonstrate the power of God's love and His amazing grace

My story is simply one sinner's portrait of God's love. We are all imperfect human beings called by God to know and love Him. Followers of Jesus are just beggars showing other beggars where the food is. God helps us to understand His power to turn sinners into saints throughout the Bible. Three of the most prominent men of the Old and New Testaments, Moses, King David, and the Apostle Paul were all murderers, yet God transformed and used them to write many of the most powerful and fundamental books of the Bible.

"Therefore, if anyone is in Christ, he is a new creation; old things have passed away; behold, all things have become new." – 2 Corinthians 5:17

God loves each of us far more than we can imagine. Regardless of who we are, what we have done or not done, what country we are from, what race or mixture of races constitutes our DNA, or what any other aspect of our life is at this moment in time, God is our loving Father. He created each of us and wants to spend eternity with all of us. He loves all of us so much, He died for us. Jesus is the ultimate expression of God's love. God became Jesus to die for us that we might have eternal life in Him.

"In this the love of God was manifested toward us, that God has sent His only begotten Son into the world, that we might live through Him. In this is love, not that we loved God, but that He loved us and sent His Son to be the propitiation for our sins." – 1 John 4:9-10

HIS STORY

The earth is a minuscule planet in relation to the universe. It spins on its axis and revolves around a sun that is just one star among an estimated five hundred billion stars in the Milky Way Galaxy, which is only one galaxy among an estimated two trillion galaxies in the universe. So, regardless of who we think we are—a student, housewife, software engineer, media darling, professional athlete, business mogul, or leader of a great nation—we are just a speck of dust in relation to the universe God created, but He deeply loves each of us and cares more about our eternal spiritual destiny than who we think we are in this temporal physical world.

"Thus says the Lord: 'Let not the wise man glory in his wisdom, let not the mighty man glory in his might, nor let the rich man glory in his riches; but let him who glories glory in this, that he understands and knows Me, that I am the Lord, exercising lovingkindness, judgment, and righteousness in the earth. For in these I delight,' says the Lord." – Jeremiah 9:23—24

Betelgeuse (pronounced "beetle-juice"), one of the brightest stars in the Milky Way Galaxy, has been estimated to be 950 times the size of our sun. As the late Pastor Chuck Smith, Founder of the Calvary Chapel movement, once pointed out in a sermon, if Betelgeuse were to be hollowed out, leaving a crust a hundred million miles thick, you could put the sun in the center and let the earth rotate around it and still have room to spare. Experts have calculated that Betelgeuse rotates at a speed of about 33,500 mph. Now, what kind of force thrusted so large a mass into orbit? A flick of God's finger.

"When I consider Your heavens, the work of Your fingers, the moon and the stars, which You have ordained, what is man that You are mindful of him, and the son of man that You visit him?" – Psalm 8:3-4

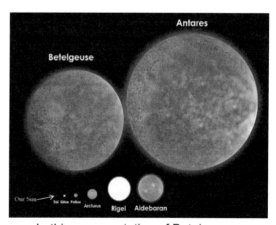

In this representation of Betelgeuse, our Sun, on the bottom far left, is barely visible [2]

"In the beginning God created the heavens and the earth."
Genesis 1:1 [1]

15

We know from the Scriptures that God is unique—different from all other beings. We also know He is perfect love and holiness—separate from all sin. Our knowledge of the history of His love and holiness is recorded from beginning to end in the Bible—the Bible is His Story.

Our first revelation of His love and holiness occurred when He spoke the universe into existence, created Adam in His image out of the dust of the earth, placed him in the Garden of Eden, and entered into spiritual fellowship with him. This unique relationship was established based on Adam obeying God's command not to eat from the fruit of the tree of the knowledge of good and evil. If Adam disobeyed, God promised he would die spiritually and his pure fellowship with God would be severed.

God then created Eve out of one of Adam's ribs and they became husband and wife. Shortly thereafter, Satan, one of the most powerful angels created by God, who had rebelled against God and was cast from His presence, tempted Eve to disobey God's command not to eat from the fruit of the tree of the knowledge of good and evil, and Adam followed suit. As a result: Adam and Eve were banished from the Garden of Eden; their flesh, rather than their spirits, began to rule their lives; mankind inherited their corrupt, carnal nature—living after the lust of the flesh and the lust of the mind; and Satan became the ruler of the world.

"We know that we are of God, and the whole world lies under the sway of the wicked one." – 1 John 5:19

As centuries passed, man's carnality increased, wickedness prevailed throughout the earth, and God destroyed mankind and every other living thing with a great flood—except for Noah, his family, and an ark full of living creatures. But God continued to reveal His love to Noah's descendants through angels, prophets, and ordinary men.

He then gave His law to His chosen people, the Israelites, and created the nation of Israel. But over the following centuries, Israel chose to disobey God's law, even persecuting and killing His prophets who foretold the coming of the Messiah, the Savior of mankind.

As a result, around the 5th century B.C., God judged the nation of Israel, dispersed the Jews throughout the world, and remained silent for about six hundred years. Then, about two thousand years ago, He revealed the ultimate expression of His love when He sent His only begotten Son to suffer and die for all of the sins, of all the people, who would ever believe in Him so that those who believe in Him are born again spiritually and become one with Him eternally.

The virgin Mary gave birth to Jesus, the Messiah. However, driven by envy, jealousy, and contempt for God's gracious gift of love and spiritual freedom, the religious leaders of Israel lived out the carnal desires of their hearts, persecuted Jesus, and begged Pontius Pilate, the Roman governor of Judaea, to order His crucifixion, which he did.

Nevertheless, throughout His life, death, resurrection, and ascension, Jesus revealed God's love in word and deed to: His apostles and disciples; the multitudes in Israel who flocked to Him; and the faithful dead who preceded Him (those who died believing the Old Testament promises of the coming Messiah). The atoning work of Jesus on the cross opened the door for direct access to God, forgiveness of sin, and eternal life, to everyone who believes in Him.

When Jesus ascended into heaven:

- God sent the Holy Spirit to dwell in the hearts of those who believe in Jesus;

- the church was formed and began to share the gospel of His love and grace with the world;

- and over the next century, by the power of the Holy Spirit, many of His apostles and disciples recorded God's word in what is now known as the New Testament.

Unlike Old Testament times, it is no longer necessary for anyone to enter into God's presence through a priest or intermediary, because the indwelling presence of the Holy Spirit gives immediate access. No longer is there any difference between Jew and Gentile in the church—all are one in Jesus. In fact, in addition to Jesus, the apostles, and His first disciples, the church began with the salvation of thousands of other Jews before the first Gentile believed.

An apostle is one of the original twelve disciples and Paul, chosen by God, who witnessed Jesus in His resurrected body. The Apostle Paul expresses the oneness of the church in the New Testament book of 1 Corinthians:

> *"For as the body is one and has many members, but all the members of that one body, being many, are one body, so also is Christ. For by one Spirit we were all baptized into one body—whether Jews or Greeks, whether slaves or free—and have all been made to drink into one Spirit. For in fact the body is not one member but many." – 1 Corinthians 12:12-14*

As most of us know, the Bible is comprised of the Old Testament and the New Testament. The Old Testament begins when God created the heavens and the earth. The New Testament begins with the genealogy of Jesus Christ. The Old Testament was written before the birth of Jesus and the New Testament was written after His death, resurrection, and ascension.

The Old Testament introduces us to Christ in many ways. In fact, after His resurrection and before His ascension, Jesus explained the Old Testament Scriptures—to His disciples—that fulfilled all that was written about Him in the Law of Moses, by the prophets, and in the Psalms. However, the most important truth in the New Testament, missing from the Old Testament, is the gospel of God's grace: Jesus died for our sins according to the Scriptures; He was buried; He rose again on the third day; and He was seen by His disciples, after His resurrection.

For the past 2,000 years, mankind has been blessed by the love of God expressed through the gospel of His grace, spoken by Jesus, recorded in the New Testament, and lived out through those who believe in Him, His church. The Apostle Paul beautifully describes God's love in one of his New Testament letters to the church. Paul's words are a mirror of self-judgment for the church and a declaration of God's immutable love for mankind:

> *"Love suffers long and is kind; love does not envy; love does not parade itself, is not puffed up; does not behave rudely, does not seek its own, is not provoked, thinks no evil; does not rejoice in iniquity, but rejoices in the truth; bears all things, believes all things, hopes all things, endures all things. Love never fails." – 1 Corinthians 13:4-8*

Remember, God created each of us with a free will. He did not create a race of robots to love Him on command; He created a race of humans with freedom of choice. We can choose to love Him, as He loves us, and we can choose to love our neighbors as ourselves. He even gave us an instruction manual on how to do both: His word, the Bible.

Dwight L. Moody, 1837-1899 [3]

Dwight L. Moody was one of the great evangelists and publishers of the 19th century. According to one of his biographers, Lyle Dorsett (Dorsett, Lyle W., A Passion for Souls, The Life of D.L. Moody – Chicago, IL: Moody Publishers, 1997, p. 192), Moody had one central message to share with people:

"Men and women are all created to be friends and lovers of God. We are made for no other end. Until we realize this, we will live lives of turmoil, confusion, and even desperation."

STUDYING GOD'S WORD IS MY favorite pastime. There is nothing I would rather do because, as in entering the oceans and the seas, every time I read His word, I discover something so new, so unique, so life-changing that I feel totally cleansed, refreshed, and alive. However, unlike the oceans and the seas, the depth of God's word is unsearchable—it is living, powerful, and sharper than any two-edged sword. It is the inspiration and power for the lives God has gifted to each of us. At the end of his life, the Apostle John elaborated on his experience living with the "Word of life":

"That which was from the beginning, which we have heard, which we have seen with our eyes, which we have looked upon, and our hands have handled, concerning the Word of life—the life was manifested, and we have seen, and bear witness, and declare to you that eternal life which was with the Father and was manifested to us—that which we have seen and heard we declare to you, that you also may have fellowship with us; and truly our fellowship is with the Father and with His Son Jesus Christ. And these things we write to you that your joy may be full." – 1 John: 1-4

I have discovered through the Bible that the same God who spoke the universe into existence and revealed Himself to the Apostle John, knew me and loved me before He created me. King David, the author of many of the Psalms of the Old Testament, expressed this truth in the following way:

"For You formed my inward parts; You covered me in my mother's womb. I will praise You, for I am fearfully and wonderfully made; marvelous are Your works, and that my soul knows very well. My frame was not hidden from You, when I was made in secret, and skillfully wrought in the lowest parts of the earth. Your eyes saw my substance, being yet unformed. And in Your book they all were written, the days fashioned for me, when as yet there were none of them. How precious also are Your thoughts to me, O God! How great is the sum of them! If I should count them, they would be more in number than the sand; when I awake, I am still with You." – Psalm 139:13-18

One of my favorite Bible preachers and commentators, Arno Gaebelein, was fluent in English, German, Hebrew, and Yiddish. Gaebelein ministered to both Jews and Gentiles in the United States and Canada during the late 19th and early 20th centuries. He states in Gaebelein's Concise Commentary on the Whole Bible:

"There was no material, no matter, out of which God could fashion the universe. It was a creation out of nothing. And there is nothing in the sinner's fallen nature which God can use; it is not a reformation, or reconstruction, but a new creation—as we read in the New Testament, 'Created in Christ Jesus.'"

Arno C. Gaebelein, 1861-1945 [4]

Gaebelein sheds light on a truth about our existence that I am beginning to absorb in an ever more profound way: there is nothing we can think, say, or do that is of any value if it is not God-generated. We are completely dependent upon God for everything. He not only provides the breath of life; His presence in our life, if we believe and follow Him, provides the power and meaning for every aspect of our life, including our relationship to Him and our relationship to everyone He connects us with.

"For I am not ashamed of the gospel of Christ, for it is the power of God to salvation for everyone who believes, for the Jew first and also for the Greek. For in it the righteousness of God is revealed from faith to faith; as it is written, 'The just shall live by faith.'" – Romans 1:16-17

God, by His infinite love, grace, and mercy, made a way to redeem sinful man. He sent His only begotten Son, Jesus, to become the Son of man. Jesus lived a perfectly righteous life on earth, suffered and died on the cross for every sin committed by those who believe in Him, and rose from the dead in a resurrected body fit for heaven.

Jesus is God's standard of righteousness. Without Him, it is impossible for anyone to enter into God's presence. God no longer sees believers as we once were, imperfect and unrighteousness carnal human beings, He sees us eternally in Jesus, perfected in His righteousness by grace through faith.

"The first man was of the earth, made of dust; the second Man is the Lord from heaven. As was the man of dust, so also are those who are made of dust, and as is the heavenly Man, so also are those who are heavenly. And as we have borne the image of the man of dust, we shall also bear the image of the heavenly Man." – 1 Corinthians 15:47-49

C.S. LEWIS, A BRITISH WRITER, lay theologian, and World War I veteran, held academic positions in English literature at both Oxford and Cambridge universities from 1925-1963. According to his autobiography, *Surprised by Joy*, in 1929, at the age of 32, he… "admitted God was God, and knelt and prayed: perhaps that night, the most dejected and reluctant convert in all England". *Surprised by Joy* tells of Lewis's conversion experience but only concerns his first thirty years because, as he wrote in the preface, "I never read an autobiography in which the parts devoted to the earlier years were not far the most interesting."

In 1941, as Hitler mercilessly rained bombs on Britain and thousands of men, women, and children were killed, maimed, and traumatized, the British Broadcasting Corporation (BBC), a government owned and operated entity, asked Lewis to deliver a series of radio broadcasts regarding God and faith. These historic broadcasts were heard by millions of British citizens. In 1943, they were published in the United States in a book titled *The Case for Christianity*. Eventually, they became available as part of a collection of Lewis's radio addresses in the now classic book, *Mere Christianity*. William O'Flaherty, on the "Anniversary of Lewis's First Broadcast Talk", August 11, 2012, shared the following:

"Lewis's first radio broadcast focused on natural law because Lewis felt the audience of his day was so lacking in their knowledge of the Bible that they didn't believe in the assumptions the Bible made about morality. Therefore, Lewis decided he must make sure there was an understanding that right and wrong exist universally. Once this truth was established, he could deal with the issue of not living up to that standard and from where such a standard originated."

THE BEGINNING

PART 1

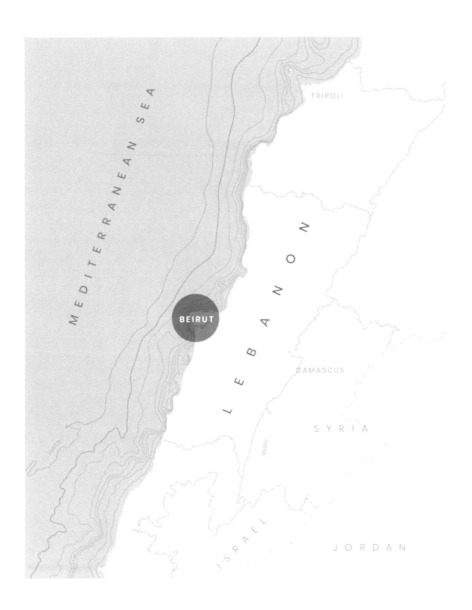

1

BEIRUT, LEBANON
33.8°N, 35.5°E

Following his Army Air Corps service as a pilot and squadron commander during World War II, as well as his Air Force service as an Inspector General during the Korean War, my dad took a job with the largest charter airline in the world, Transocean, to help launch a new airline in the Middle East: Air Jordan. As a result, in 1954, my family was living in Beirut, Lebanon. I was five years old.

Early days of Air Jordan,1954 – passengers and crew preparing to board a DC-3
for an inaugural flight from Amman to Aqaba, Jordan (my dad is second from the right) [1]

AMMAN - JERUSALEM - MA'AN*(Petra) - AQABA				
TUES FRI		DC-3		TUES FRI
AJ 900				AJ 901
10.15	d	AMMAN	a	17.15
10.45	a	JERUSALEM	d	16.45
11.15	d		a	16.15
12.15	a	MA'AN*(Petra)	d	15.15
12.45	d		a	14.45
13.15	a	AQABA	d	14.15

(*) MA'AN FLAG STOP ONLY - (MIN. BOOKING FIVE)

Air Jordan – DC-3 flight schedule, 1954 [2]

Mom and Dad, World War II –
Marseilles, France, 1945 [3]

Our family consisted of my mom, my dad, and my older sister, Linda. My mom was an Army dietitian and captain during World War II. She met my dad, a major, during the invasion of North Africa and they were married in Marseilles, France, by the Mayor of Marseilles, at the end of the war.

They were a great complement to one another and loving parents. My dad was an astute businessman, had a great sense of humor, and was the best joke and storyteller I have ever known. He had a tender heart, was a master carpenter, and could fix anything. My mom was an incredible cook, a quintessential hostess, and a rock of wisdom and patience. They enjoyed hosting and entertaining family and friends, traveling, playing golf and bridge, and acquiring antiques. They also enjoyed a cocktail or two before dinner, especially a bourbon old-fashioned.

Dad was born and raised in the small town of Monmouth, Illinois. His parents were solid midwestern Swedes. My paternal grandfather was a baker, my paternal grandmother a homemaker, and they raised a family of five, whom I grew to know and love.

Mom was born and raised in Woburn, Massachusetts, a suburb of Boston. Her heritage was English. My maternal grandfather had a farm in Woburn and sold wholesale vegetables in Faneuil Hall, the historic 18th century public market located in downtown Boston. My maternal grandmother was a homemaker, and they raised a family of three, whom I also grew to know and love.

Faneuil Hall – Boston, Massachusetts – early 1900s [4]

At the end of WWII, my dad was released from his command and returned to the States before my mom. When he arrived on the East Coast, he met my mom's parents for the first time. Very early the next morning, my grandfather drove him to Faneuil Hall in his full-dress uniform, which my grandfather insisted he wear.

When they arrived, my grandfather proudly introduced his new son-in-law to the men he worked with in the adjacent market stalls. They, in turn, poured him a stiff whiskey. When their visit ended, my dad could hardly stand to walk out.

My maternal grandfather, Alden Cummings, holding up a crate of his farm-grown vegetables and surrounded by some of the men he worked with at the Faneuil Hall public market in downtown Boston, Massachusetts [5]

Sketch of my dad having a drink at
the Beirut Commodore Hotel, 1958 [6]

For Linda and me, our mom was the cement that held our family together during our formative years through high school, because our dad was traveling around the world on business about sixty percent of the time.

My sister Linda on the day I was born,
December 9, 1948, at La Guardia Airport, NY,
on her first solo flight to Boston, MA,
to stay with our maternal grandparents [7]

My dad and I – Beirut, 1954 [8]

During our years in Beirut, we belonged to the Eden Rock Resort and Swim Club situated on a cliff overlooking the Mediterranean Sea just south of the city. We would drive to the club from our downtown apartment and my dad would teach me to swim and dive off the one-and three-meter springboards. When he felt I was comfortable swimming and diving, we descended the cliff to the sea, where he introduced me to saltwater and waves.

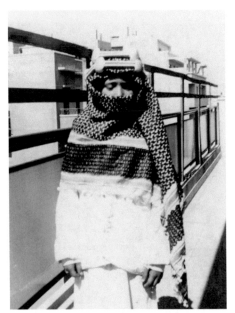

Me – Beirut, 1954 – age five –
dressed in an Arab robe and headscarf
made by my dad's Sudanese
bodyguard's wife [9]

I was born in Rockville Centre, New York, in December of 1948. My first home was located in Mineola, a small village located on the peninsula of Long Island. In 1950, our family moved to California because my dad was recalled from the Air Force Reserves to serve in the Korean War. During this time, we lived in Novato, near Hamilton Air Force Base.

Shortly after his return from Korea in 1954, my dad interviewed for a job with Transocean and was hired to establish an operational base in Kabul, Afghanistan. Because Afghanistan in 1954 was not the healthiest country in the world for a five- and seven-year-old, my mom took my sister and me to the Transocean headquarters infirmary, located in a hangar at Oakland Airport, and we each received a series of about a dozen vaccinations.

Flying from San Francisco to Kabul was a long trip. Unlike today, when frequent flyers don't give a second thought to flying half-way around the world on a jumbo jet nonstop, in the early 1950s, we began our journey by flying on a four-engine, piston-driven, double-decker, Boeing B377 Pan American Stratocruiser, which carried us across the continental United States to New York.

When we arrived at Idlewild Airport in New York (renamed John F. Kennedy International Airport in 1964), we boarded a Trans World Airlines (TWA) Constellation, commonly known as a "Connie", for a 15-hour flight to London, with refueling stops in Greenland and Ireland. We spent two nights in London to help adjust to the time change and then boarded another Connie to Rome.

Pan American World Airways (PAA) Boeing Stratocruiser (early 1950s) –
San Francisco Bay Bridge (background) [10]

TWA "Connie" at London Airport –
(Since renamed Heathrow Airport) – 1954 [11]

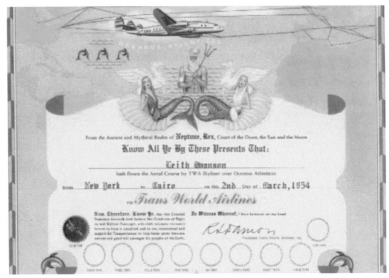

Trans World Airlines First Certificate of Flight – March 2, 1954 [12]

When we landed in Rome, my dad received a cable (a paper telegram) from Transocean instructing him to cancel our onward trip to Kabul and to travel instead to Amman, Jordan, where he would assist King Hussein (at that time known as the "Boy King," as he was 18 years old) and the Jordanian government in merging two competing air carriers, Arab Airways Jerusalem and Air Jordan, to form Air Jordan of the Holy Land.

We spent the night in Rome before boarding another "Connie" to Cairo, Egypt, where we stayed several days, before flying on to Amman. When we arrived, we moved into the Amman Club Hotel, the nicest hotel in Amman at the time and lived there for about six months prior to moving permanently to Beirut, Lebanon, known then as the Paris of the Middle East.

Life in Beirut was an interesting experience for a five-year-old. We lived in a series of hotels for the first few months, where I was introduced to room service and enjoyed French cuisine, like chateaubriand, frog legs, and escargot. My parents eventually leased a sixth-floor penthouse apartment in the fashionable Hamra District, all of our household furnishings arrived by ship from California, and we moved in.

My mother frequently hosted formal cocktail parties for their friends and my dad's business associates. Most of the people who attended these parties worked for the American Embassy, TWA, Pan American World Airways (Pan Am), Bechtel Corporation, the Arabian-American Oil Company (Aramco), and other companies that were involved in the business of oil exploration and production. I didn't realize it at the time, but I was learning to interact with adults at a young age, which served me well later in life when I was traveling the world as a young adult and working with people two or three times my age.

Family photo – Beirut apartment – 1954 [13]

St. George Hotel – Beirut, Lebanon, mid 1950s –
(You could swim in the Mediterranean in the morning
and snow ski in the Cedars of Lebanon in the afternoon.) [14]

This was the time my mom, Linda, and I began to see less and less of my dad, week to week, month to month, and year to year, until he finally retired after we were grown up and out of the house. My dad's passports looked like hundred-page novels, with countless pages added for visas (an endorsement on a passport indicating that the holder can enter, leave, or stay for a specified period of timc in a foreign country).

My mom was a trooper. She organized the house, shopped in the Arab souks (markets) for our groceries, enrolled Linda and me in a grammar school for international children located on the American University of Beirut campus, and basically created a life for us that was as comfortable and loving as one could expect in the Middle East in the 1950s.

Although this was a fairly unstable time in the Arab world, I pretty much wandered the streets without worry. I had a close friend, Bill Works, whose father was the military attaché to the American Embassy (a military attaché is a military diplomat attached to a government embassy). Bill lived several blocks away, and we would walk to one another's homes without supervision.

On Sundays, we attended a Presbyterian church located on the campus of the American University of Beirut. In retrospect, going to church was more of a superficial religious ritual practiced on Sundays than a devoted, heartfelt life of worship lived out every day of the week. Nevertheless, my parents were always loving and nurturing to my sister and me. They always exemplified kindness to others, and I don't think I ever heard them fight or argue with one another.

We prayed before dinner, but I don't remember reading the Bible at home. Like many churchgoers today, my parents were practicing a Sunday ritual rather than living a life of faith dedicated to God every day of the week. They were wonderful, loving parents, but they were unwittingly substituting a Christian religious observance for a deep and abiding relationship with Jesus Christ.

Old Beirut cafe and souk – circa 1950s [15]

Religion is man attempting to reach up to God through self-inspired works. Faith-inspired Christianity, better defined as following Jesus, is God reaching down to man and imputing His righteousness to those who believe that Jesus died for man's sin and God raised Him from the dead. Faith and belief in God are expressed by the attitudes and actions of those who believe in Jesus, known in the Bible as works. Works in Jesus do not save us, but they demonstrate our faith and belief in the One who can empower us to do the works He inspires us to do.

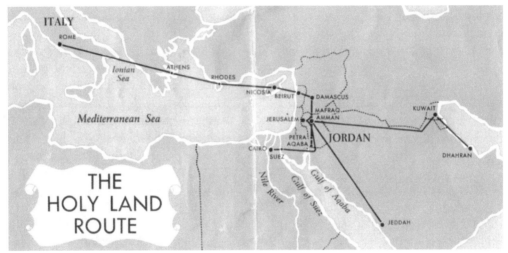

"The Holy Land Route" – Air Jordan airline [16]

After church, our family tradition was to drive downtown to Uncle Sam's, the only restaurant in Beirut that served an American hamburger. This was the treat of the week for me. I could hardly wait for Sunday to roll around! When you are five years old and growing up on powdered milk, hummus, and tabbouleh, a hamburger is as good as it gets.

There were some sketchy moments. One Sunday afternoon, while we were enjoying our hamburgers at Uncle Sam's, we began to hear a cacophony of metal doors slamming down on the sidewalks all along the street. Every retail store and restaurant in downtown Beirut has a heavy metal door that rolls down over the windows for protection at night. It was unusual for them to be rolled down early in the afternoon.

The reason for the closures was a street riot protesting the invasion of Egypt by Israel in 1956, otherwise known as the Suez Crisis. The proprietor of Uncle Sam's immediately instructed us to flee out of an upper kitchen window in the back. My dad crawled out the window and ran to retrieve our car. When he returned, the kitchen staff helped lift my mom, Linda, and me up and out the window. Thankfully, we made it home safely.

A few nights later, there was a huge explosion across the street from our apartment building. A group of Arab nationalists bombed the British Bank of the Middle East, and the concussion blew out some of the windows of our apartment building facing that side of the street.

On another occasion, my mom and dad woke us up in the middle of the night because there was a huge earthquake that shook all of Lebanon. We walked down six flights of stairs and spent the night in our car, which my dad had parked in a vacant lot across the street. We learned later that the Chim Earthquake had destroyed 6,000 homes and killed 136 people.

Besides family trips to the Holy Lands (Israel, the Palestinian territories, western Jordan, southern Lebanon, and southwestern Syria), hanging with Bill Works, and spending weekend afternoons at the Eden Roc Resort and Swim Club, one of our family highlights each year was an R&R (rest and recreation) trip back to the good old USA, where we stayed with my mom's parents in Woburn, Massachusetts, and visited my mom's friends on Cape Cod.

During these R&R's, Linda and I relished the finer things in life unavailable in Beirut, like whole milk, peanut butter and jelly sandwiches, television, and movie theatres featuring English-speaking cartoons, newsreels, and movies.

IN 1957, AFTER MY DAD had fulfilled his assignment to help launch Air Jordan, we returned to the United States and my parents bought a home in Alamo, California. At the time, Alamo was a small rural community located in the East Bay area of San Francisco, sandwiched between Danville and Walnut Creek.

My sister and I were enrolled in the local grade school for about a year before my dad came home from work one evening in 1958 and announced that we were moving to Tripoli, the capital of Libya, a North African country that borders the Mediterranean Sea on the north, Tunisia on the west, Egypt on the east, and Niger, Chad, and Sudan on the south.

An analogy of God's orchestration of our lives can be seen in an art form known as needlepoint, which has been popular for thousands of years. Multicolored yarn is stitched through a stiff open weave canvas, creating beautifully detailed portraits, landscapes, and other subject matters. These creations are typically framed and hung on a wall. However, if you were to remove a framed needlepoint and turn it over, you would see a mishmash of colored yarns with no discernable pattern or purpose. Sometimes that's the way our lives look to us, but God always sees the perfect outcome because He alone knows the end from the beginning.

An unknown 17th century British cleric, speaking about divine providence, was quoted as saying:

"God nothing does, nor suffers to be done, but you yourself would do, could you but see the end of all events as well as He."

In retrospect, I can see God's waves of grace overflowing my life, although at the time I was oblivious to His love and divine involvement in every aspect of my existence. I was nine years old in 1958 and a move to Tripoli didn't seem that unusual after living in Mineola, Novato, Amman, Beirut, and Alamo. I didn't feel a pull to remain in Alamo, because home to me was in an airplane flying around the world. God was orchestrating my life in a way that I can see clearly now—over sixty years later.

WAVES OF GRACE

Little did I know it at the time, but God was preparing me for experiences later in life, that would require the ability to meet and interact with people from a variety of different cultures and national backgrounds, eat a variety of exotic foods, and adjust my circadian rhythm to various time zones. He was also orchestrating a moment in my life when I would meet my future wife, Judy De Jager, who would lead me to Jesus through her love and faithfulness.

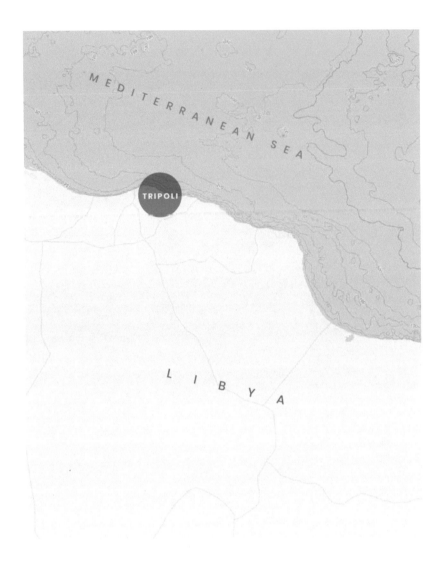

2

TRIPOLI, LIBYA
32.8 °N, 13.1°E

We moved to Tripoli and once again lived near the sea. This was a time when Libya was a kingdom ruled by King Idris under Italian oversight. It was also a country where the United States had established its largest strategic air command in the world: Wheelus Air Force Base. My sister and I attended school at Wheelus AFB, which was about a 90-minute drive from our villa.

We belonged to a club on the Mediterranean not far from our "villa" (basically, a cement home with a wall around it) that featured a golf course (sand fairways and sand greens rolled with oil), as well as a beautiful reef off the beach that heightened my fascination with the sea and the creatures that dwelt there.

These first experiences snorkeling in the Mediterranean were like entering another world. Years later I learned that many astronauts, when asked to describe space travel, compared it to snorkeling and scuba diving because they were afloat in a weightless environment surrounded by sensory input otherwise invisible to the human eye. Both environments served as catalysts to transport them to an alien world, seemingly beyond time and self-consciousness.

I didn't realize it at the time, but I was skimming the surface of a reality that would transform my life many years later; God's creative and amazing design of the universe—from the nucleus of an atom to the endless expanse of space—from time to eternity.

At this stage in my dad's career, Transocean had become insolvent and he co-founded his own aviation company, International Aviation Development Corporation (IADCO). IADCO provided air charter services to the oil and gas companies that were developing oil and gas concessions in North Africa and the Middle East (a concession is a grant awarded by a sovereign country to a multi-national corporation that provides the corporation with the rights to explore and develop natural resources in a designated area of the country).

I had several American friends who lived nearby whose dads were also involved in the oil and gas industry. We were all ten or eleven years old, and we all owned pellet guns. One of our favorite things to do was to hike with our guns to some huge sandstone caverns, that had been used by the Germans during World War II to shelter tanks and ammunition from allied bombers. In the late 1950s they sheltered large bats that hung from the ceilings.

We carried flashlights and glass jars into these caverns, shot the bats from the ceilings, and carried them home in our jars as trophies. One day, shortly before Christmas, I winged a bat that dropped to the sand floor, quite alive but unable to fly. I placed it in my jar, and on the way home spotted an American kindergartener licking a candy cane and holding a second one in his other hand. He was fascinated by my bat, so I traded my bat for the candy cane—a real trophy!

Hanging bat in a cave [1]

IN RETROSPECT

When my dad announced our move to North Africa, I had visions of swinging on jungle vines that hung down in our backyard and living among lions, elephants, and huge pythons. When our plane touched down at Tripoli Idris International Airport in 1958, one of my dad's drivers met us in a VW bus to drive us to our hotel in downtown Tripoli. On the drive to town, I was disappointed to see that we were going to be living in a desert, not a jungle, environment.

We lived in the seafront Hotel Casino Uaddan for six months, which featured a first-class Italian restaurant and a popular casino. Linda and I woke up early on weekday mornings to catch a bus for the hour-and-a-half ride to Wheelus Air Force Base to attend school. Upon our return in the late afternoon, my mom would often take us to the hotel bar, where we enjoyed bottles of cold Pepsi and freshly baked potato chips. Dinner was usually room service featuring Italian cuisine.

Weekends were spent sneaking into the casino when it was closed, taking carriage rides with my mom through the city streets and visiting Roman ruins like the Leptis Magna archaeological site on the North African coast. As we had in Beirut, we listened to the Muslim call to prayer at all hours of the day and night. To this day, whenever I hear these wailing prayers of the Islamic faith in a movie theatre or elsewhere, I am reminded of the sights and smells of growing up in the Middle East and North Africa.

Seafront Hotel Casino Uaddan (center – left) – Tripoli, Libya – circa 1960s [2]

Roman ruins – Leptis Magna, Al-Khums, Libya –
(80 miles east of Tripoli on the Mediterranean Sea) [3]

After our sojourn at the Uaddan Hotel, we moved to a villa located in the Giorgimpopoli suburb of Tripoli, home to many American and British expatriate families (a family living outside its native country) working in Libya.

There was an abandoned quarry, a few steps from our villa, that I used as a shortcut to visit a friend. One afternoon, after returning home from school, my mom gave me some cookies and I set out to visit my friend. As I circled the quarry, a group of Arab teenagers jumped out from behind a rock, surrounded me, grabbed my cookies, and shoved me to the ground. I took off running, and when I looked back to check my progress, I was hit in the forehead with a rock. Fortunately, I wasn't badly hurt, but I never used that shortcut again.

On Sundays after church, we usually stopped off at a British fast-food restaurant for take-out of the best fish and chips I can remember eating. On special occasions, when my dad was home, we frequented a seafront restaurant that specialized in serving calamari, a squid dish popular in the United States today, but little known then.

As I reminisce about these years in Tripoli, some of the high-lights include: snorkeling on the Mediterranean reef not far from our villa; watching the film *Around the World in 80 Days*, when our grammar school at Wheelus Air Force Base hosted a special screening; and flying co-pilot with my dad in a DC-3 over the Sahara dessert. I can also remember walking down a sand street, not far from our villa, where an elderly Arab man sat on his haunches frying grasshoppers for sale on an old frying pan held over a small stick fire.

I can also reflect on the certainty that God had His hand of protection over me. The Arab teenagers who shoved me down by the quarry and hit me with the rock could have just as easily thrown me over the edge down a hundred-foot drop-off. I could have contracted any number of diseases from the bats I shot, the food I ate, or the water I drank, but we moved from Libya to Germany in 1959 and I was in perfect health

Poster for *Around the World* in 80 Days [4]

WAVES OF GRACE

Looking back now, watching "Around the World in 80 Days" in 1958 was a harbinger of a chapter in my life when I would repeatedly travel around the world in about the same amount of time, meet my wife of now fifty years, and be introduced to Jesus.

3

WIESBADEN, GERMANY
50.0 °N, 8.2°E

In 1959, as my dad's company began to expand, we moved to Wiesbaden, Germany, and at eleven years of age, I began to swim competitively and to platform dive off 5-, 7.5-, and 10-meter platforms. Swimming competitively was a natural progression because I loved the water and had confidence in my ability to flow through it; however, it would be the 1970s before I fully discovered my passion for the oceans and the seas. Thanks to my dad, my ability to swim and dive has played a deep and abiding role in the successive ways I embraced ocean sports later in life.

Rio 2016 – Olympic diving platforms –
(1, 3, 5, 7.5, and 10 meters) –
Photo: Jonas de Carvalho [1]

Living in Germany was a stark contrast to living in the Middle East and North Africa. There was little to notice of the ravages of World War II, but there were reminders. The home of the American family who lived across the street from us was a former Nazi Party official residence. It featured a conference room with padded walls and a padded door, all covered in rich green leather to prevent anyone from eavesdropping on secret meetings.

Down the tree-lined street from our home was a beautiful park, lake, and casino: the Kurhaus. We would rent row boats at the Kurpark behind the casino, cruise the lake, and buy tasty ice cream cones and the original German gummy bears (Gummibärchen).

Front of the Kurhaus Casino and Restaurant –
Wiesbaden, Germany [2]

Kurhaus Park (back of Casino and Restaurant) –
Wiesbaden, Germany – Photo: Pedelecs [3]

We didn't have television, just a radio that could be tuned to the American Armed Forces Radio Network. We listened to 1950s radio shows like *Fibber McGee and Molly* and *Amos 'n' Andy*, or occasionally caught a championship boxing match, like the one that featured Floyd Patterson fighting to retain his world championship title. One spring, we drove to Holland on vacation and one Christmas, my dad gave me an airline ticket to accompany him on a business trip to Rome.

There was a large American military presence in Wiesbaden at this time, and both Linda and I attended U.S. Air Force and Army base schools nearby. I played Pop Warner football, organized basketball, Little League baseball, joined the Boy Scouts and the National Rifle Association, and learned to play golf at a U.S. military facility, Rhineblick Golf Course. One Christmas, I learned to ski with some school friends on a ski trip to Lech, Austria, sponsored by our grammar school.

We attended church on Sunday and usually had lunch afterwards at the Civilian Club, a U.S. military officer's club located in a beautiful old mansion in a quaint area of the city. Although we were civilians, my mom and dad were recognized for their military service and were accorded certain privileges commensurate with their rank.

U.S. Army Rhineblick Golf Course –
Wiesbaden, Germany [4]

These were the formative years of my life. By the time I graduated from seventh grade, I had lived in five countries; attended six schools; studied English, Arabic, and German; eaten all kinds of foods; gazed upon horribly deformed beggars on Arab streets selling Chiclets chewing gum to survive; smelled the pungent mixture of exotic spices sold in Arab souks; and swum with maimed Nazi World War II veterans in German public swimming pools.

I had flown tens of thousands of miles on very loud propeller-driven airplanes, like Boeing Stratocruisers, Lockheed Constellations, and Boeing DC-3's, DC-4's, and DC-6's. Commercial aircraft, prior to the introduction of jet aircraft in the early 1960s, featured piston-driven engines. The drumbeat of those engines for seven or eight hours at a time was deafening.

I had visited cities like San Francisco, Chicago, Boston, New York, Gander, Shannon, London, Copenhagen, Rome, Cairo, Amman, Tripoli, Frankfurt, and Amsterdam, but I was always homesick for the States. I can remember thinking, on an R&R flight back to the U.S., that I would kneel down and kiss the airport tarmac when the plane landed. In those days, there were no enclosed "airways" for disembarking passengers, just "gangway" stairs that were rolled into place once the captain shut down the engines.

The Pan American Stratocruisers had an upper and lower deck. The upper deck was all passenger seating. The lower deck, reached by a spiral staircase, consisted of a bar with lounge seating. Once the aircraft reached cruising altitude most of the adults descended to the bar and my sister and I had the upper deck to ourselves. We would snatch every pillow we could from the unenclosed overhead racks, lug them back to our seats, and build forts. By the way, everyone smoked everywhere in those days—including on commercial airplane flights.

We flew for free on Transocean on a space-available basis and accepted the seats we were offered. One time, my mom, sister, and I slept overnight in the waiting lounge at London Airport (renamed Heathrow Airport in 1966), only to board a smelly Transocean DC-6 cargo plane bound for New York, that had just delivered a cargo of Belgian Congo monkeys to the Frankfurt Zoological Garden in Germany. It had a handful of passenger seats located toward the front of the aircraft behind the cockpit. We were assigned those seats and this flight ranks at the top of my list as one of the worst and smelliest flights I have ever experienced.

MY LIFE WAS ONE OF constant change, displacement, and adaptation. I never knew what it was like to grow up in one community, attend the same schools, and hang with the same friends from kindergarten through high school. At the time, I thought everyone lived a life like the one I was living because I didn't know anything else. I didn't give a second thought to my mom leaning out over the railing of the balcony of our sixth-floor apartment in Beirut and selecting a live turkey from an Arab merchant shepherding a flock of turkeys down the middle of the street. I thought it was normal when the merchant grabbed the one my mom selected, chopped its head off, and threw it in the bucket our Arab maid had lowered down to him on a rope. It never occurred to me that it wasn't standard operating procedure for our maid to gut and clean a turkey in the kitchen sink and cook it—or that most families didn't have a maid. I thought everyone boiled their water and drank powdered milk, because the tap water was filthy and the only milk available was unpasteurized, and dangerous to drink.

When our American refrigerator arrived from the U.S., I didn't think it was unusual when an Arab laborer—probably fifty years of age or older and weighing no more than 120 pounds—wrapped a strap around the back of the refrigerator, placed the strap across his forehead, leaned the front door of the refrigerator on to his back and carried it up six flights of stairs to our apartment because it was too big to fit in the elevator. I probably assumed all kids had an opportunity to play on the swing set King Farouk built for his children at his palace in Cairo before he was deposed—or to visit the city of Bethlehem and tour the Church of the Nativity.

Linda and I riding a camel near the Pyramids – Cairo, Egypt – 1954 [5]

King Farouk's Abdeen Palace – Cairo, Egypt – Photo: Leonid Andronov [6]

I never gave a second thought to meeting Arab dignitaries at cocktail parties my mom and dad hosted—or thought it unusual when my dad's 6'2", 230-pound Sudanese bodyguard opened his thobe (robe) to display ammunition belts that crisscrossed his chest, revolvers slung under each arm, and curved knives tucked into his belt. It never crossed my mind that most kids my age didn't have the opportunity to visit an Arab grade school classroom, with their second-grade class, and see Arab second graders sitting on a dirt floor covered with flies from head to foot.

When we were living in Wiesbaden, Germany, I was elected president of my seventh-grade class and was asked to represent our school in delivering the food and clothing our school had collected for an impoverished neighborhood. We drove to this neighborhood in a large U.S. Army truck. When we arrived, I jumped up on the rear platform and helped hand boxes down to the soldiers gathered below. As I did, I began to realize how privileged I was to be where I was, doing what I was doing.

From left: Orvis Nelson, Founder and President of Transocean, me, my dad's Sudanese bodyguard, Orvis's mother, and my sister Linda [7]

WAVES OF GRACE

When we moved back to the United States and I started eighth grade, I was a self-confident twelve-year-old, comfortable interacting with kids my own age and with adults. I knew how to order food in French, Italian, and Arabic restaurants, and I could easily adapt to new schools and new cultures. I was as relaxed boarding an airplane for a transatlantic flight as I was crossing the street. In a few brief years I had grown up a lot experientially, but not spiritually.

In retrospect, self-confidence was probably the major stumbling block that prevented me from finding Jesus. Self-confidence can lead to pride, and pride is the hallmark of a life lived in opposition to God. Pride gives birth to arrogance, and in the extreme, narcissism. It was only by God's grace that I was eventually able to overcome my self-confidence, although pride is still a sin I struggle with because Satan, the devil, who is pride personified, knows my weaknesses and will tempt me with them any time he can.

4

ALAMO, CALIFORNIA

37.8 °N, -122.0°W

In 1961, our family moved back to our home in Alamo. I attended eighth grade in Alamo and high school in Danville. With few exceptions, all of my friends in Alamo and Danville had grown up together. They had played Little League and Pop Warner Football together, joined the same Cub Scout and Boy Scout packs, attended the same birthday parties, and generally bonded as kids do.

I was the new kid on the block and had to adjust. One of the most difficult adjustments was not being able to share my life experiences with other kids for fear of being perceived as bragging. Although my life was all I had known up to that point in time, I began to realize that it was a very different life from everyone else I knew. I didn't know it at the time, but I had had a very unusual and privileged upbringing. Fortunately, I had learned to adapt to my surroundings. I was used to being the new-kid-on-the-block, because I had always been the new-kid-on-the-block.

Not fitting in wasn't so bad in eighth grade, but high school was a different matter. However, by God's grace, I had a loving family, and despite the occasional fight behind the backstop of the baseball field after school to stick up for myself, I readily adjusted to growing up in Alamo: hanging with some close friends; dove and quail hunting; sneaking onto farms and ranches to rope and ride horses; competing in AAU (American Athletic Union) swimming competitions; playing competitive golf on the Northern California junior circuit and on my high school golf team; and dating a bit.

San Ramon High School
Golf Team – 1965 [1]

My summers were spent working as a gas station attendant, lifeguard, golf caddie, and caddie shack flunky. One summer I commuted an hour and a half each way to Stockton, California, to work at my dad's FAA (Federal Aviation Administration) approved airframe and engine overhaul facility at Stockton Airport, sandblasting aircraft engine pistons, sweeping the floors, and sorting used aircraft nuts and bolts.

The following summer, in the days before automated sprinkler systems, I memorized every sprinkler head location at Round Hill Country Club, an eighteen-hole golf course in Alamo, California. I then watered the course, from eight at night to four in the morning, driving a jeep loaded with sprinkler heads, back and forth, between the front nine holes and back nine holes.

One of the highlights of those years was caddying eighteen holes at Round Hill CC for Joe DiMaggio and Lefty O'Doul, one bag on each shoulder. Another was being photographed for a Round Hill CC promotional brochure. During a practice session on the driving range, as I prepared to hit a drive, the club professional and a photographer walked over with Jayne Mansfield, the famous actress, and asked if she could take a picture with me. When I readily assented, she leaned over me from behind, with her arms and hands overlapping mine, and the photographer snapped the shot. I was fifteen years old at the time and had little appreciation for the fact that Joe DiMaggio was an American icon and that Jayne Mansfield was fast becoming one.

Although these years were relatively uneventful compared to what I had been used to, I had some excellent teachers, made good friends, and did my best to fit in. In 1966, when I graduated from high school, the war in Vietnam was beginning to escalate, the free speech movement was in full swing at University of California Berkeley (about a half-hour drive from our home), and sex, drugs, and rock and roll were beginning to frame the culture of our generation.

In that volatile environment, my dad wisely took me on a trip to visit his alma mater, Monmouth College, in Monmouth, Illinois, where he had been born and raised. I think he realized that my uprooted upbringing might leave me vulnerable to the unsettled cultural shifts occurring around us. He probably thought it would be beneficial for me to experience the fertile ground of his Midwestern roots. I met his sisters and their families in Chicago and Galesburg, Illinois, loved them, and decided to leave California and attend Monmouth College.

Family reunion with my dad's sisters – 1981 [2]

Wallace Hall – Monmouth College –
Photo: Jason Lonsberry [3]

WASHINGTON, D.C.

38.9 °N,-77.0°W

I spent my freshman year and the first two quarters of my sophomore year at Monmouth College, before being selected during the third quarter to participate in a special studies program in Washington, D.C., which was affiliated with American University. This program had a three-fold curriculum: one, write an independent study paper on a topic concerning the federal government; two, meet with various federal government leaders for a series of lectures; and three, study art and architecture with the Curator of the National Gallery of Art.

There were three significant events that occurred in my life that spring. The first was the result of an assignment given by the Curator of the National Gallery of Art. We were instructed to tour the National Cathedral to study the architecture. A small group of us decided to visit on a Sunday morning in order to combine our assignment with the opportunity to hear the acoustics of the church during a service.

When we arrived the morning of March 31, 1968, we noticed a team of technicians assembling sound and camera equipment and we asked them why. They shared that Dr. Martin Luther King, Jr., would be delivering the sermon. We decided to stay for the entire service and we were privileged to hear one of the most moving messages I have ever heard.

The cathedral filled with people and many others gathered outside to listen on loudspeakers. We had the best seats in the house. Dr. King's sermon was titled "Remaining Awake Through a Great Revolution" (Congressional Record, 9 April 1968) and much of what he shared was timeless:

"Somewhere we must come to see that human progress never rolls in on the wheels of inevitability. It comes through the tireless efforts and the persistent work of dedicated individuals who are willing to be co-workers with God. And without this hard work, time itself becomes an ally of the primitive forces of social stagnation. So, we must help time and realize that the time is always ripe to do right."

National Gallery of Art, West Building
– Washington, D.C. – Photo: Kunar Klack [4]

He ended his sermon:

"Thank God for John, who centuries ago out on a lonely, obscure island called Patmos, caught a vision of a new Jerusalem descending out of heaven from God, who heard a voice saying, 'Behold, I make all things new; former things are passed away.' God grant that we will be participants in this newness and this magnificent development. If we will but do it, we will bring about a new day of justice and brotherhood and peace. And that day the morning stars will sing together, and the sons of God will shout for joy. God bless you."

When we returned to our brownstone house, not far from the Washington Hilton in the Northwest African American section of town, I immediately sat down and wrote several letters to family and friends sharing my experience. Dr. King's sermon had impacted my heart, but not in a spiritual conversion, "Come to Jesus" way. Instead, he began to open my understanding of what it was like to be born and raised an African American in the 20th century.

The second event occurred later that week on the evening of Thursday, April 4, when President Lyndon Baines Johnson was scheduled to speak at the Washington Hilton. I walked over in the rain to watch his entourage arrive and catch a glimpse of him exiting his limousine.

As I huddled with several others across the street, under the covered entry to an office building, I was startled by the scream of an African American woman standing next to me. She had a transistor radio glued to her ear and shared that Dr. Martin Luther King, Jr., had just been assassinated in Memphis, Tennessee. It turned out we had watched him deliver his last sermon.

The third event occurred the morning of the next day, April 5. As we exited the main doors of the National Gallery of Art, after our class with the curator, we stepped outside and witnessed what seemed like every police car in the nation's capital speeding down Pennsylvania Avenue with their sirens blaring. We watched in amazement as about forty patrol cars peeled off Pennsylvania Avenue, block by block in groups of four, and raced up the numbered streets to the Northwest African American section of town where we lived.

Dr. Martin Luther King, Jr. –
1964 [5]

We then noticed gangs of African American youth running through the streets with baseball bats and tire irons, breaking shop windows, and stealing anything they could lay their hands on. At the same moment the entrances to the federal government office buildings, that lined Pennsylvania Avenue, flew open and thousands of employees stampeded out the doors pushing aside pedestrians who were in their way. The federal government had declared an emergency and ordered all federal employees to leave downtown immediately, and head for the safety of their homes in the suburbs.

There were four guys and eight girls in the Monmouth College Washington House program that quarter, and the guys shepherded the girls back to our brownstone house. Once we safely arrived, we learned that the International House, just a few blocks away from our brownstone, where we normally walked to dinner, would be closed indefinitely. We also noticed that our neighbors were spray painting their cars with "Soul Brother" or "Soul Sister", a premonition of what was about to explode.

The four of us guys decided to walk to a local grocery store and buy food for the next few days. On the way back from the store, we noticed several African American young men walking towards us on the same side of the street. We quickly sidestepped across the street, and as they walked past us on the other side, one them yelled out, "You better be in by nightfall, white boys!"

That night, we watched from our rooftop as the Northwest section of Washington, D.C. burned across the skyline. It looked like the London blitzkrieg. We watched through our front windows as dozens of African Americans carried stolen TV's, washers, dryers, boxes of liquor, and other loot down the sidewalk and into their homes.

The next day, President Johnson ordered a curfew from six at night to six in the morning. National Guard troops were stationed on street corners throughout the city and machine gun emplacements were set up in front of the White House and on the Capitol Hill steps. I had seen this type of rioting overseas, but never thought I would experience it in our nation's capital. It made me realize how fragile our democracy is and how few of us truly appreciate the freedoms we take for granted. I was beginning to understand that Americans live in an imperfect country with a checkered history, but it is the best country on earth when, according to The Pledge of Allegiance, it is "one nation under God".

April 5, 1968 – car parked in front of our brownstone [6]

Soldiers set up a machine gun emplacement
on the steps of the U.S. Capitol – April 1968 [7]

Soldiers standing guard on the corner of 7th and N Street NW in
Washington, D.C. with the ruins of buildings that were destroyed
during the riots that followed the assassination of
Dr. Martin Luther King, Jr. – April 1968 – Photo: Warren K. Leffler [8]

ROME, ITALY

41.9 °N, 12.4°E

After completing my studies in Washington, D.C., I spent my junior year abroad in Rome, Italy, with Loyola University of Chicago. About two hundred students, from many different colleges and universities throughout the United States, lived in a dormitory on the campus of a beautifully landscaped former Papal residence situated on the highest hill overlooking Rome, Monte Mario.

Many of our classes were taught by Jesuit priests. All of us studied Italian and we enjoyed long weekends exploring Rome and the surrounding Italian countryside. On extended holidays we planned trips and pooled resources to explore various European countries.

During the Easter holiday, I led a group of four other students on a photo safari through East Africa. I had never liked zoos and wanted to know what it was like to experience wild animals in their natural environment, like fish in the sea. We camped out every night in the bush (the wild) and visited most of the major game reserves in Kenya and Tanzania.

Entrance to the Loyola University of Chicago,
Rome Center campus on Monte Mario – 1968 [9]

East African skyline and our Land Rover – April 1969 [10]

Standing with a park ranger on a plateau
overlooking the Maasai-Amboseli Game Reserve – Kenya, April 1969 [11]

On our last night out, we decided to set up camp in a remote area of the Tanzanian Serengeti National Park. At that point in our safari, we had traveled about a thousand miles and observed all of the major game animals. We pitched our tent, built a campfire, cooked our dinner, and retired for the night. Our Land Rover slept two, our tent slept three, and we rotated every night.

Around midnight, those of us in the tent heard the roaring of a lion, which steadily increased as others in the pride (a family of lions) joined in. They sounded like they were just a few yards from our tent, but the guys in the Land Rover were sound sleepers and unaware of the danger. We were unarmed except for the few spears, shields, and knives we had acquired by barter from Maasai tribesmen in Kenya, and they were in the Land Rover. We were defenseless.

After repeated efforts to wake our friends by raising our voices without provoking the lions, they finally got the hint, backed the Land Rover up to the front entrance of the tent, and as we threw up the flap, they simultaneously swung open the back door, and we jumped in. The five of us spent the night in the Land Rover scared to death. The next morning, when the sun was well up and over the horizon, we scrambled out, threw all our camping equipment into the back of the Land Rover, and hightailed it back to Nairobi, Kenya.

EAST AFRICAN TYPES   MASAI WARRIORS   903

Maasai Warriors – postcard – 1969 [12]

IN RETROSPECT

As I look back on these memories today, I realize that each of us possesses an old and possibly a new testament. I also know that our lives are recorded in our memories to a degree, but they are precisely and comprehensively chronicled in the mind of God.

There is not a thought, word, or deed in our entire lives that is unknown to God and one day all of us will be held to account for everything we have thought, said, or done. When that day unfolds, we will either stand before God in our own self-righteousness or we will stand in the amazing grace and righteousness of Jesus Christ, who paid the price for all of our sin.

> *"My little children, these things I write to you, so that you may not sin. And if anyone sins, we have an Advocate with the Father, Jesus Christ the righteous. And He Himself is the propitiation for our sins, and not for ours only but also for the whole world." – 1 John 2:1-2*

The truth about Jesus is that He died for the sins of everyone who believes in Him—and by simply believing in Him, we are eternally alive in Him. If we believe in Jesus, God sees and loves us as He sees and loves Jesus, not as the imperfect, sinful people we are. By simply believing that Jesus died for our sins we are a new creation and we have a new testament or testimony in Him.

> *"He who believes in the Son has everlasting life; and he who does not believe the Son shall not see life, but the wrath of God abides on him." – John 3:36*

In retrospect, I have learned that there was nothing I could have done to earn my way into heaven; it was all done by Jesus. Now that I know Him, I have discovered that I can never endear myself to Him by "making up my mind" that I'm going to do this or that to please Him. Any attempt I make to practice righteousness by my own strength is fruitless. I can do nothing without Him.

> *"I am the vine, you are the branches. He who abides in Me, and I in him, bears much fruit; for without Me you can do nothing." – John 15:5*

Legend tells of an elderly preacher from Scotland who, as he lay dying, was asked, "What are you doing now?" He responded, "I am just gathering all my good works up together, and I am throwing them all overboard; and I am lashing myself to the plank of free grace, and I hope to swim to glory on it." In essence, he was sharing an eternal truth—no man or woman is worthy of salvation.

Once we begin following Jesus, growing in faith is a lifetime adventure on earth that ends when we join Him in heaven. Since beginning this journey, I have grown in my realization that there is nothing I can do of my own volition to please God and there is nothing I can do to make Him love me any less. He loves me as He loves Jesus, perfectly and eternally. I cannot earn His love, nor can I do anything to diminish it

"For by grace you have been saved through faith, and that not of yourselves; it is the gift of God, not of works, lest anyone should boast." – Ephesians 2:8-9

Anything I think I have done for God, that I think places Him in my debt, like going to church on Sunday or practicing some other religious ritual is worthless. God refuses to accept ritualistic sacrifice—it is an abomination to Him. Afterall, He created everything, owns everything, and needs nothing. I entered God's kingdom through a prayer of faith, and from that moment on, I am one with Him eternally by His presence in my heart. As I trust in Him and surrender myself to Him, He directs my path. This is why His word is so important to me. The Bible teaches that faith comes by hearing and hearing by the word of God, whatever is not of faith is sin, and without faith it is impossible to please God.

Our encounter with the pride of lions in Tanzania brings to light a key spiritual truth that should awaken both believers and unbelievers. Satan, our archenemy, prowls about like a roaring lion, seeking whom he can rip apart and murder. In addition to being the father of lies and doctrines of demons (false teaching), he is a murderer by nature and his endgame is to spiritually murder everyone on earth—relegating them to hell, where they will join him and his demonic host for eternity. Believers can be tempted and attacked by Satan, but they can never be separated from God and lose their eternal salvation. Unbelievers are subject to his schemes.

A lion on the prowl emits a roar that freezes, in fear, the prey he is about to devour—like a deer in the headlights. Likewise, in the spiritual realm, we must be constantly aware of Satan's schemes to destroy mankind through lies, fear, and wickedness. We know, through Scripture, that Satan can transform himself into an angel of light, with all power, signs, and lying wonders. He knows he is on borrowed time and he is doing everything in his power, as the ruler of the world, to tempt mankind into fatal depths of fear and wickedness. Believers, by the power of the Holy Spirit dwelling within them, can escape Satan's temptations through God's faithfulness:

"No temptation has overtaken you except such as is common to man; but God is faithful, who will not allow you to be tempted beyond what you are able, but with the temptation will also make the way of escape, that you may be able to bear it." – 1 Corinthians 10:13

Throughout history, ungodly nations and empires have succumbed to Satan's wiles and fallen into God's judgment—forever extinguished and forgotten. God's word and the signs of the times clearly reveal that the world is now falling under God's judgment and the United States is leading the way. Through the mechanism of a manufactured presidential election, God has allowed unbridled Satanically-inspired depravity to flourish globally—exposing a depth of wickedness that far surpasses anything we could have imagined just a few years ago—and it will only grow worse. It will grow tragically worse after the church is raptured—an unknown future moment in time when Jesus returns for His church and all believers, dead and living, join Him eternally in heaven (see Chapter 27).

"All nations before Him are as nothing, and they are counted by Him less than nothing and worthless." – Isaiah 40:15

We are living in a day and age when believers should be vigilant in prayer and unbelievers should seek the God of the Bible who created them and loves them. Only God knows the moment He has appointed for each person to die. His heart desire is that all should be resurrected to everlasting life in heaven with Him—not an eternity of shame and contempt in hell with Satan. Time is of the essence. Before leaving this world, unbelievers should: recognize they are sinners; realize Jesus died for their sins on the cross; turn from their sinful life to God; and—with a heartfelt prayer—confess Jesus as their personal Lord and Savior.

"Behold, I stand at the door and knock. If anyone hears My voice and opens the door, I will come in to him and dine with him, and he with Me." – Revelation 3:20

WAVES OF GRACE

During my sophomore year of college, my mom and dad moved to the island of Malta, where my dad and his partner established an FAA certified airframe and engine overhaul base for their growing fleet of charter aircraft. Malta is a small island, approximately 9 by 17 miles, that is strategically located in the center of the Mediterranean Sea: 50 miles south of Sicily, 200 miles north of Libya, and 180 miles east of Tunisia. During summer months and school breaks I lived and worked there,
nurturing my love for the sea.

5

MALTA

35.5°N, 14.2°E

    I learned to scuba dive at a small aquatic center located in St. Julian's, Malta, on a finger of land that featured the Dragonara Casino, a former palace. My instructor, a retired British Royal Navy demolition diver, in turn, introduced me to members of the Royal Navy demolition team stationed on the island.

Until 1964, Malta had been part of the British Commonwealth. It was a strategic allied naval base during World War II. As a result, it was heavily bombed by the Germans during the war and to this day, fighter planes, naval vessels, and bombs litter the surrounding sea. The British demolition team defused any live bombs left over from the war.

Dragonara Casino, St. Julian's, Malta – Photo: Tony Hisgett [1]

Siege of Malta – World War II – The heavily bomb-damaged Kingsway Street in Valletta, Malta – April 1942 [2]

I was privileged to dive with these demolition experts on their off days. They knew the best dive sites and we dove on German fighters that had been shot down and on sunken naval vessels.

We drove out to the dive sites in a couple of vintage Rolls Royce's that were owned by the team members.

Maltese fort located at the entrance to the Grand Harbor – Port of Valletta [3]

Prepping for a dive with one of the British Royal Navy demolition team members on a sunken World War II British naval vessel – Port of Valletta's Grand Harbor, Malta – 1968 [4]

One afternoon, we strapped on our scuba gear, grabbed our spearguns, entered the sea, and swam about a quarter mile off the coast to a Nazi Messerschmitt fighter in about fifty feet of water. As we descended, my mind filled with images of a skeleton sitting in the cockpit slumped over the controls. The pilot had disintegrated long before, but we recovered a machine gun, which we donated to the local pub to be placed on the mantel over the bar.

Malta, 1968 – just prior to diving on a Nazi Messerschmitt Bf. 109 fighter aircraft [5]

Nazi Messerschmitt Bf. 109 [6]

The Maltese are a blended mix of cultures that have occupied the island for millennia. Their roots can be traced to North Africa, the Middle East, and Southern Europe. They speak Maltese, which is a guttural Arabic-sounding language interspersed with Italian and English-sounding words. Most Maltese can also speak broken English. Highly educated Maltese are typically fluent in English and Italian.

In the 1960s, Malta was 100% Roman Catholic, most of the sixty-eight chartered towns had a patron saint, and every patron saint was celebrated annually on a certain holiday. The townspeople honored their patron saints like Americans observe the Fourth of July, with parades and fireworks. The celebratory processions were led by men marching through the streets carrying religious icons. I always knew the day of a local celebration by the fireworks that exploded at daybreak and woke me up. These were not colorful fireworks as Americans know them, but countless missile-like bombs that exploded with a thunderous boom.

Living among the Maltese deepened my impression of Christianity as something for the masses: interesting, but not appealing to me. I share this because during these formative years I simply tried to follow a certain set of rules and regulations, as opposed to entering into a personal relationship with God based on my faith and trust in Him, and His eternal love for me.

MY EXPOSURE TO THE CHRISTIAN religion, Protestant or Roman Catholic, was purely on a surface level. I now realize that man can be blinded by his religion. As Pastor Chuck Smith, once said:

"When God is seeking to establish a vital life-changing relationship, people try to formalize it into a religious system."

Roman Catholic celebration and procession – Silema, Malta [7]

As we covered in the "Essentials" introduction, when a person trusts and believes in Jesus: they are indwelt by the Holy Spirt; they become alive in Jesus spiritually; and they are complete in Him eternally. The free gift of salvation originated in God's heart—outside of time and space—and is gracefully revealed to believers in a moment of time predetermined by God through His gift of faith.

The process of salvation unfolds in three phases: justification—repenting from sin and turning to faith in Jesus; sanctification—the life-long process of being separated from sin and conformed into the image of Jesus; and glorification—upon death, instantaneously passing from this world into the heavenly presence of Jesus; eternally glorified, holy, and free from all sin.

God takes no pleasure in the death of the wicked. He created His church at Pentecost for one reason—to glorify Him by proclaiming His love and the gospel truth of His word to both Jew and Gentile. The salvation of God in Jesus is freely available to everyone until death do us part. No one will enter heaven by following a system of works or by believing in the ideologies and philosophies of men. We were all born in sin, we will all die in sin, and we will all go to hell in sin, without believing in the gospel truth—and Satan, the ruler of the world and the father of lies, is masterfully orchestrating worldly deceit to shield the lost from the gospel.

> *"Beware lest anyone cheat you through philosophy and empty deceit, according to the tradition of men, according to the basic principles of the world, and not according to Christ. For in Him dwells all the fullness of the Godhead bodily; and you are complete in Him, who is the head of all principality and power." – Colossians 2:8-9*

One of the most formidable religious systems in the world is Roman Catholicism. Its dogmas and doctrines were created over the centuries by Ecumenical Councils of the Roman Catholic priesthood (a hierarchy of popes, bishops, cardinals and priests) and then memorialized in the *Catechism of the Catholic Church*. The creation of the Roman Catholic *Catechism* is reminiscent of the creation of the Jewish *Talmud*—a book of laws created by men (rabbis) during the 2nd–5th centuries A.D. to interpret the Jewish *Torah*—a list of 613 commandments, given by God to Moses, and taken from the first five books of the Old Testament.

Central to the Roman Catholic belief system is the celebration of the Mass and Eucharist, also known as the ceremony of transubstantiation. Transubstantiation is performed by a priest who supposedly reaches up into heaven, takes Christ down to earth, turns Him into bread and wine, and sacrifices Him on an altar for the sins of the living and the dead. This ceremony is not only past belief, it is also antithetical to God's word, which clearly teaches Jesus offered Himself once for all.

> *"...we have been sanctified through the offering of the body of Jesus Christ once for all." – Hebrews 10:10*

Where do we find the hierarchy of the Roman Catholic priesthood, transubstantiation, purgatory, Mary worship, and other Roman Catholic dogmas and doctrines in the Bible? We don't. Just like we don't find the Jewish Talmud or the philosophical, psychological, social, religious, and political traditions of men—which are now accepted as special revelations of God by many contemporary Protestant denominations and evangelical churches. The Roman Catholic *Catechism* is sprinkled with God's word—and some are saved—but many are misled or blinded from the pure truth of God's word. The question we must all ask ourselves is: Where have we placed our trust—in ourselves, in Christ alone, or in Christ plus the tradition of men?

> *"Every word of God is pure; He is a shield to those who put their trust in Him. Do not add to His words, lest He rebuke you, and you be found a liar." – Proverbs 30:5-6*

My paternal grandfather, grandmother,
and me – Monmouth, Illinois – 1949 [8]

I ATTENDED PRESBYTERIAN SUNDAY SCHOOL almost every weekend growing up, but it was simply something I was forced to do. During my years in Beirut, from first to third grade, my parents would take me to my Sunday school classroom and give me a few piasters (Lebanese coins) for the offering. As soon as they left for "big church," my best friend, Bill Works, and I would walk to a small Arab grocery store and buy candy with the offerings our parents had given us.

Recently, I learned from my oldest living aunt that my paternal grandfather and grandmother, who both passed into heaven while we were living overseas, were raised in strong, faith-based, Christian homes. I'm sure they both prayed over their children and grandchildren, and I think their prayers and God's grace kept the door of my heart open to knowing Jesus. I also believe there were other relatives and family friends who prayed for me.

God can and does direct experiences and events in our lives that demand our attention and can lead to our conversion. One of the most commonly known is called a "fox-hole conversion." This refers to when a soldier at war realizes the fuse of his life is about to burn out. However, it doesn't need to be war that God uses to draw us to Him; it can also be drugs, alcohol, divorce, death of a loved one, family tragedy, or simply hearing His word for the first time, like the thief on the cross hanging next to Jesus.

When I didn't find the skeleton of a German fighter pilot in the Messerschmitt, I didn't give a second thought to what had happened to him. When you're nineteen years old—strong, healthy, and full of life—the thought of death rarely enters your mind. I had no idea how fortunate I was to be where I was, doing what I was doing. Today, I would choose the word blessed rather than fortunate, because today I know that God was involved in every facet of my life. Little did I know that His hand of grace and mercy was directing my ways, despite my ignorance of Him.

There's a good chance that somebody we know has prayed and/or is praying for us. It might be a mom, dad, close friend, or someone we hardly know. It might have been a grandfather or grandmother who prayed for us when we were an infant or even in our mother's womb. Believing in Jesus can be God's answer to their prayers or it can occur in other ways. Each of us is unique and God knows how to touch each of us uniquely with His love.

The good news is that God, in His timeless and eternal wisdom, has a plan. His plan is forgiveness. Forgiveness is a life-changing word. When Jesus taught His disciples to pray, He emphasized forgiveness. Look around. Unforgiveness and bitterness run rampant. People obsessively cling to the most insignificant perceived abuses of their space, from the person that cuts in line at the supermarket, to the driver on the freeway we might meet on our way to work tomorrow. The consequences of unforgiveness can be tragic and we hear about them every day in the news. Unforgiveness will destroy us, whereas forgiveness will build us up. If we are harboring bitterness and unforgiveness, we are hurting ourselves far more than the other person. G. Campbell Morgan, a great man of God and famous Bible commentator said:

"The final proof of greatness is ability to forgive. This is true of God, and therefore must be true of men."

Every day we hear or read about a murder that defies imagination. The impact of these tragedies reaches far beyond the person upon whom the crime was perpetrated. Like a rock thrown into a still pond, the ripple effect reaches waves of family members and friends, causing untold suffering, pain, and often, a life-long bitterness that has generational consequences. Occasionally, rather than embracing the bitterness created by a tragedy like this, the surviving loved one(s) will forgive the murderer and pray for his or her salvation. Only God can inspire a person to do this and I don't think it is an uncommon occurrence, only underreported. But it is up to the murderer to repent and be saved.

Repentance is heartfelt remorse for past sin demonstrated by becoming the opposite of what we were. It is a God-given conviction of wrongdoing leading to a 180° turning from it. In the mid-twentieth century, Oswald Chambers, a renowned Scottish preacher, defined this process in his famous devotional book, *My Utmost for His Highest* (first published in 1935 by Dodd, Mead, & Co., New York, and titled The Golden Book of

Oswald Chambers: *My Utmost for His Highest*):

"The entrance into the kingdom of God is through the sharp, sudden pains of repentance colliding with man's respectable 'goodness.' Then the Holy Spirit, who produces these struggles, begins the formation of the Son of God in the person's life. This new life will reveal itself in conscious repentance followed by unconscious holiness, never the other way around. The foundation of Christianity is repentance. Strictly speaking, a person cannot repent when he chooses—repentance is a gift of God."

When God sent Jesus to become God in the flesh, to suffer and die for all of the sins, of all the people, who would ever believe in Him, He expressed the absolute pinnacle of forgiveness. As Jesus hung on the cross, suffering one of the most painful executions devised by man—and experiencing the full fury of God's wrath for the sins of all who would ever believe in Him—He did not judge the Jews and Romans who placed Him there. On the contrary, He prayed for them because of their ignorance.

"Then Jesus said, 'Father, forgive them, for they do not know what they do.'" – Luke 23:34

God answered His prayer a few weeks later on the Day of Pentecost (the day on which the Holy Spirit descended upon the apostles and disciples, which occurred fifty days after Jesus ascended to heaven following His resurrection), when the Apostle Peter, filled with the Holy Spirit, shared the word of God with the same multitudes and about 3,000 Jews believed and were spiritually reborn. We, too, are the recipients of God's amazing grace, if we will hear and believe His word.

"The Lord is not slack concerning His promise, as some count slackness, but is longsuffering toward us, not willing that any should perish but that all should come to repentance." – 2 Peter 3:9

WAVES OF GRACE

I returned to Monmouth College in the Fall of 1969 for my senior year. One afternoon, in the spring of 1970, shortly before graduation, as I was walking through the student center, I noticed a table had been set up by some visiting representatives of Chapman College (now Chapman University) to promote their World Campus Afloat (WCA) program, now known as Semester at Sea (SAS). I stopped and asked one of the Chapman representatives if they hired Resident Assistants to help monitor the students aboard the ship and he replied affirmatively. I took one of their flyers and decided to consider this opportunity again, after I completed graduate school, because I had been accepted to the Thunderbird Graduate School of International Management, near Phoenix, Arizona, beginning in the Fall of 1970.

6

PHOENIX, ARIZONA

33.4°N, -112.0°W

After graduating from Monmouth, I traveled to Malta for the summer to work for my dad before starting at Thunderbird. In May of 1971, just before graduating from Thunderbird, I reported to the local office of the Selective Service System of the United States government for my draft physical. Up to that point in time, like many draft-age men, I had utilized student deferrals to avoid the draft and the Vietnam War. My chances of avoiding it now were miniscule, because a draft lottery had been established and it was the luck of the draw.

In December of 1969, every day of the year was imprinted on a plastic ball, placed in a container, and randomly selected. My birthday ball was the 23rd selected—a sure ticket to Vietnam if you were physically fit. Although I was probably in the best physical condition of my life, I had seriously injured my lower back playing football during my freshman year of college. The resultant x-rays revealed a congenital spinal deformity. In hindsight, this was one of a series of life experiences with eternal consequences.

In May of 1971, a Selective Service physical involved sitting at a desk in a room with forty or fifty other draft-eligible men and filling out a questionnaire about all aspects of your physical health. The guys around me checked every box they could think of. I checked one box about my back. When we finished, we were instructed to strip to our underwear and form a line in another room with a dozen or so inspection stations. We were then poked, prodded, and questioned by nurses and medical corpsmen.

The last station was manned by a doctor who reviewed the files of the tests we carried with us. I presented the doctor with my file and he solemnly reviewed it. He then stated that I was in perfect health and asked if I had anything else to share about my back. I handed him a letter from my doctor about my spinal deformity. After carefully reading it, he looked up at me and said, "Mr. Swanson, you are permanently disqualified from the Armed Forces of the United States."

Congressman Alexander Pirnie (R-NY)
drawing the first capsule for the Selective Service Draft Lottery –
December 1, 1969 [1]

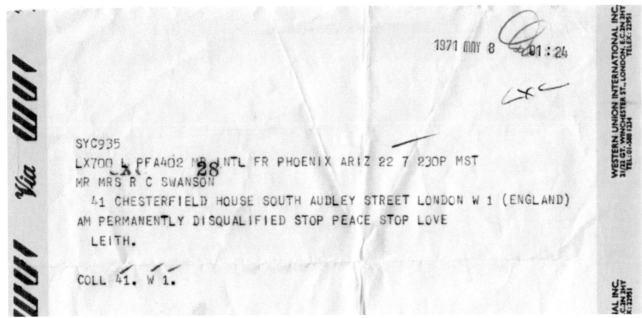

SYC935

LX700 L PFA402 MB NTL FR PHOENIX ARIZ 22 7 230P MST

MR MRS R C SWANSON

 41 CHESTERFIELD HOUSE SOUTH AUDLEY STREET LONDON W 1 (ENGLAND)

AM PERMANENTLY DISQUALIFIED STOP PEACE STOP LOVE

 LEITH.

COLL 41. W 1.

Transatlantic Western Union cable to my mom and dad – May 8, 1971 –
at the time, we didn't have any idea how transformative a moment this was. –
(The word STOP inserted at the end of a sentence in a cable equals a period.) [2]

This created a major turning point in my life because, in April of 1971, I had signed a contract with the Chapman College World Campus Afloat program (WCA) to be their Advance Agent for the Fall Semester 1971 sailing. I had applied to be a resident assistant, but upon reviewing my resume, they asked if I would consider being the Advance Agent for a new program, they were creating in partnership with C.Y. Tung, the Chairman of Orient Overseas Lines—the sixth largest shipping company in the world, headquartered in Hong Kong.

Prior to my employment, Chapman had leased a ship for several years from Holland America Line. However, in 1970, Holland America Line went through a reorganization and withdrew its ship from the program. Tung came to the rescue. He had a passion for international education and bought the *R.M.S. Queen Elizabeth*, sister ship to the *R.M.S. Queen Mary* (now a tourist attraction in Long Beach, California) for several million dollars.

He then towed her from Port Everglades, Florida—where she had sat idle in mothballs as a failed tourist attraction—to Hong Kong, where he completely refurbished her—at a cost of several more millions of dollars and—at minimal cost—agreed to lease her to Chapman College for the WCA program. He renamed her *Seawise University*, a play on his initials, C.Y. At the time, the *Queen Elizabeth* was the largest operational passenger liner in the world, with a capacity of 3,200, including crew, and a draft (the depth from her waterline to the bottom of her hull) of 38 feet.

There were only a handful of harbors throughout the world that could accommodate the Queen dockside due to her deep draft. Because of this, we were going to have to use tenders, otherwise known as ferry boats, to transfer students and staff to shore at almost every port. This would be a logistical nightmare for the in-port programs we had planned, that involved loading and unloading hundreds of students and faculty onto dozens of buses parked by the ship's berth in each port.

R.M.S. Queen Elizabeth – Photo: Roland Godefroy [3]

R.M.S. Queen Elizabeth – The Main Lounge,
featuring a painting of Queen Elizabeth [4]

One of Thunderbird's graduation requirements was fluency in a foreign language and I had selected French. The summer after I graduated, I moved to France to polish my fluency, and while living there, learned that the retrofit of *Seawise University* had been delayed until the Spring Semester 1972. As a result, C.Y. Tung bought another ship out of mothballs in Baltimore, Maryland, the *S.S. Atlantic*, and renamed her the *S.S. Universe Campus*.

Just weeks prior to the fall 1971 departure from Long Beach, California, Tung began a refurbishment process at sea, as the *Universe Campus* sailed down the East Coast from Baltimore through the Panama Canal to Long Beach, where she would take on hundreds of students, faculty, and staff, before departing for Honolulu to circumnavigate the world for the first time.

Little did I realize it at the time—but by God's grace and my family upbringing—He had used my living and traveling abroad to gift me with this amazing job. Had I been inducted into the army; I probably wouldn't be writing this book. More than likely, I'd be dead or wounded, physically or psychologically, or both, as were many I knew who served. Those who survived were heroes, but they were treated like lepers by the 1960s and '70s American counterculture.

Chapman College, World Campus Afloat, *SS Universe Campus* [5]

ANOTHER EVENT THAT OCCURRED DURING this time involved a suicide. When I returned to Southern California from Paris in August of 1971 to begin my contract, I arrived to a WCA program in crisis. Not only were there major concerns about accommodating six hundred students, faculty, and staff, on a ship that was on its way through the Panama Canal, the Dean of the Ship, the person with overall responsibility for the success or failure of the program, and the person who had hired me, committed suicide the week before I arrived.

In addition, for some reason unbeknownst to anyone, he had kept all of the key files dealing with the 10-15 academic programs scheduled and organized for each port of call at his home. Due to certain questionable circumstances surrounding the cause of his death, his home had been impounded by the police. The files were under lock and key and inaccessible to Chapman officials.

Chapman reached out to a retired veteran of the WCA program, Dr. Desmond Bittinger, and contracted with him to replace the Dean. Little did I know this was a divine turn of events, not only would Desmond and I work closely together throughout the world, but in two years he would officiate at my wedding.

Dr. Bittinger and his wife, Irene, were seasoned world travelers. Desmond had received his PhD from the University of Pennsylvania in Anthropology and Sociology. He had been a Church of the Brethren minister, professor at McPherson College, President of McPherson College for fifteen years, and Chancellor of Chapman College. He and Irene had participated in eleven World Campus Afloat voyages.

Dr. Desmond and Irene Bittinger [6]

Desmond and Irene had served as missionaries to Nigeria from 1930-1938 and raised three of their four children there. They ministered to the local tribespeople, translated their spoken language into written word, and then translated their written word into the Bible. They also started a leper colony. Desmond hunted big game to feed their growing family. In 1956, many years after their return to the United States, the state of Kansas named Irene "Mother of the Year".

In August of 1971, Desmond and I met for the first time at the Chapman College campus in Orange, California. At the time, he was what many followers of Jesus might call one of the godliest people on earth and God was about to weave him into my life. God had providentially introduced us to one another and we were tasked with rebuilding a broken program. He was in his late 60s and a survivor of over a dozen surgeries necessitated by the various diseases he had contracted while living in Africa. He was a tough cookie. I was twenty-two years old and looked sixteen.

I'm sure Desmond took one look at me and wondered what he had gotten himself into. Nevertheless, he embraced me with his loving, gentle manner, and together—in the space of a few weeks—we did our best to piece together an around-the-world educational program, without the knowledge and benefit of much of what had previously been planned and organized.

On the night before the ship was scheduled to sail, with a full complement of over six hundred students, faculty and staff safely aboard, Desmond and I sat in his office on the ship with several key Chapman staff and Orient Overseas Lines executives. We were discussing last-minute arrangements when there was a knock on the door. Several United States Coast Guard officers entered and informed us that they were not going to allow the ship to sail due to certain safety concerns about the ship's seaworthiness.

We were able to allay their concerns by explaining how these items would be corrected during the first day at sea, so they gave us the green light to depart as scheduled. Desmond and I became close friends during the next several months of this journey. We worked together to provide the best shipboard experience we could create for the participants. Little did I know it at the time, but God was using Desmond to share the love of Jesus with me. I'm now certain I was a regular subject of Desmond and Irene's prayers.

Wilkinson Hall – Chapman University – Photo: Tracie Hall [7]

75

A BIBLICAL EXAMPLE OF HOW God works—in ways unimaginable to us—occurred during the formation of the early church in Jerusalem. A Jew named Saul was a member of the Sanhedrin—the Jewish Supreme Court responsible for executing civil and criminal jurisdiction in Israel. Saul's Jewish lineage and ancestry were impeccable:

> *"If anyone else thinks he may have confidence in the flesh, I more so: circumcised the eighth day, of the stock of Israel, of the tribe of Benjamin, a Hebrew of the Hebrews; concerning the law, a Pharisee; concerning zeal, persecuting the church; concerning the righteousness which is in the law, blameless." – Philippians 3:4-6*

Saul hated Christians, persecuted them mercilessly, and was complicit in the stoning to death of Stephen, one of the seven deacons of the early church appointed by the apostles. Saul was also one of the most educated Jews of his day. He was a student of Gamaliel—one of the premier teachers of the law in the first century—and was intimately familiar with the Old Testament and the ways of both the Hebrew and Greek Jewish cultures that comprised the nation of Israel. Shortly before he completed a journey down the road from Jerusalem to Damascus—where he had been sent by the Sanhedrin to persecute Christians—God saved him. It seems that—in God's eyes—Saul's upbringing, educational background, temperament, and life experiences, were perfectly suited to spread the gospel throughout the world.

Many years later—during the first of three missionary trips throughout the Roman empire—Saul adopted his Roman name, Paul, and went on to become the greatest evangelist in the history of the world. (An evangelist is a person, like Billy Graham or Greg Laurie, who seeks to convert others to the Christian faith, especially by public preaching. The gift of evangelism is one of the innumerable gifts God bestows upon select believers to share the gospel.)

Towards the end of his life and ministry—shortly after he had been shipwrecked on the island of Malta, while being transported from Caesarea to Rome, as a prisoner to appear before the Roman Emperor, Caesar Nero—Paul was delivered to the captain of the guard in Rome by a centurion, Julius, who had accompanied him on this voyage. At this stage of his imprisonment, Paul was permitted to dwell by himself with the soldier that guarded him. Three days after his arrival in Rome, Paul called the Jewish leaders of Rome to meet with him. At this point in time, we pick up the rest of the story—as related by Luke, Paul's physician—in the last chapter of the book of Acts:

> *"So when they had appointed him a day, many came to him at his lodging, to whom he explained and solemnly testified of the kingdom of God, persuading them concerning Jesus from both the Law of Moses and the Prophets, from morning till evening. And some were persuaded by the things which were spoken, and some disbelieved. So when they did not agree among themselves, they departed after Paul had said one word: 'The Holy Spirit spoke rightly through Isaiah the prophet to our fathers, saying,*

> *"Go to this people and say: 'Hearing you will hear, and shall not understand; and seeing you will see, and not perceive; for the hearts of this people have grown dull. Their ears are hard of hearing, and their eyes they have closed, lest they should see with their eyes and hear with their ears, lest they should understand with their hearts and turn, so that I should heal them.'"*

> *"Therefore let it be known to you that the salvation of God has been sent to the Gentiles, and they will hear it!" And when he had said these words, the Jews departed and had a great dispute among themselves." – Acts 28:23-29*

COSTA MESA TRAVEL

Date	Place	Itinerary
9/6/71	Lv Los Angeles	Western # 610 6:00pm
	Ar Honolulu	8:10pm
9/14/71	Lv Honolulu	American # 71 2:15pm
	Ar Pago Pago	6:30pm
9/22/71	Lv Pago Pago	UTA #591 7:00pm
9/23/71	Ar Aulkand	10:35pm
9/24/71	Lv Aulkand	Air Newzealand # 855 9:00am
	Ar Sydney	10:10am
9/25/71	Lv Sydney	Trans Australia # 1304 7:00am
	Ar Port Morsby	11:45am
10/1/71	Lv Port Morsby	Trans Australia # 1305 1:15pm
	Ar Brisbane	3:50pm
10/2/71	Lv Brisbane	Trans Australia # 522 9:30am
	Ar Darwin	1:30pm
10/6/71	Lv Darwin	BOAC # 807 4:25pm
	Ar Hong Kong	9:15pm
10/7/71	Lv Hong Kong	Cathay # 793 8:30am
	Ar Bali	12:40pm
10/12/71	Lv Bali	Garuda Indonesian # 685 1:25pm
	Ar Singapore	7:00pm
10/17/71	Lv Singapore	Malaysia Singapore # 585 8:45pm
	Ar Colombo	10:15pm
10/23/71	Lv Colombo	Air Ceylon # 321 9:00am
	Ar Bombay	11:05am
10/31/71	Lv Bombay	East African # 871 10:15am
	Ar Nairobi	5:05pm
Open	Lv Nairobi	East African
	Ar Mombasa	
Open	Lv Mombasa	East Afircan
	Ar Nairobi	
Open	Lv Nairobi	East African
	Ar Mombasa	
Open	Lv Mombasa	East African
	Ar Nairobi	
11/13/71	Lv Nairobi	BOAC #029 8:40am
	Ar. Jo-Berg	11:25am
	Lv Jo-Berg	South African # 142 4:00pm
	Ar Lourenco Marques	5:15pm
11/18/71	Lv Lourenco Marques	Deta # 483 4:00pm
	Ar Jo-Berg	4:50pm
	Lv Jo-Berg	South African # 327 7:30pm
	Ar Capetown	9:25pm
11/28/71	Lv Capetown	South African # 326 8:15pm
	Ar Jo-Berg	9:55pm
11/29/71	Lv Jo-Berg	Pan Am # 183 9:30am
	Ar Lagos	3:30pm
11/30/71	Lv Lagos	Waac Nigeria # 963 2:00pm
	Ar Freetown	6:30pm
12/8/71	Lv Freetown	UTA # 842 11:25am
	Ar Paris	6:15pm
12/9/71	Lv Paris	Air France # 2007 10:15am

My flight itinerary – Chapman College "World Campus Afloat" – Fall Semester, 1971 [8]

Some of the postcards sent to my mom and dad –
Fall Semester, 1971 –
(Top) Pago Pago, American Samoa,
(Middle) Bali, Indonesia,
(Bottom) Columbo, Ceylon (Sri Lanka) [9]

WAVES OF GRACE

When the SS Universe Campus sailed the next day, I spent the night at a hotel next to Los Angeles International Airport (LAX), boarded a flight to Hawaii the following day, and met the ship about a week later at the Aloha Tower pier in Honolulu harbor. I then flew on to Pago Pago, American Samoa; Auckland, New Zealand; Sydney, Australia; and Port Moresby, New Guinea. Upon landing in each city, I organized the logistics for the ship's stay; met with foreign officials, dignitaries, and the press; greeted the ship upon arrival; briefed the leadership and students about what was happening in that port; and then scrambled to catch a flight to the next port of call.

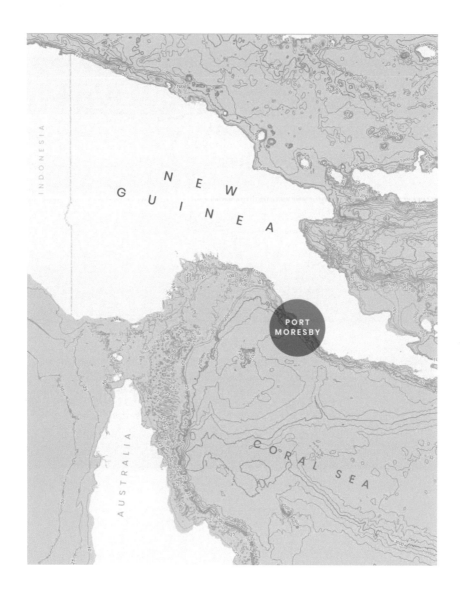

7

PORT MORESBY, NEW GUINEA

-9.4°S, 147.1°E

New Guinea is the second largest island in the world after Greenland, with a current population of about eleven million. In 1971, the eastern half of the island, including the capital, Port Moresby, was an Australian territory named Papua New Guinea and the western half was an Indonesian territory named Irian Jaya.

New Guinea is located in the Pacific Ocean north of Australia, east of Indonesia, south of Japan, and west of the Solomon Islands. It gained global recognition during World War II (WWII) when Japan invaded New Guinea to use it as a springboard for an invasion of Australia. American and Australian armed forces counterattacked, and from 1942-1945, fought one of the most brutal campaigns of WWII.

In the early 1960s, New Guinea was once again placed in the global spotlight when Michael Rockefeller, the fifth child of Nelson Rockefeller and a fourth-generation heir to the Rockefeller fortune, disappeared. A boat he was using to explore the island overturned and he attempted to swim to shore. His body was never found, but many speculated he was taken alive and eaten by tribesmen still practicing cannibalism.

When my flight from Australia landed at Port Moresby Airport in 1971, one of my first items of business was to confirm the arrangements for an anthropology program—Desmond and I had planned and scheduled—that included an overnight stay in the Central Highlands, a range of mountains located to the northeast of Port Moresby.

The town we were scheduled to visit, Mt. Hagen, was located in the Western area of the Central Highlands and was first visited by zoologists and explorers during the 1930s. In 1971, it was known for its coffee plantations and an indigenous population still living a Stone Age existence. This was the first time the World Campus Afloat program had visited New Guinea and I needed to fly to Mt. Hagen to finalize our program arrangements with an Australian patrol officer, otherwise known as a kiap, who was stationed there and would lead our students and faculty on a tour and study of the region.

The day after my arrival in Port Moresby, I boarded a four-seat Cessna 172 and flew up to Mt. Hagen's Kagamuga Airport, located at an elevation of 5,000 feet. When we landed, the Australian patrol officer, Ian, picked me up in his Land Rover and we proceeded to tour the countryside. As we drove along the spectacular mountain range and through lush valleys, it was not unusual to observe native tribesmen walking down the side of the road wearing nothing but a koteka, otherwise known as a penis gourd, that serves as a sheath for their penises. According to the tribesmen, it is not considered a sexual symbol, simply a covering.

Downtown Port Moresby, New Guinea – Photo: M Schlauch [1]

Australian patrol officers (kiaps) working with
indigenous tribesmen – Papua New Guinea [2]

Ian put me up for the night at his home and invited me to accompany him and one of his indigenous workers to visit members of various tribes who had walked in from their villages for a meeting nearby. There are hundreds of social groups or tribes that populate the island of New Guinea; some number in the thousands and some in the hundreds, and each speaks a unique language or dialect.

When we arrived, we entered a one-room thatched roof hut with a firepit in the center and a hole in the roof that allowed smoke from the fire to draft up and out. There were also some bamboo mats spread out on the dirt floor surrounding the fire and those in attendance stood up and welcomed us. We then sat down and joined them in a circle on the mats.

When our discussions began, Ian would turn to me and explain in English the topic he was about to discuss before turning to his indigenous worker and explaining the topic to him in Pidgin English, a cross between the common local dialect and English. Ian's worker would then translate the topic into the dialect of the tribesman Ian was directing his question to. The tribesman would then respond through Ian's worker, repeating the translation process in reverse.

Traditional thatched-roof hut – Papua New Guinea [3]

As we sat and talked like this late into the night, Ian turned to me and shared that he had just learned from one of the tribesmen that he lived next to a tribe that still practiced cannibalism, and Ian invited me to question the tribesman about this subject. One of the questions I asked was why the tribe he lived next to cannibalize their enemies.

When he responded, I was surprised by his answer. He shared that cannibalism was not practiced by the tribe to satisfy a hunger for food, it was practiced as a spiritual ritual. If a noted warrior or tribal leader of a rival tribe was killed in battle, the opposing tribe would cannibalize different parts of his body for certain enviable traits: if he was known for his wisdom and intellect, they ate his brain; for his courage and bravery, they ate his heart; for his skill with a spear, they ate his eyes and the muscles of his throwing arm.

I'll never forget sitting in this small hut, in the Central Highlands, conversing with Ian and these tribesmen around a fire until late at night—and learning about their respective cultures, customs, and lifestyles. Physically, they were thin and short of stature, averaging about five feet tall, but they were wiry and friendly. Each of them was very open and transparent as they answered our questions and openly discussed their everyday problems and concerns. At an early age, I was again privileged to experience the extraordinary diversity of God's creation.

THE NEXT MORNING, AS WE ate breakfast, Ian encouraged me to buy a book written by an Australian patrol officer about their early work in New Guinea. I bought a copy and read a story that occurred in the 1930s in the Western Highlands, when two Australian patrol officers flew their two-seat biplane into a remote jungle clearing in order to convene a peace conference between two warring tribes.

When the patrol officers landed their biplane in the clearing, one stayed behind in a small hut while the other flew on to pick up the first of the two warring chieftains. After he returned with the first chieftain, he took off again to pick up the second one.

In each instance, once he had landed at the respective village and led the chieftain to the biplane, he carefully coached him about how to board the plane and how to put on and take off his seat belt. He also explained how they would fly high in the sky above the jungle, before descending to the treetop canopy to land in a clearing.

After landing to pick up the second chieftain, the patrol officer climbed into the cockpit, took off, flew high over the jungle, dropped down to the treetop jungle canopy, landed in the clearing, taxied to the hut, cut the engine, set the brake, and turned to help the chieftain out of his seat. To his surprise, he wasn't there!

The patrol officer climbed out of the plane, walked over to the hut where his fellow patrol officer was sitting outside with the first chieftain, and asked if they had seen the second chieftain exit the plane. When he learned they had not, they began to discuss what might have happened, when they heard a shout from the edge of the jungle and spotted the missing chieftain—limping along dragging a leg.

As they ran over to help, they noticed one of his arms was contorted in a grotesque way and that he was cut and bleeding all over his face and body. They gently assisted him over to the hut and laid him down to treat his injuries.

When they asked him what had happened, he explained in his dialect that when the plane had descended from high in the sky to the top of the jungle canopy, he thought it was time to unbuckle his seat belt and climb out. When he did, he fell like a rock through the trees and broke his arm and hurt his leg when he hit the ground. He added that he didn't want to fly anymore because the landings were too rough!

IN RETROSPECT

About ten years after my visit to the Western Highlands, Pastor Chuck Smith also had the opportunity to visit the Highlands. While there, he was invited to a tribal feast as the guest of honor and following the feast, he was approached by the tribal chieftain. Chuck shared what happened next in a sermon he preached in the early 1980s about church unity (Smith, Chuck, "Through the Bible", C2000 Series Bible Studies, Audio, Genesis Through Revelation, 1979-1986, Acts 28):

"At the end of the dinner, the chieftain came up to me and he had some spears in one hand; he had a translation of the Bible in his own language in the other hand. And he said, 'Before the white man came and brought us this (holding up his translation of the New Testament), we used to use these (the spears) to kill men. But now that I have this (holding up again his translation of the Bible), I don't need these anymore. I want to give them to you.' And he gave me these spears that they had used in their fights to kill one another, not needing them anymore because they had the Word of God now.

"I tell you; my heart was bonded to that primitive chieftain. We embraced each other, and just cultures apart, yet there was a bond between us. 'For there is neither Jew nor Greek, Barbarian, Scythian, bond or free: but Christ is all, and in all, Colossians 3:11.' There was this bond between us, and my heart was bonded to him as I could feel his heart bonded to me. It was just a beautiful experience. I felt right at home among these people because I realized they're all a part of the family of God.'"

I've had the privilege to hear Pastor Chuck preach on several occasions and shake his hand after the services, but I have never had the opportunity to sit down and talk with him. I look forward to meeting him again in heaven. I don't know the background about how this remote tribe was first touched by God's love or the story of how this tribal chieftain became a follower of Jesus, but the fact that he did, and that he and Chuck bonded together as one in Jesus in the Highlands of New Guinea, is testimony to the universal power of God's word and the diligence of His church to share His word with the world.

> *"And Jesus came and spoke to them, saying, 'All authority has been given to Me in heaven and on earth. Go therefore and make disciples of all the nations, baptizing them in the name of the Father and of the Son and of the Holy Spirit, teaching them to observe all things that I have commanded you; and lo, I am with you always, even to the end of the age. Amen.'" – Matthew 28:18-20*

WAVES OF GRACE

From 1971-1973, the SS Universe Campus frequently visited port cities located along the east, west, and south coasts of the African continent, as she circumnavigated the world with 525 students (from 200 universities and colleges) and a faculty and staff of 75. I fell in love with the indigenous Africans. They walked with a natural but unassuming dignity, and for the most part, were quick to smile and had a great sense of humor. One of our ports of call during the Fall Semester of 1971 was the capital of Mozambique, Lourenço Marques, now renamed Maputo. In 1971, Mozambique was a Portuguese colony located south of Tanzania on the Indian Ocean across the Mozambique Channel from the island of Madagascar.

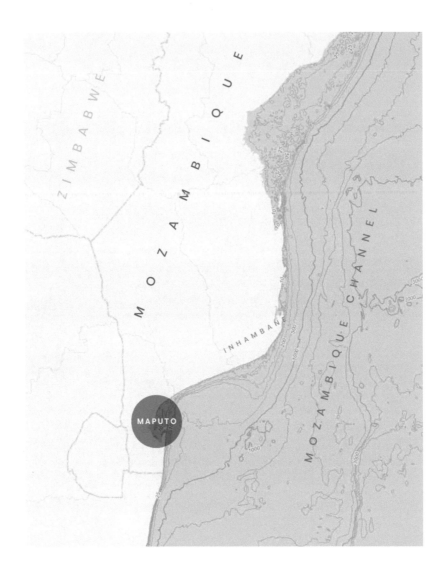

8

LOURENÇO MARQUES (MAPUTO), MOZAMBIQUE
-25.8°S, 32.6°E

The owner of the company that handled the travel arrangements for our in-port programs in Mozambique, Manual Ramoz, was a red-headed Portuguese national with a fun-loving, wild, and adventuresome spirit. On the Sunday before the ship was scheduled to arrive from Mombasa, Kenya, Manual invited me to visit the Maputo Game Reserve, just a ferry ride away from the capital.

As I shared previously, this was not my first experience with African game reserves. In 1969, I had spent several weeks on safari in East Africa (the former British colonies of Kenya, Tanzania, and Uganda). The wild animals in the East African game reserves were familiar with the sounds and smells of the VW buses and Land Rovers, that transported tourists to these protected reserves (vast tracts of land where hunting is prohibited), but I had no idea how unusual my excursion with Manual would be.

Maputo Game Reserve was very different from East African game reserves. In 1971, Mozambique had very little tourism because a guerrilla war against Portuguese rule had been escalating since 1961, eventually resulting in the country's independence in 1975. Due to this war-time environment, only a handful of vehicles entered this vast reserve each year. On the Sunday that Manual picked me up, with a picnic lunch and

an indigenous local armed with an elephant gun, we were the only vehicle to enter the reserve. With Manual at the wheel, we spent the entire day driving through this reserve and never saw another person.

The scenery was spectacular, but the animals were wild and aggressive and so was Manual. My first taste of his fearlessness, the outcome of having been born and raised in Mozambique, occurred shortly after we entered the reserve, when we came across a huge black rhinoceros. As soon as Manual spotted this rhino, he drove up to it and stopped the Land Rover about thirty yards away. I was petrified, and to my surprise, as soon as we stopped, Manual jumped out, left the engine running, took off his shirt, and started shouting and waving his shirt at the rhino. Rhinos are nearsighted, and as Manual shouted and waved his shirt, the rhino turned and started to charge him.

Port of Mombasa, Kenya – Fall Semester 1971 –
Watching the ship arrive from Bombay (Mumbai), India,
prior to sailing to the next port-of-call, Lourenço Marques (Maputo), Mozambique –
From left: Charles Abramidis, Ralli Brothers (shipping agency) Director
and S. Jagani their Mombasa port agent, me, and
CY Tung Owner's Representative for Africa, Jack Williams [1]

Charging Black Rhino – Photo: Bernard Dupont [2]

Manual leaped back into the driver's seat and started to play a game of chicken with this two-ton armored tank. As he accelerated the Land Rover from 5 to 10 to 35 kph (kilometers per hour), the rhino ran alongside us, and every time it dipped its head and its three-foot long horn into the side of the Land Rover to smash us, Manual would gleefully steer away, only to turn back again.

This went on for about a half-kilometer until the animal was exhausted and Manual had had his laughs. I was terrified, visualizing the Land Rover on its side in the middle of nowhere with no way to communicate with the outside world and a giant rhino trying to kill us. Little did I know that this was just a precursor of what was to follow.

As we continued on, Manual drove down into a dry riverbed with embankments that ranged from three to ten feet in height. As we proceeded along, the local riding shotgun pointed out something ahead of us to Manual in Portuguese. Manual turned to me and shared that the gunman had spotted a herd of elephant not yet visible to Manual or myself.

Indigenous Africans, especially those familiar with the bush and game reserves, have amazing eyesight. They can see wild animals in the distance long before we can. Manual handed me a pair of powerful binoculars, and sure enough, I could see a herd of about forty elephants feeding near the tree line of a nearby forest.

As we approached this herd from the riverbed, the gunman shouted, and I noticed through the binoculars that the leader of this herd, a giant bull, had raised his trunk like a periscope, turned it in our direction, and caught our scent. It let out a wild trumpet blast, and before we knew it, led the entire herd on a stampede towards us.

Elephants Charging – Photo: JMx [3]

On a normal road we could have easily outrun them, but we were in a riverbed filled with rocks, ruts, and steep sidewalls, with no way out. When Manual u-turned the Land Rover, we were only able to creep up to 5-15 kph, and the herd quickly began to gain on us.

When the gunman leaned out his window with the elephant gun, and tried to take a bead on the bull as we bounced along, I knew we were in trouble. But just at that moment, we hit a patch of washboard (a flatter, rutted surface) and picked up our speed to about 30 kph. When we finally reached a section of riverbed with a low embankment, Manual raced out onto the African plain and sped away, laughing maniacally at the wheel.

FREETOWN, SIERRA LEONE

8.4 °N, -13.2°W

One of the challenges we faced during the first semester voyage occurred in the West African port of Freetown, Sierra Leone, toward the end of the voyage. Freetown was our second to last port of call before the ship crossed the Atlantic and returned to the United States. Early one morning, as usual, I boarded the ship off the coast of Freetown with the port pilot, health officer, immigration officer, and customs officials. The port pilot assists the ship's captain to guide the ship safely through the harbor to its berth.

After climbing the rope ladder up the side of the ship at sea with the other officials, I sat opposite Desmond at his desk in the Dean's office. As we went over the details of the Freetown visit, we suddenly heard a horrible crunching sound and I was launched from my chair into the front edge of the desk.

The ship's pilot, as it turned out, was also an alcoholic. He was in no condition to guide the ship to its berth and had given the captain erroneous instructions regarding the relationship of the ship's speed to the harbor currents, which resulted in the ship plowing directly into the cement pier and creating a large hole in the bow. Even worse, we discovered shortly thereafter, the pilot also owned the only ship repair facility in Freetown.

By now, having taken the ship around the world and in and out of many third world counties, none of this surprised me. Desmond and the captain of the ship were able to work their way through this challenge, as they had many others, by utilizing the expertise of our shipping agent to negotiate and apply pressure on the ship's pilot and his repair facility to expedite the repair.

The ship completed its circumnavigation of the world with a transatlantic crossing to New York, and I was none the worse for wear. God used Desmond Bittinger to touch my life in many ways throughout this voyage. His selfless faith in God was reflected in his love and kindness to me, to the entire shipboard community, and to all of the dignitaries and indigenous people he interacted with in each port.

Daily life in Freetown, Sierra Leone – West Africa – Photo: UNMEER [4]

IN RETROSPECT

When I completed my first semester as Advance Agent, Chapman asked me to sign a second contract for the Spring Semester of 1972. My first semester had been a trial by fire. The job of Advance Agent involved hundreds of responsibilities in each of the twelve to fourteen ports visited each semester.

The basics included: organizing the in-port programs designed to complement each student's academic curriculum (usually 15-20 programs per port for the students, faculty, and staff); monitoring all the shipping logistical work involved with the arrival and departure of a 20,000 ton, 800-passenger ship (including a Taiwanese crew of 200); and acting as ambassador for the program to the government officials, media, and various dignitaries of each country.

The job sounds exciting and romantic and in many ways it was. It was also physically and mentally taxing. For four months at a time, every few days, I slept in a different bed, in a different country, in a different time zone, used different currency, ate different food, and interacted with different people, who spoke different languages, and possessed different levels of English comprehension. At the time, I had a basic understanding of French, Italian, and German, but transacting business in many African and Asian countries always posed a challenge. I quickly learned that I was better off

sticking to English in business situations, because everyone I worked with had at least a basic familiarity with English and I realized that I was placing myself at a disadvantage trying to utilize my rudimentary language skills in situations that required a level of fluency I didn't possess. So, rather than struggle with my language deficiency I stuck to English, which more often than not provided the leverage I needed to negotiate and achieve what I was trying to accomplish.

Casablanca –
Spring Semester 1972 [5]

Although I didn't have a God-given giftedness to learn and speak different languages fluently, I did have the ability to listen to the level of English comprehension of the person I was interacting with and gauge my vocabulary, and sentence structure, to their level of English comprehension. After several years of traveling around the world doing this, whenever I returned to the United States, I often found myself stumbling to express myself in fluent English, because I had spent so much time speaking broken English with the people I worked with in foreign ports.

Flying around the world to over twenty major international cities in less than four months and landing in a different country every few days is a unique experience. Each time the airplane made its approach and descended in altitude, I was mesmerized by the sight of vast population centers that dotted the earth's surface, each a magnet for millions of people living in close quarters and striving to survive. It's hard to imagine a more eye-opening way to overview the diversity and magnitude of the earth's population.

As an example, when my flight descended into Johannesburg, South Africa, on my way to Cape Town, I was amazed to see a major network of freeways crisscrossing the countryside and skyscrapers lining the horizon. I was expecting to see a metropolis of shanty towns and crumbling colonial buildings, like most of the other major cities I had visited on the African continent. From the air, it looked like we were landing in a modern American city.

I learned later that the freeways were little used. They had been built as a strategic network of runways by the South African government to land military aircraft. Each runway included underground ammunition and fuel depots, thus enabling the military to expeditiously dispatch soldiers by air, at a moment's notice, in the event of an indigenous uprising.

In the early 1970s, apartheid (segregation on grounds of race) was at its peak in South Africa. It was the only country in the world on our itinerary where we were forbidden to hire a private travel company to arrange our in-port programs for the students. Instead, we were required to use the South African Government, Department of Information, to handle all WCA program implementation.

The government wanted our students to see what they wanted to show them and nothing else. In fact, I had to meet with the president of the South African student government association clandestinely, in order to arrange secretive excursions for our students to visit the townships. Until apartheid was outlawed in 1994, townships were segregated suburban areas located on the periphery of towns and cities, that were reserved for Non-Whites (Indians from Asia), Africans (indigenous blacks), and Coloreds (people of mixed-race).

Unbeknownst to me, the South African Secret Service had bugged my hotel room phone, which I had used to communicate with the student government leaders, who were anti-government and anti-Apartheid. Early one morning, I was summoned to the office of the American Ambassador, who had been informed by the Secret Service of my activities. They had directed him to compel me to end my "nefarious" meetings immediately.

However, since turnabout is fair play, I had an idea. In most ports there was always a bevy of dignitaries invited to meet the ship when she docked. In Cape Town, these dignitaries included high ranking officials from the Department of Information, the Mayor of Cape Town, and the distinguished academic and departmental heads of the University of Stellenbosch (with whom we had planned several in-port educational programs).

What these officials and dignitaries did not know, because I hadn't mentioned it, was that the WCA student body president was African American. When the ship docked and the WCA deans, executive staff, and student leaders descended the gangway, these officials and dignitaries stood to attention in their cloaks, gowns, and Sunday best, but they were dumbfounded when I introduced them to the student body president!

ON ANOTHER OCCASION, I HAD to overnight in Lagos, Nigeria, in order to connect to another flight, the next day. At the time of this voyage, my dad's company, IADCO, had a contract to provide charter aircraft for certain American oil companies operating in Nigeria. My dad had traveled to Lagos on several occasions and warned me to be very careful during my stay.

One of the things he mentioned was, that when you disembarked and began your walk from the aircraft to the terminal, a person dressed in the uniform of a customs official would occasionally approach you on the tarmac, request your passport, and walk away with it, promising to return it when you cleared customs.

My dad informed me that this "official" was an imposter. These imposters would bribe their way through airport security, request your passport, and then abscond with it, leaving you stranded. This would be a dire circumstance for me because my passport contained over a dozen visas previously secured for me to enter many of the countries on the ship's itinerary. Sure enough, when my plane landed, as I was walking to the terminal with the other passengers, one of these "officials" approached me and requested my passport. I ignored him.

Once I cleared customs, I was on my guard. In 1971, Lagos was probably one of the most dangerous and filthiest cities I have ever visited. On the drive from the airport to my hotel in downtown Lagos, I noticed a dead man lying on the side of the road. When I returned to the airport

the next morning, he was still there. At the time I thought, "If there is hell on earth, this is it."

Every time my plane landed in a foreign country; I was like an astronaut landing on another planet. I presented my passport and entry card to the passport control officer, cleared customs, and looked for my name on a sign someone was carrying, that had been sent to meet my flight by the travel company we had appointed to handle the ship's in-port program. At that point in time, this person was my only link to otherwise being alone and unknown.

At times I experienced a loneliness I have never felt before or since, despite interacting with dozens of different people in each port. I was somewhere on the planet, out of reach of everyone I was close to, and without the benefit of a smartphone, a laptop, or even a computer to connect with them. My only source of communication with those I knew and loved was a brief written cable or an international telephone call, which involved a service that was often garbled and always prohibitively expensive. Little did I know, that although I was unaware of my Creator and Lord, He was aware of me.

In retrospect, I was probably able to manage my loneliness by sharing my travel experiences through correspondence with family and friends. One of the most important items transported out to the ship in each port, by our shipping agent on the pilot boat, was the mail pouch. I now know that a loving family and close friends are priceless in this temporal world we live in. They are the foundation of mental, physical, and emotional health, especially if we don't know Jesus. I also know, from my study of the Bible, that loneliness is one of the most horrific features of hell (see the following explanation and Chapter 26).

WHAT IS HELL AND WHERE is it? The Bible provides a glimpse of this unseen spiritual reality in terms of the past, present, and future, often comparing believers to unbelievers. Through the Scriptures we learn that what is commonly referred to as hell is actually an intermediate realm of spiritual existence for the unbelieving dead. In the New King James Version (NKJV) of the Bible, Jesus refers to hell, hell fire, and *Hades* (in New Testament Greek), fifteen times in the gospels. Following is my understanding of hell from the Scriptures and several Bible commentaries listed in the Bibliography.

Past – In Old Testament times, the abode of the spirits (or souls) of the dead was known in Hebrew as *Sheol* and was comprised of two compartments located in the lower parts of the earth or, as stated by Jesus in the Gospel of Matthew, in the "heart of the earth". One compartment was for wicked, self-absorbed unbelievers, *Hades*, a place of torment, and one compartment was for God-fearing believers, *Abraham's bosom*, a place of comfort for those who trusted God for a future heavenly reality.

In the Gospel of Luke, Jesus describes these two compartments in a story about a rich man and a beggar:

> *"There was a certain rich man who was clothed in purple and fine linen and fared sumptuously every day. But there was a certain beggar named Lazarus, full of sores, who was laid at his gate, desiring to be fed with the crumbs which fell from the rich man's table. Moreover the dogs came and licked his sores. So it was that the beggar died, and was carried by the angels to Abraham's bosom. The rich man also died and was buried. And being in torments in Hades, he lifted up his eyes and saw Abraham afar off, and Lazarus in his bosom.*
>
> *"Then he cried and said, 'Father Abraham, have mercy on me, and send Lazarus that he may dip the tip of his finger in water and cool my tongue; for I am tormented in this flame.' But Abraham said, 'Son, remember that in your lifetime you received your good things, and likewise Lazarus evil things; but now he is comforted and you are tormented. And besides all this, between us and you there is a great gulf fixed, so that those who want to pass from here to you cannot, nor can those from there pass to us.'*
>
> *"Then he said, 'I beg you therefore, father, that you would send him to my father's house, for I have five brothers, that he may testify to them, lest they also come to this place of torment.' Abraham said to him, they have Moses and the prophets; let them hear them.' And he said, 'No, father Abraham; but if one goes to them from the dead, they will repent.' But he said to him, 'If they do not hear Moses and the prophets, neither will they be persuaded though one rise from the dead.'"* – Luke 16:19-30

Notice several things in this story about *Sheol*, that Jesus shares prior to His death and resurrection:

- The spirits of unbelievers go to a place of conscious torment and intense pain.

- Unbelievers experience no rest or peace.

- Unbelievers are alone in total isolation and without hope.

- The spirits of believers go to a place of conscious comfort.

- Believers are in fellowship with other believers.

- Everyone goes to one of these two specific destinations.

- Death is separation, never extinction.

- People consciously know each other—we do not lose our identities, memories, consciousness, or senses when we die.

- God is not a respecter of persons—in God's eyes there is no difference between a rich man and a poor man.

- Our personal heritage means nothing in the afterlife.

- We take nothing material from this world with us.

- There is no second chance to repent of our sins and receive the free gift of forgiveness and eternal salvation in the afterlife.

- There is no way to pass from *Hades* to *Abraham's bosom* or vice versa.

- Death for an unbeliever means eternal separation from God.

After Jesus was crucified and buried, some Bible scholars believe He descended to the "heart of the earth", emptied *Abraham's bosom*, and ascended to heaven with the believers who dwelt there. Others believe that when these believers died, they went immediately into the presence of God. Only God knows for sure.

Present – In New Testament times when those who believe in Jesus die their spirits immediately pass from earth to heaven. When the rapture of the church occurs—an unknown future moment in time when Jesus returns for His church and all believers, dead and living, join Him in heaven—

they will receive new bodies designed to experience eternal life in heaven. They will then appear before the judgment seat of Christ to receive rewards (crowns) proportionate to their faithful service.

> *"For the Lord Himself will descend from heaven with a shout, with the voice of an archangel, and with the trumpet of God. And the dead in Christ will rise first. Then we who are alive and remain shall be caught up together with them in the clouds to meet the Lord in the air. And thus we shall always be with the Lord. Therefore comfort one another with these words." – 1 Thessalonians 4:16-18*

When unbelievers die their spirits join the spirits of those in *Hades* and remain there until the "great white throne" judgment. (See Chapter 27 for more on the chronology of the rapture of the church and the "great white throne" judgment.)

Future – The "great white throne" judgment is a future and final judgment that occurs at the end of the thousand-year reign of Jesus on earth, when unbelievers are resurrected in bodies designed to experience the "second death" and are cast into the "lake of fire". The "second death" is a spiritual death that occurs when unbelievers are eternally separated from God. The "lake of fire" is a future hell prepared for Satan, his demonic angel host, and all unbelievers. As J. Vernon McGee shared in his five-volume Bible commentary, *Thru the Bible with J. Vernon McGee*, Volume 4, page 321:

"Hell, as we think of it, is a place that has not yet been opened for business."

WAVES OF GRACE

In late December of 1971, following Christmas with family and friends in the United States, I once again began the process of obtaining visas and organizing flight and hotel reservations for another trip around the world beginning in January 1972. This time the ship would sail in the opposite direction, from Port Everglades, Florida, to Long Beach, California. Unbeknownst to me, this sailing would begin to take my life in the opposite direction, from self to hope, from this world to heaven.

9

CASABLANCA, MOROCCO

33.5°N, -7.58°W

I began each semester's circumnavigation of the world by flying from the East Coast of the U.S. to a West African port or from the West Coast of the U.S. to Hawaii, followed by a South Pacific or Asian port. In addition to ports previously mentioned, other ports of call included: Casablanca, Morocco; Dakar, Senegal; Monrovia, Liberia; Luanda, Angola; the Seychelles Islands; Bombay and Madras, India; Colombo, Ceylon; Hong Kong; Penang, Malaysia; Singapore, Bangkok, Thailand; Manila, Philippines; Bali, Indonesia; Taipei, Taiwan; and Kobe, Japan.

Announcing
the Maiden Voyage of SEAWISE
(formerly the R.M.S. Queen Elizabeth)
75-day Circle Pacific Cruise.

Sailing from Los Angeles on April 24, 1972. Rates from $30 a day first class.

Sailing from Vancouver, B.C. on April 18, 1972

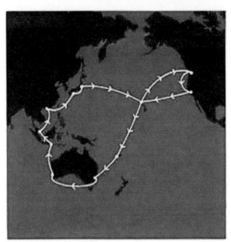

	ARRIVAL DATE	DEPARTURE DATE
Los Angeles		April 24 PM
Honolulu	April 29 AM	May 3 AM
Suva	May 10 AM	May 12 PM
Sydney	May 16 AM	May 18 PM
Fremantle	May 23 AM	May 25 AM
Bali	May 28 noon	May 31 AM
Singapore	June 2 AM	June 5 AM
Hong Kong	June 8 AM	June 11 AM
Kobe	June 14 noon	June 16 PM
Yokohama	June 17 AM	June 20 AM
Honolulu	June 26 noon	June 29 AM
Vancouver	July 4 noon	July 6 PM
Los Angeles	July 9 AM	

Ports of call and dates subject to change without notice.

Advertisement for the maiden voyage of *Seawise University* that was not to be. [1]

As things turned out, the *Seawise University* retrofit continued to experience delays and the maiden voyage was postponed again. After I signed a new contract to be the Advance Agent of the *Universe Campus* for the Spring Semester 1972 voyage, I flew to London in late December 1971 and then on to Zermatt, Switzerland, to spend a few days skiing with a friend, before flying on to Casablanca to meet the ship. While I was in Zermatt, I picked up the *International Herald Tribune* newspaper one morning, looked at the front page, and was startled to see that *Seawise University* had burned and sunk in Hong Kong harbor.

Seawise University burning in Hong Kong Harbor –
January 9, 1972 [2]

Remains of *Seawise University* –
Hong Kong Harbor – 1972 [3]

I learned several months later, from an Orient Overseas Line executive, that at the time of the fire, C.Y. Tung, a Nationalist Chinese, was negotiating with Chiang Kai-shek, the President of Taiwan, to place *Seawise University* in Taiwanese registry (commercial ships that sail to foreign ports are registered with a specific country and fly that country's flag for tax purposes and other reasons).

The leadership of the communist Chinese union construction crews, who were performing the final refurbishment work on the Queen (*Seawise University*), hated the Taiwanese. When they received word of these secret negotiations, they decided to sabotage the ship.

At the time of the fire, the refurbishment work was nearly complete and the ship had passed several sea trials (sailing a newly outfitted ship into the open ocean in order to test its operational integrity). She was almost ready to be recommissioned, when the union crews strategically placed oil and gas cannisters throughout the ship, lit them, and burned her to a black hulk, completely destroying one of the most beautiful ships in the world.

Following the destruction of *Seawise University*, the *Universe Campus* would go on to become the permanent home of the World Campus Afloat/Semester at Sea program. She was the longest-serving ship in the program's history and was retired from service in 1995. The Fall Semester 1971 maiden voyage had a turbulent start, but by the grace of God we were able to introduce a new ship to the program and to the world.

COLOMBO, CEYLON (SRI LANKA)

6.9 °N, -79.8°E

During the second semester voyage, as the *Universe Campus* sailed from Bombay (renamed Mumbai in 1996), India, to Colombo, Ceylon (renamed Sri Lanka in 1972), a revolution occurred on the day my plane was scheduled to arrive. I had no idea that the government had placed a curfew on the entire island from eight at night to six in the morning. When my flight landed, at eleven that night, I was asked by a customs agent if I would like to stay overnight at the airport.

I thought this was an odd request because, as usual, I had already made preparations to be met by a representative of the travel company we had contracted to handle our in-port program arrangements. When I looked around, I could see him through a window holding up a sign with my name on it.

I declined the custom agent's offer, exited the secured arrival area, and was greeted by Bobby Arnolda, President, Darlene's Travel Service. I asked Bobby what was going on and he told me about the revolution, adding that he, along with certain key medical personnel and governmental officials, had a pass that allowed him to drive at night. He then cautioned me that we would need to go through three military checkpoints on our sixty-kilometer drive from the airport to my hotel in Colombo, the capital.

We walked outside into the balmy jungle air, climbed into a monstrous 1960 Chrysler Imperial Crown Convertible, and headed for the first military checkpoint. As we walked to his car, Bobby shared that this was the first revolution a lot of the young soldiers assigned to the checkpoints had experienced. The troops were therefore on edge and highly emotional, calming their anxieties by drinking a home-made alcoholic beverage. But Bobby advised me not to worry.

We proceeded safely through the first checkpoint. Then, about twenty kilometers further down the jungle road, when Bobby slowed the car for the second checkpoint, I watched in terror as two soldiers raised their machine guns and charged our car. Bobby stopped immediately.

1960 Chrysler Imperial Crown Convertible –
Photo: Sicnag [4]

Our windows were down due to the muggy air. One of the soldiers ran to my side of the car and rammed his machine gun through the window, as I dove to the floorboard. Fortunately, the soldier at Bobby's window was slightly less aggressive and Bobby was able to diplomatically talk our way through. He assured them we were not rebels intent on killing them in the middle of the night, but simply a travel agent and a tourist on our way from the airport to Colombo. We proceeded to my hotel without further incident.

The next day, I met with the American ambassador to assess the wisdom of bringing the ship into port with 600 Americans during a revolution. To cancel the visit and readjust our itinerary would create a monumental logistical nightmare. After a long discussion, weighing the pros and cons, we decided to go for it. The ship arrived, the students behaved and observed the curfew without incident, and the ship departed safely.

Indian soldier instructs young Ceylonese soldiers on how to fire a machine gun [5]

IN RETROSPECT

In retrospect, I now see these incidents as several in a series of life experiences where God intervened and rescued me from a violent death. What is important to remember, in all of life's circumstances, is that God is intimately involved with every aspect. This includes the next breath we take, the eyes we are using to read these words, and the brain that enables us to comprehend them. We are not melting from the heat of the sun or spinning off the earth because of a lack of gravity.

The following narrative, based on a true story, provides poignant insight into the depth of love God has for each of us. It was originally written in 1967 by Dennis E. Hensley, *To Sacrifice a Son: An Allegory*, and published in the Michigan Baptist Bulletin. There have been numerous versions circulated since. The following is my abridged interpretation of a version shared on the *Bible Answer Man Broadcast* radio program that aired April 5, 2010:

"During the depression years of the 1920s, John Griffith brought his eight-year-old son, Greg, to work with him. John's job involved operating a drawbridge on the Mississippi River. As the day progressed, John and Greg walked down the ravine below the control house to have lunch. Following lunch, John glanced at his watch, saw that it was 1:07 PM, remembered that the bridge was still raised, and realized that the *Memphis Express* was due to cross the bridge in a few minutes.

"John calmly instructed Greg to stay put and ran back up to the control house. As John looked down from the control house to check the river traffic, he saw to his horror that Greg was trapped in the gears that raised and lowered the bridge. Greg had evidently decided to follow his dad back up the hill, tripped, and fallen into the giant gear box. At that moment, John heard the train whistle. He frantically searched his mind for a solution and immediately realized there wasn't time to save both his son and the four hundred passengers thundering toward the bridge.

Mississippi River drawbridge [6]

"He weighed the lives of the passengers with the life of the son he loved with all his heart and knew there was only one thing to do. And so, burying his face under one arm, he plunged the lever down with the other. The cries of his son being crushed to death were drowned out by the sound of the bridge as it slowly lowered into position. With only seconds to spare, the *Memphis Express* roared out of the trees and across the bridge.

"John lifted his tear-stained face and looked into the windows of the passing train. A businessman was reading the morning paper, a uniformed conductor was glancing at his pocket watch, ladies were sipping their afternoon tea in the dining car, and a small boy was eating a dish of ice cream. Many of the passengers seemed to be engaged in idle conversation or careless laughter. No one looked his way. No one cast a glance at the giant gear box that housed the mangled remains of his hope and dreams.

"In anguish John pounded the glass of the control room and cried out, 'What's the matter with you people? Don't you know? Don't you care? Can't you see I've sacrificed my son for you? What's wrong with you?' And then, as suddenly as it had happened, it was over, and the train disappeared, moving rapidly across the bridge and out over the horizon."

This story only touches the surface of the love God expressed for us, because the crucifixion of Jesus, unlike Greg's death, was not an accident. In the eternal counsels of heaven, before the creation of the universe, God the Father, God the Son, and God the Holy Spirit, foreordained this miraculous moment in history, when Jesus would sacrifice His life for all of the sins, of all who would ever believe in Him, and fulfill at least 332 Old Testament prophecies concerning His life, death, and resurrection—including those prophesied over six hundred years before by the prophet Isaiah:

> *"He is despised and rejected by men, a Man of sorrows and acquainted with grief. And we hid, as it were, our faces from Him; He was despised, and we did not esteem Him. Surely He has borne our griefs and carried our sorrows; Yet we esteemed Him stricken, smitten by God, and afflicted. But He was wounded for our transgressions, He was bruised for our iniquities; the chastisement for our peace was upon Him, and by His stripes we are healed. All we like sheep have gone astray; we have turned, every one, to his own way; and the Lord has laid on Him the iniquity of us all." – Isaiah 53:3-6*

It is impossible for us to begin to comprehend the physical suffering and pain Jesus endured when He shed His blood and freely gave His life for the sins of all who would believe in Him—let alone the spiritual horror of experiencing the full fury of God's wrath. Although He was terribly humiliated and horribly tortured by both Jews and Romans, before He was brutally crucified, His supreme sacrifice was separation from God. Sin always separates man from God, but by believing in God's sacrifice of His only begotten Son, we can be separated unto God by grace through faith.

When Jesus, the One through whom the universe was created and is sustained, was judged by God for the sins of all who would ever believe in Him, His co-existence, fellowship, and Oneness with God the Father was severed, but God raised Him from the dead and He now sits at the right hand of God with all power and authority over heaven and earth.

> *"He is the image of the invisible God, the firstborn over all creation. For by Him all things were created that are in heaven and that are on earth, visible and invisible, whether thrones or dominions or principalities or powers. All things were created through Him and for Him. And He is before all things, and in Him all things consist. And He is the head of the body, the church, who is the beginning, the firstborn from the dead, that in all things He may have the preeminence." – Colossians 1:15-18*

As we consider the suffering and pain Jesus experienced on the cross, we must also consider the suffering and pain God the Father experienced as Jesus hung there. As any parent will share, one of the most difficult experiences a mother or father will know is to watch a son or daughter suffer when they are sick or hurting, but the death of a son or a daughter is beyond the comprehension of anyone who has not experienced it.

God's immeasurable love for us was never more transparent than when He sacrificed His only begotten Son on the cross for our sins. It's inconceivable for us to imagine the horror of having every sin ever committed by saved mankind laid upon Jesus. If we choose to reject God's salvation, we will spend eternity in hell. If we choose to receive His salvation—by repenting of our sins and inviting Him into our hearts as our personal Lord and Savior—we will never be forsaken by God and we will live eternally with Him in heaven. Our choice is not irreversible until we breathe our last breath and pass into eternity, with or without Him.

> *"...I am the way, the truth, and the life. No one comes to the Father except through Me." – John 14:6*

WHAT IS HEAVEN, WHERE IS it, and what is it like? Although a comprehensive answer is far beyond our imagination and comprehension, we can begin by saying it is a place where God dwells with His angelic host and all redeemed believers that have died. The Apostle Paul who once visited heaven referred to it as the "third heaven". In other words, heaven surrounds the entire universe God created; a universe that He will dissolve with fire and recreate at the end of the millennium.

> *"Now I saw a new heaven and a new earth, for the first heaven and the first earth had passed away. Also there was no more sea." – Revelation 21:1*

What will heaven be like? First of all, consider the fact that when a believer is saved, he or she is a new creation. God sees all believers as He sees Jesus—perfectly holy and righteous, spiritually, in Jesus. Although we are still alive in earthly bodies at war with our new spiritual nature, we are the temple of God (Father, Son, and Holy Spirit) and we are being sanctified into the image of Jesus. When we die, we will instantaneously enter heaven glorified in perfect spiritual holiness and righteousness. Then, when the rapture occurs—prior to His second coming and the millennium—our physical bodies will be resurrected in perfection and eternally joined to our perfected spiritual being. How? Only God knows.

> *"For this we say to you by the word of the Lord, that we who are alive and remain until the coming of the Lord will by no means precede those who are asleep. For the Lord Himself will descend from heaven with a shout, with the voice of an archangel, and with the trumpet of God. And the dead in Christ will rise first. Then we who are alive and remain shall be caught up together with them in the clouds to meet the Lord in the air. And thus we shall always be with the Lord." – 1 Thessalonians 4:15-17*

Every believer, in a predetermined moment of time, will live eternally in a glorified and incorruptible body in heaven—similar to the body of Jesus after His resurrection. We will be as recognizable individually in heaven as He was on earth and we will be able to fly through heaven as He did when He ascended into heaven. Although our finite human minds are incapable of even beginning to imagine the wonders of heaven, I believe the crowning glory of our heavenly life will be the unending joy of worshipping God forever—and communing with Him in perfect fellowship with every other believer and God's angelic host.

WAVES OF GRACE

As I look back now, over fifty years later, I realize that Bobby Arnolda and I could have just as easily been shot to death as survived our encounter with the drunken soldiers in Ceylon.

Over and over and over again, I can recount memories, some good, some bad, where I know God rescued me. God is good all the time and He was about to show me how good in the middle of the Pacific Ocean.

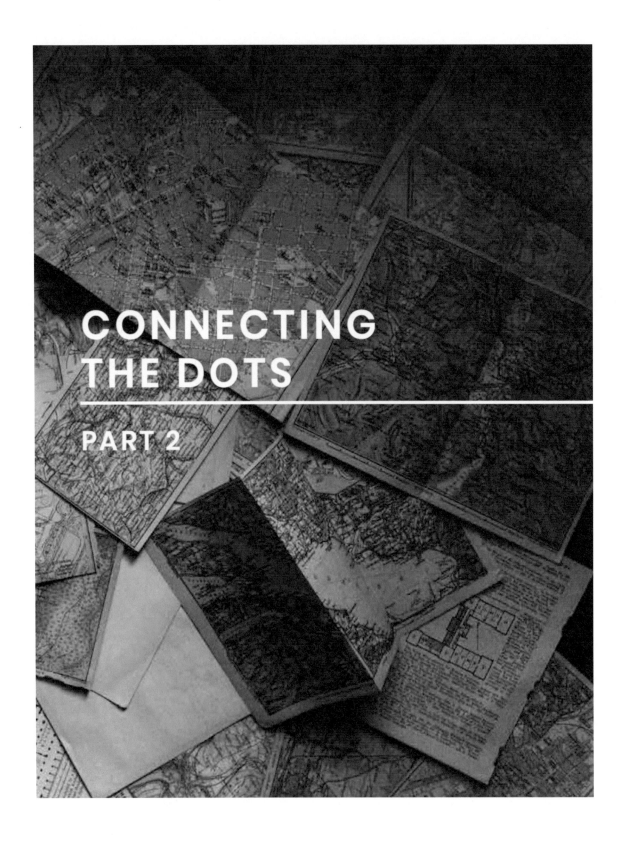

CONNECTING THE DOTS

PART 2

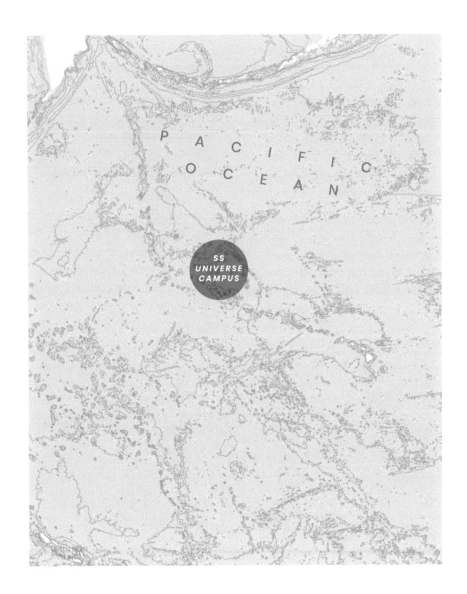

10

THE PACIFIC OCEAN

28.2 °N, -177.3°E

The final port of my second semester circumnavigation was Kobe, Japan. My contract always expired with the last foreign port and I could either cruise back to California on the ship or catch a commercial flight home to Los Angeles (LAX) and Laguna Beach. I was exhausted and anxious to get home, but decided to rest up and cross the Pacific aboard the ship.

Little did I know that this would be one of the most important decisions I would make in my life. Even though I didn't believe in God, at this stage in my life, I now realize He loved me and was orchestrating the circumstances of my life beyond anything I could ask, think, or imagine.

One morning, about halfway across the Pacific, I woke up and headed down to the student cafeteria to grab a cup of coffee. As I reached for the coffee pot, a hand intercepted mine, and a very attractive coed, Judy De Jager, offered to pour me a cup and introduced herself.

It turned out that one of my good friends from graduate school knew Judy growing up. When my friend learned that Judy had been accepted by Chapman for the spring 1972 voyage, he suggested she look me up.

Although Judy bided her time introducing herself, I think it was love at first sight for both of us. We spent time getting to know one another over the remaining days crossing the Pacific, and when the ship arrived, we enjoyed our first date on the outdoor patio of Chuck's Steakhouse, at Waikiki's Outrigger Hotel, overlooking the beach.

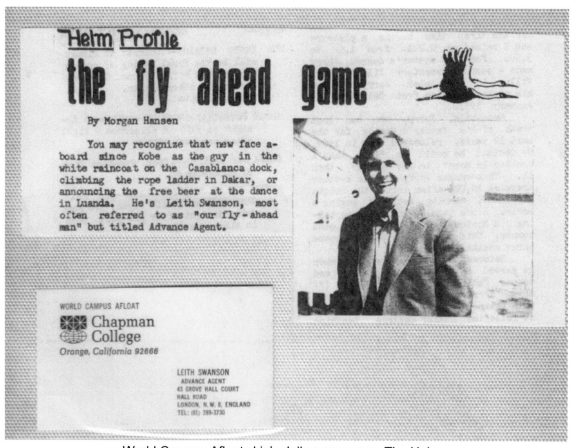

World Campus Afloat ship's daily newspaper, *The Helm* – Spring Semester – 1972 [1]

Judy – May 1972 – a few days after we met at sea –
SS Universe Campus approaching Hawaii [2]

I then flew back to Southern California and we reconnected a few weeks later at a World Campus Afloat alumni party near Chapman College. We dated that summer, each taking turns driving from our respective homes in Chino and Laguna Beach to spend time together.

Judy was a follower of Jesus and assumed I was too, because our family attended church. Unfortunately, I was not. As previously mentioned, church for our family was basically a religious ritual that consisted of a Sunday morning service followed by business-as-usual Monday through Saturday, not a 24/7 personal relationship with God. Jesus' presence in Judy's life, and her faithful love for me, would ultimately lead to my salvation fifteen years later! By the grace of God, Judy saw something in me that empowered her to share her life with a lost soul.

> *"Wives, likewise, be submissive to your own husbands, that even if some do not obey the word, they, without a word, may be won by the conduct of their wives, when they observe your chaste conduct accompanied by fear." – 1 Peter 3:1-2*

We became inseparable, and one summer evening, I asked her to marry me. To my delight, she readily accepted. When my parents heard the news, they flew from London to meet her for the first time. Upon their arrival, they invited us to meet them at one of the nicest restaurants in Laguna Beach for dinner. It was love at first sight for them as well, but my dad couldn't resist an opportunity to reveal his sense of humor.

When the waiter arrived to take our order, my dad and I both ordered escargot, one of our favorites. Other than her World Campus Afloat experience, Judy had never traveled abroad; she had led a fairly sheltered life. When she asked my dad what escargot was, he replied they were snails. He then added, to Judy's amazement, that when they were served you had to keep an eye on them, so they wouldn't crawl off your plate. Judy was shy and trusting and believed every word!

Engaged – Fall of 1972 [3]

Late that summer, I began working on a consulting basis for a helicopter manufacturing company in Phoenix, Arizona (see Chapter 16). I drove back and forth, from Phoenix to Chino, to see Judy most weekends, and in the meantime, I was asked to sign another contract with Chapman for the 1973 Spring Semester voyage. I agreed to do so, with the stipulation that they also provide a job for Judy. Chapman obliged and Judy became the publications secretary for the ship's daily newspaper, *The Helm*.

Left to right: my dad and mom,
and Judy's mom and dad [4]

We were married in Chino, in November of 1972 by Desmond Bittinger, spent our honeymoon at the Mark Hopkins Hotel in San Francisco, lived a few weeks in Phoenix, and then flew to London on helicopter business and to spend Christmas with my family.

After celebrating our first New Year's Eve together in London, we returned to Chino to spend a few days with Judy's family, before I flew to Casablanca, the first port of call for the spring semester. The day after I flew to Casablanca, Judy flew to Port Everglades, Florida, to join the ship for the transatlantic crossing. We rendezvoused about a ten days later in Casablanca.

Early in the morning on the day of the ship's scheduled arrival to each port, I would board the pilot boat, a small seaworthy vessel that transports the port pilot, customs officials, public health officer, immigration officers, and shipping agents, to meet the ship, usually several miles out to sea.

The ship's crew would hang a rope ladder down the port side of the ship from a small door. The various port officials, pilot, and I would then climb up the rope ladder to this open door. In bad weather or stormy seas, climbing the rope ladder up the side of an 800-passenger, 20,000-ton ship was a dangerous undertaking.

The jump from the pilot boat to the rope ladder had to be timed to match both the roll of the ship and the roll of the pilot boat in open-ocean swells. A miss-judged jump could mean serious injury or death, as you could get smashed between the two vessels or swept underneath one or the other.

Judy would always be at the entry door to greet me, because she had checked with the ship's Captain the night before to determine the time the pilot boat was scheduled to arrive. After I briefed the Dean of the Ship, on a variety of matters pertinent to a specific port of call, I would occasionally be asked to speak to an assembly of students and faculty, particularly when there was a political situation in the country we were visiting, that warranted it.

Usually in each port of call, Judy and I would enjoy a few days to ourselves before I boarded a flight for the next port. We basically had a four-month extended honeymoon, because the various executives of the travel companies whom I had worked with and befriended, rolled out the red carpet to celebrate our marriage. They often arranged a beautiful hotel room, a car and driver, and dinner at first-class restaurants!

Pilot boarding a ship at sea prior to entering a harbor –
Photo: Danny Cornelissen [5]

IN RETROSPECT

Looking back at the moment Judy approached me on the ship, I'm in wonder at God's amazing grace and divine orchestration of our lives. After He had transplanted me from country to country during my formative years, I ended up attending graduate school in Glendale, Arizona. At that point in time, in my mind's eye, I was there to earn a degree in international business and find a job. In God's eternal kingdom, I was there to meet another Thunderbird student, Arlen, whose Dutch family lived near Judy's family growing up.

Judy was raised in the community of Bellflower, California, a suburb of Los Angeles. In the 1950s and '60s, Bellflower was primarily a community of Dutch immigrants who owned and operated dairy farms. They attended the same churches, their children attended the same Christian schools, they usually married within the local Dutch population, and fathers passed along their dairy farms to their sons from generation to generation. Judy's mom and dad exemplified faithfulness to God, family, and country.

Judy's upbringing was about as different from mine as different can be, but for some reason known only to God, Judy had an interest in seeing the world and applied to attend the 1972 Spring Semester of the Chapman College World Campus Afloat program. When she was accepted and Arlen heard about it, he encouraged Judy to look me up. In retrospect, if I hadn't been on a ship in the middle of the Pacific Ocean, if Judy hadn't grown up in Bellflower, and if Arlen and I hadn't become friends, Judy and I might not have met.

Our story is only one story among innumerable millions, that testifies to God's amazing grace and divine orchestration of our lives. It is a testimony to the truth that God's ways are not our ways—they are much higher than our ways and they are always perfect. God is love and He will always do everything possible to demonstrate His love to everyone on earth, because He wants everyone on earth to know that He loves them despite any circumstances in which they might find themselves.

Laguna Beach, California – Summer of 1972 –
Photo: Vince Streano [7]

WAVES OF GRACE

As you will read in subsequent chapters, fifteen years later, after God blessed me with the seed of faith to invite Jesus into my heart as my personal Lord and Savior, He also blessed Judy and me with the birth of a child, the most wonderful gift in the world.

11

LAGUNA BEACH, CALIFORNIA

33.5 °N, -117.7°W

The early years of our marriage were characterized by my search to reconcile married life and its attendant responsibilities, with a former lifestyle punctuated by international travel and an independence that was self-centered. My life up to the point of our marriage had been one of constant travel, change, and plans centered on what I wanted to do, when I wanted to do it. The reality of settling down and finding an eight-to-five job, to support Judy, hit me like a ton of bricks.

After completing my last contract with Chapman, in the late spring of 1973, we moved to Walnut Creek in the San Francisco Bay Area. I found a job recruiting engineers for one of the largest global engineering companies in the world, Bechtel Corporation, headquartered in San Francisco, and hated it. I felt compressed and stunted by the corporate bureaucracy, and I dreaded the long commute from our home in Walnut Creek to the *City* and back. I wasn't prepared mentally for the changes I was experiencing and fell into a deep depression.

My dad suggested I visit my childhood pastor from Danville. I called his office, arranged an appointment, and he suggested I read the Bible. I returned home and randomly opened Judy's Bible to a passage I no longer remember. Reading that passage helped pull me through this depression, although I continued to struggle with periodic depressive episodes, until I invited Jesus into my heart many years later and began to read God's word with spiritual discernment (see Chapter 17).

> *"… the natural man does not receive the things of the Spirit of God, for they are foolishness to him; nor can he know them, because they are spiritually discerned." – 1 Corinthians 2:14*

After working for Bechtel for a couple of years, I eventually quit, obtained my California real estate sales and brokers licenses, and decided to try my hand at residential real estate.

Just as I began to pursue this new career, Judy's dad, Garry, had his Cessna 210 aircraft stolen. At this time, Garry had a very successful hay brokering business, Dairyland Hay Company, and he used this aircraft to fly his dairy farm customers from Chino to the hayfields of the Imperial Valley and elsewhere to inspect hay.

Garry was a mechanical genius and set his mind on inventing a device to prevent his Cessna from ever being stolen again. In 1975, he successfully patented his Wheelock anti-theft locking device and asked Judy and me to move back down to Southern California to help him market it. The opportunity to move back to Southern California enticed us enough to pack our bags and return to Laguna Beach, the seaside community where we had courted during the summer of 1972 before we were married.

In addition to our day jobs, we managed a small apartment complex, located directly across the Pacific Coast Highway from Laguna's Main Beach, in exchange for living at a reduced rent in the penthouse apartment. Our bedroom window looked out over the ocean, and when I began to appreciate the ocean was my backyard, I began bodysurfing with fins and loved it. Our bed was too low to look out over the window sill without getting up, so I built a bed out of 4x4 and 6x6 wooden structural posts and lag bolts, that was twice as high as a normal size bed, in order to roll over in the morning and check the surf.

Main Beach – Laguna Beach, California – Photo: SunflowerMomma [1]

At daybreak, one summer morning in 1976, I woke up and witnessed a hurricane-generated south swell slamming the coast off Laguna's Main Beach. I grabbed my fins and entered the ocean a few minutes later. The wave faces were 8-10 feet, the current was sweeping north, and there was no one else out. This was my first taste of the great power and energy God can create in the ocean. I was addicted. I fell in love with the rhythm of the ocean and its moods. The tidal swings, the beauty of a breaking wave, and the challenge of becoming one with the wave's energy, all served to draw me to a life-long embrace of ocean sports.

FOR THOSE UNFAMILIAR WITH HOW ocean waves form, an explanation is in order without getting too technical. When storm events like hurricanes occur in the open ocean, they generate powerful winds that create friction on the ocean's surface. This friction results in deep ocean waves, often barely discernible on the ocean's surface, due to the deep depth of the ocean at the point of origination. Such storm-driven waves travel distances ranging from hundreds to thousands of miles in sets or intervals, that consist of one or more waves per set, before terminating at a shallow beach break or some other coastal land formation.

Surfers refer to the arrival of waves as a swell, and depending on the size and force of the swell, it can last a morning, an afternoon, a day, or several days. There are also various complex factors that determine the power, height, and shape of waves that arrive from a swell, with two of the most important being the depth and topography of the ocean floor where the swell terminates.

An excellent example of the forces at play in the creation and termination of an ocean swell is what occurs at a reef break called the *Banzai Pipeline*, or simply Pipeline or Pipe. Pipeline is located on the North Shore of the Hawaiian island of Oahu. During winter swells the waves formed at Pipeline are considered by many to be the best surfing waves on the planet. They are renowned for their huge, hollow, and thick barrel shape.

Hurricane Linda – September 1997 – Tracking up the coast of Mexico and generating powerful waves along the coasts of Mexico, the Baja Peninsula, and Southern California [2]

Barreling Wave – Photo: peterjamesanthony [3]

Pipeline is famous for possessing some of the most dangerous waves on the planet because of the unforgiving maze of nearshore reef formations, that can permanently cripple or kill surfers who wipe out or fall from their board. There is also a sandy ocean floor weaving through these reef formations that is constantly being reshaped by shifting ocean currents and seasonal weather patterns. Picture Oahu as a mountain peak sticking out of the middle of the Pacific Ocean. As a wave arrives at Pipeline, the energy of the wave suddenly transitions from the deep ocean to the shallow sea bottom, where it grows in height and is shaped by the reef and sandy bottom into a grinding barrel.

The waves at Pipeline are also shaped by many other constantly changing variables, including the direction of the swell and the wind, and tides that swing from high to low twice daily. When Pipeline is firing, only professional surfers and talented locals familiar with the interplay of all of these factors have the skill to surf it and survive. In December of 1998, I had the opportunity to attend the Pipeline Masters surfing championship, the premier event of professional surfing's annual World Tour. It is an event comparable to what the Masters is to golf or the Tour de France is to bicycling.

During the preliminary elimination heats, as 10- to 15-foot waves broke or closed out close to shore, the force and power of their impact would actually shake the beach like a small earthquake. (10- to 15-foot Hawaiian waves equate to 15- to 20-foot waves in other areas of the world, because Hawaiians measure the height from the back of the wave, rather than from the front.)

A closeout occurs when a wave folds over itself, all at once, from end to end. When that happens, a surfer caught in the closeout cannot ride the wave any further because it does not offer a non-vertical face that can be ridden. If the bottom over which the wave closes out is a shallow reef formation, it can be life-threatening, because the force of the closed-out wave typically forces the surfer uncontrollably down to the bottom.

THE OCEAN, LIKE LIFE, IS everchanging. It can be as calm as a pond one moment or as horrifically violent as a hurricane the next. It is always a reflection of the forces of the universe that God holds in His hands. If you love ocean sports, or simply delight in the beauty of an ocean sunrise or sunset, you have been touched by the power and majesty of His creation.

"The earth is the Lord's, and all its fullness, the world and those who dwell therein. For He has founded it upon the seas, and established it upon the waters." – Psalm 24:1-2

According to the ESA (European Space Agency), in the NGC 2775 image above: "Millions of bright, young, blue stars shine in complex, feather-like spiral arms, interlaced with dark lanes of dust. Complexes of these hot, blue stars are thought to trigger star formation in nearby gas clouds and the overall feather-like spiral patterns of the arms are then formed by shearing of the gas clouds as the galaxy rotates."

According to God:

"'To whom then will you liken Me, or to whom shall I be equal?' says the Holy One. Lift up your eyes on high, and see who has created these things, who brings out their host by number; He calls them all by name, by the greatness of His might and the strength of His power; not one is missing." – Isaiah 40:25-26

NGC 2775 – A spiral galaxy located 67 million light-years away in the constellation of Cancer
Image: ESA/Hubble & NASA, J. Lee and the PHANGS-HST Team;
Acknowledgment: Judy Schmidt (Geckzilla) [4]

Bodysurfing with fins, like board surfing, requires positioning yourself to ride a wave right or left and precisely timing when you will connect with the wave. Bodysurfers, with fins, will use the power of their kick, the rotation of their body, and the stretching out of an arm, to conform to the face of the wave and surf it.

Bodysurfing skillfully, with fins, necessitates a deep knowledge of and respect for the ocean. Two champion caliber bodysurfers, and all-round watermen, are Mike Stewart and Mark Cunningham. They can catch, bodysurf, and exit a wave of almost any size effortlessly and with style. Their grace, agility, and fearlessness stand on par with professional athletes of any sport.

Bodysurfing with family is the best!
Powerhouse Park, Del Mar, California –
July 1994 – Session with nephews:
Little Leith (left) and Brandon (right) [5]

Surfing is a passion. Once you have achieved the ability to connect to the power of a wave, it is addictive. It often dictates the rhythm of your life. Tidal swings, cycles of the moon, weather forecasts, swell direction, and a myriad of other variables will frequently determine when and where you surf that day. Surfing encompasses board surfing, stand-up paddle surfing, boogie boarding, bodysurfing, kite surfing, wind surfing, and many other variations of wave or ocean connections.

Like a spectacular sunrise or sunset, surfing comprises moments of intense and fleeting connections with the energy of God's universe that totally engulf your senses. Likewise, if we know Jesus, there are moments when God's presence will so deeply touch us that we know we have tasted heaven.

God's love for us is all-encompassing. One of the ways He derives gratification is watching us enjoy His creation. He designed us with five senses to fully absorb and relish the beauty of His imaginative majesty, which constitutes an act of worship and thanksgiving—if we believe in Him.

When asked what surfing meant to him, Aaron Gold, a follower of Jesus and professional big wave surfer, who holds the Guinness Book of World Records for paddling into and surfing a 63-foot wave, shared:

"As soon as I hit the water, that's like my sanctuary where I go for my quiet time. That's where I'm most comfortable. All the things in your life just kind of fade away because you're forced to be in that moment."

Aaron Gold – Guinness World Record paddle-in 63-foot wave – January 15, 2016 – Jaws, Peahi, Maui, Hawaii – Photo: Erik Aeder [6]

God has not only created every unique wave throughout history, He has created billions of human beings, each unique and each uniquely loved by Him. Each of us is as precious to God as anyone who has ever walked the face of this planet. He knows and loves each of us personally and intimately. He has also gifted each of us in special ways to enjoy Him and His creation.

We often grasp for the fleeting happiness of this temporal world by seeking fame, fortune, and self-gratification. This type of happiness comes and goes depending on our state of mind, because it is an emotional condition predicated on pleasurable outward circumstances. True happiness is the eternal joy of God's presence that resides deep in the hearts of those who believe in Jesus and follow Him—it never changes.

> *"Jesus Christ is the same*
> *yesterday, today, and forever." –*
> *Hebrews 13:8*

In the film *Chariots of Fire*, Olympic runner Eric Liddell says:

"I believe God made me for a purpose, but he also made me fast, and when I run, I feel God's pleasure."

After winning the gold medal in the 1924 Paris Olympics, men's 400 meters, Eric Liddell, who was born in China to Scottish missionary parents, returned to China as a missionary teacher from 1925-1945. In 1932, he became an ordained minister and in 1934 married Florence Mackenzie of Canadian missionary parentage. They had three daughters—the last of whom Eric would never see.

In 1941, when life in China became extremely dangerous due to the Japanese invasion, Florence, who was pregnant, returned to Canada with their children. In 1943, Eric, along with many other expatriates, including members of the China Inland Mission, was interned in a Japanese concentration camp. He became a leader and organizer of the camp and—through His selfless commitment to God and others—became an inspiration to all who suffered there.

In 1945, he was diagnosed with an inoperable brain tumor and died five months before liberation. The entire camp was stunned by his death and deeply missed his presence. According to a fellow missionary, Liddell's last words were, "It's complete surrender", in reference to his walk with Jesus. He was buried in a garden behind the Japanese officers' quarters—his grave marked by a small wooden cross.

> *"Do you not know that those who run in a race all run, but one receives the prize? Run in such a way that you may obtain it. And everyone who competes for the prize is temperate in all things. Now they do it to obtain a perishable crown, but we for an imperishable crown." – 1 Corinthians 9:24-25*

"The Story of Eric Liddell" – inspiration for the film
"Chariots of Fire" – [7]

WAVES OF GRACE

In the Fall of 1978, I accepted a job designing international education programs for United States International University (USIU) in San Diego, California. Judy and I moved from Laguna Beach to San Diego and needed to find a place to live. At the same time, some close friends, Jerry and Gail Rice, both accomplished sailors, asked us if we would consider cruising around the world with them. Little did we realize it at the time, but their question precipitated a complete change in lifestyle.

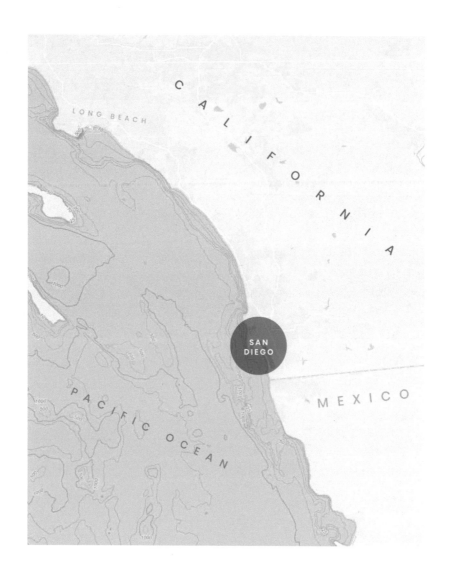

12

SAN DIEGO, CALIFORNIA

32.7°N, -117.2°W

Neither Judy nor I had ever sailed before, so we decided to buy a sailboat and live aboard in the San Diego port community of Point Loma, which would solve our housing issue and help us decide if we should accept Jerry and Gail's offer. We wandered into a yacht brokerage on Shelter Island and met a broker named Bob Welles.

Shortly thereafter, we learned that Bob was probably the most accomplished sailor in San Diego at that time. He was a trust fund baby and had inherited a substantial amount of money at a very young age. In the early 1960s, Bob, his wife Sylvia, and their four young sons, moved to Auckland, New Zealand, where they custom-built a 57-foot ketch, the *Sylvia*, to sail around the world.

When we met Bob, he and Sylvia had just returned to San Diego after cruising 50,000 miles. Their boys were grown, they were nearly out of money, and Bob was in bad shape physically. He had just taken a job brokering sailboats when we randomly walked into the yacht brokerage office where he was working.

Bob found us a 1962 mahogany stripped-planked Lapworth 40 with a 13-foot beam (40-feet long and 13-feet in the middle from side to side), the *Seven Seas*, which was one of the last of the wooden Transpac (Transpacific Yacht Race) racing boats. The *Seven Seas* had a full keel and beautiful lines. In layman's terms, a full keeled sailboat features a keel that runs much of the length of the hull, below the waterline, as opposed to a fin keel, which is much smaller and centrally placed between the bow and stern.

Living on the *Seven Seas* meant that Judy and I each possessed about three changes of clothes, no telephone, no refrigeration, and no running water. We snuck up to the hotel next to our marina each night to rifle ice cubes from the ice maker for our cooler and Judy used a foot pump by our sink to draw cold water from the boat's tank to wash the dishes.

Seven Seas – full keel [1]

Repairing our dingy – Fall 1978 –
Harbor Island Marina, San Diego, California [2]

Seven Seas interior [3]

Along with Bob and Sally (Sylvia's nickname), we participated in the "Beer Cans" every Wednesday evening in the summer—sailing San Diego Bay, drinking beer, and taking turns bombarding other sailboats with water balloons. Bob and Sally taught us to sail, and we sailed the *Seven Seas* on our own for the first time on Thanksgiving Day 1978.

SOUTHWEST OF MECCA, SAUDI ARABIA ON THE RED SEA

21.3 °N, 39.8°E

My first assignment for USIU was to tour Europe and the Middle East to assess international education opportunities. One of my friends from college, Dan Thompson, a consummate adventurer, was living and working in Saudi Arabia at the time and invited me to stay with him at his villa in Riyadh, the capital, during this trip.

One weekend, Dan organized a dive trip for me and another American expatriate, Ken, who was also living and working in Saudi Arabia. The three of us and Dan's wife, Sandy, flew from Riyadh, located in central Saudi Arabia, to Jeddah, a port city located on the Red Sea. We rented a car at the airport, picked up scuba gear from Dan's storage unit, shopped for supplies, and drove about 150 kilometers south and west of Jeddah, skirting Mecca along the way.

We drove the last 30 kilometers to the Red Sea through an unmarked sandy wilderness, dug the rental car out of the sand several times when we got stuck, and ended up on a totally isolated beach completely on our own. At the time, you could not travel to Saudi Arabia as a tourist; you had to be formally invited by a Saudi Arabian sponsor. We camped on a beach next to what looked like an underwater aquarium, that would be the envy of any scuba or freediver in the world (freediving is diving with only a mask, snorkel, fins, and a deep breath of air).

On our second night there, at midnight under a full moon, Dan, Ken, and I entered the Red Sea on a freediving expedition to hunt lobster. We had scuba dove this area for two days and had used up our compressed air. We had also experienced the exhilaration of exploring three amazing reef formations, that paralleled each other from the beach out to sea, each separated by stretches of pure white sandy bottom. The western edge of the third reef dropped off hundreds of feet into deep blue oblivion.

The three of us swam in formation close to the sandy bottom at depths varying from twenty to thirty feet. We aimed and angled our respective dive lights upwards toward the surface, where they converged under the night sky and refracted down, illuminating the ocean floor in front of us. As we headed over the sandy patch on our way to the first reef, we developed a rhythm of surfacing together for a breath and then diving down again in unison.

The reefs teemed with brilliant coral and sea life, including large tiger sharks. Viz (visibility) during our day dives was typically a couple hundred feet. We were headed for the third reef, where Dan had noticed a lot of lobsters tucked away that liked to crawl around at night.

Red Sea coral and marine life – Photo: (Vlad61) [4]

Suddenly, the entire sandy bottom in front of us began to undulate, as a beautiful manta ray with a twenty-foot wingspan, disturbed by our dive lights, slowly began to rise from the bottom, shedding the cloak of sand it had burrowed itself into. We were mesmerized, as it gracefully lifted offand began to sail out in front of us like a stealth bomber.

Little did any of us know that God would orchestrate the three of us meeting again, several years later, when Dan, his brother Keith, Ken, and I, all collaborated to launch a helicopter manufacturing company.

Tiger Shark – Photo: (N. Hammerschlag) [5]

Underside of a Manta Ray [6]

128

SAN DIEGO, CALIFORNIA

32.7 °N, -117.2°W

Once we learned to sail, Jerry and Gail, our friends that had invited us to sail with them around the world, visited us from Eugene, Oregon, and we introduced them to Bob and Sally, who in turn invited us for a summer afternoon sail aboard the *Sylvia*. Early in the evening, following a fun afternoon off the coast of Point Loma, we began to enter San Diego harbor.

Bob was at the helm (wheel), and after lighting a cigarette, turned to Sally with a mischievous grin, and asked her to take it from him. He then turned to the rest of us and announced that it was a *Sylvia* tradition to load and fire the brass cannon at a select target (usually a U.S. Navy ship or submarine docked nearby) whenever the *Sylvia* reentered the harbor. Just as these words left Bob's mouth, he turned and saw a tall ship (a large, traditionally-rigged sailing vessel), *The Californian,* sailing towards us, stuffed to the gills with tourists hanging from the rails.

Bob quickly opened a storage hatch, brought out the largest miniature brass cannon I had ever seen, and mounted it with bolts to a wooden platform on the stern. He then proceeded to pack it with a double charge of gunpowder and toilet paper (nothing that would hurt anyone) before instructing Sally and the rest of us to come about, which would swing the stern directly in front of the starboard (right) side of *The Californian*.

The Californian – San Diego Harbor – Photo: (Dale Frost) [7]

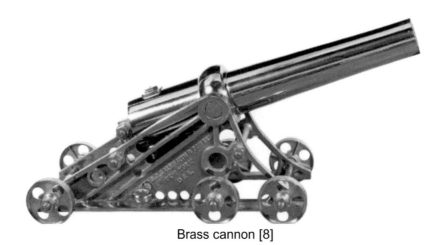

Brass cannon [8]

Sally spun the wheel and shouted commands to trim the sails. Bob waited until we were perfectly positioned, about fifty yards away, and lit the fuse with his cigarette. The explosion was so powerful that the force blew the cannon off its mount and sent it careening backwards down the teak deck, grazing Gail's leg. Fortunately, she wasn't badly hurt, but the deck of the *Sylvia* was damaged, the people on *The Californian* were screaming, and all of us were surrounded by a cloud of white smoke.

A few minutes later, a Harbor Police patrol boat powered up to the *Sylvia*, demanded through their bull horn that we heave-to, pulled alongside, boarded the vessel, arrested and handcuffed Bob, and escorted him unto their boat. It turned out that the skipper of *The Californian* knew and disliked Bob, had radioed the Harbor Police, and had charged Bob with attempted murder.

Jerry, Gail, Sally, Judy, and I were left in the middle of San Diego Bay. We sailed the *Sylvia* back to her slip, at the San Diego Yacht Club, and I drove down to police headquarters and bailed Bob out with my MasterCard—and eventually all charges were dropped.

Recently, well known evangelist and pastor/teacher, Greg Laurie, wrote a book titled *Steve McQueen: The Salvation of an American Icon*, which focuses on the fact that McQueen, one of Hollywood's most famous leading men during the 1960s and '70s, placed his faith in Jesus Christ about six months before being diagnosed with terminal cancer. God took him home about a year after he learned he was terminally ill.

After his conversion, McQueen expressed a desire to meet Billy Graham. A few days before McQueen passed away, in a Mexican medical clinic following surgery, Graham visited him in California, prayed with him, and gave him his personal Bible. A few days later, when McQueen's son, Chad, arrived at the clinic in Mexico, shortly after his passing, he found McQueen clutching Graham's Bible to his chest.

Steve McQueen - 1930-1980 –
Photo: (Kate Gabrielle) [9]

Near the end of his life, McQueen shared that he regretted living most of his life on earth without Jesus and thus missing the opportunity to use his stardom to glorify God. Several years ago, I learned that Bob Welles had passed away. I have no idea where Bob is today, but like Steve McQueen, I regret that so many years of my life were wasted on myself and not on sharing the love of Jesus with those I knew before my conversion.

IN 1980, I STARTED A consulting business, Transcontinental Services. I leased office space on Shelter Island in Point Loma, not far from where our boat was berthed. One of my first assignments was serving as a real estate consultant to one of the seven brothers of the King of Saudi Arabia, a prince who was interested in acquiring a home in Southern California.

One of his advisors asked me to help find a suitable property and arrange for an extended visit to Southern California by his family and their entourage. I worked closely with them during their visit, showing them luxury homes in La Jolla, Beverly Hills, and Bel-Air, as well as arranging hotel accommodations, off-duty Los Angeles police security, limousines, etc.

During this time Judy became friends with one of his daughters (a princess), and when she married, she and her husband invited us to travel with them extensively throughout the United States and abroad. It fascinated us to witness the evolution of a culture only a few generations removed from their Bedouin desert roots, now living a lifestyle of the rich and famous. They had everything materially most of us dream about, but they were trapped between two worlds.

When they were in Saudi Arabia, their behavior and freedom to move about publicly was governed by the strict observance of their Islamic faith. The women never left the palace compound unless they were chaperoned, veiled, and covered from head to foot. They were never allowed to drive or be alone with a man.

Although the men could drive, their freedom of behavior was greatly limited to the privacy of their palace. For most of them, when they traveled abroad, everything changed. If they were flying to Europe or the United States, as soon as the aircraft left Saudi airspace and leveled off at cruising altitude, the women usually headed for the first-class restrooms and changed into fashionable Western clothing.

Once they reached high school or college age, many of the male royals were educated in Europe and/or the United States. They were quite fluent in English and Western customs. Both the men and the women were always heavily guarded. They never knew the freedom of movement most of us take for granted, much like a Hollywood movie star or a famous professional athlete.

FAST FORWARD FORTY YEARS AND the Saudi's are in the process of building the tallest building in the world, "Jeddah Tower"—a 167-story structure over a half-mile high and located on the Red Sea in the port city of Jeddah. Some of the brightest engineers and architects in the world are building this monument to man, in the birthplace of Islam, utilizing state-of-the-art scientific and mathematical disciplines established by Bible-believing scientists centuries ago, including:

Isaac Newton (1642-1727) – Law of Gravity, Calculus, and Dynamics; Charles Babbage (1792-1871) – Computer Science; Lord Rayleigh (1842-1919) – Dimensional Analysis and Model Analysis; Leonardo da Vinci (1452-1519) – Hydraulics; Bernard Riemann (1826-1866) – Non-Euclidean Geometry; and Ambrose Fleming (1849-1945) – Electronics (all are listed in *The Biblical Basis for Modern Science* by Dr. Henry M. Morris).

All people are God's children regardless of their wealth, power, influence, culture, nationality, or religion. I now know that the only thing separating a follower of Jesus from a member of the Saudi Royal Family or, for that matter, from anyone else on the face of the earth not following Him, is God's grace.

The Rendering of Jeddah Tower [10]

John MacArthur, pastor-teacher, Grace Community Church, Sun Valley, California, mentioned the construction of "Jeddah Tower" in a sermon he preached, August 21, 2022, titled "Why You Can Trust Scripture", wherein he illustrates God's design of the universe and the immutable physical and material laws God created, that demonstrate the absurdity of man's attempts to change the climate.

MacArthur shares that the physical universe operates through a system of fixed laws (astrological, geological, biological, mathematical, etc.). As an example, he uses Newton's Law of Gravity, coupled with measurements from the National Aeronautics and Space Administration, to demonstrate that wherever you are on earth at this moment in time, you are 1.6 million miles from where you were yesterday at the same time, because:

- the earth is spinning on its axis at 1,000 miles per hour;

- our solar system is moving around the sun at 67,000 miles per hour;

- our galaxy and the galaxies around us are moving across space at 490,000 miles per hour;

- and the known universe is moving towards the Great Attractor, a region of space 150 million light years away (one light year equals six trillion miles), and the mass of the Great Attractor is one quintillion time's greater than our sun, and has a span of 500,000,000 light years.

How is it that that everyone on the face of the earth is not spinning uncontrollably off the planet? Because we're moving at exactly the same speed as the atmosphere that surrounds us. Nevertheless, globalist elites and the world leaders they influence are now blindly focused on creating economic and political policies and regulations, premised on controlling the earth's climate—as if they are in charge of the universe—which amounts to pure lunacy and the rejection of God.

WAVES OF GRACE

Judy and I lived on our sailboat through 1981, but as we spent more time at sea, I realized I tended to become seasick if I wasn't topside. Whenever I went below deck out in the open ocean, I immediately experienced some degree of nausea. It became obvious to both of us that we weren't destined to circumnavigate the world on a sailboat. God was taking us in another direction, and He was leading me to a saving knowledge of Jesus Christ.

13

LA JOLLA, CALIFORNIA

32.9°N, -117.2°W

Early one morning, in 1981, on a cold January day, I drove to La Jolla High School with Judy to run a few miles on the track before an ocean swim at La Jolla Cove. After the run, we drove to the cove and I began swimming out to the half-mile buoy. As I rounded the buoy to head back to the cove, I raised my head slightly and squinted my eyes to get my bearings (in the early 1980s I rarely wore goggles when open ocean swimming).

Early morning – La Jolla Cove – La Jolla, California –
Photo: Jeff Shewan [1]

A minute later, head down and swimming hard with eyes closed in about 50 feet of water, I got slammed on my right side. I instinctively reacted by flipping with a half-twist to face what had hit me. At that point, I didn't know if I had been injured. When I surfaced, I found myself face-to-face with a cute baby California sea lion pup about three feet away.

As it wiggled its whiskers and looked at me with adoring eyes, I realized it had butted my side to establish a parental bond because it had been separated from its mother. As I headed to shore, it followed along brushing my side from time to time. When I walked out on the beach and looked back the pup was staring at me from the water with an expression of abandonment.

California sea lion pup [2]

IN RETROSPECT

As I reflect on my encounter with this sea lion pup, I am reminded that despite my attempts to turn from God, my choosing to ignore His love, mercy, grace, and protection, He has always been constant in His passion and love to draw me to Himself. In retrospect, this sea lion pup could have been a great white shark and the opportunity of freely receiving the gift of eternal life, that I now possess, might have evaporated in a moment.

The Bible shares in many passages that wisdom begins with the fear of the Lord. This is not fear as we commonly think of it, such as being afraid of someone or something, but a reverence for and heartfelt appreciation of our Creator and Lord.

"The fear of the LORD is the beginning of wisdom, and the knowledge of the Holy One is understanding." – Proverbs 9:10

If you're reading this book and have not yet trusted in Jesus as your personal Lord and Savior, many Biblical words and concepts will be indecipherable, because they can only be spiritually discerned. Knowing something supernaturally by the revelation of the Holy Spirit, that would not be known by natural deduction, is one of God's many gifts to those who know and believe in Him.

The words wisdom, knowledge, and understanding are prime examples. In this temporal world we live in these words are often associated with someone's age, academic qualifications, or unique life experiences. But from God's eternal perspective, human wisdom, knowledge, and understanding amount to nothing, compared to His omnipotence, omnipresence, and omniscience… God knows everything!

SHORTLY AFTER THE GREAT FLOOD, when God destroyed all human life on the face of the earth except Noah and his family, it did not take long for humans to display their carnal self-importance in response to God's command to Noah and his sons to populate the earth.

"So God blessed Noah and his sons, and said to them: "Be fruitful and multiply, and fill the earth." – Genesis 9:1

At the time of God's command, all of Noah's descendants spoke the same language. Nimrod, Noah's great-grandson through Ham, one of Noah's three sons, decided to disobey God and make a name for himself and his Hamitic followers. They established the city of Babel, southeast of where the ark had landed after the flood, and built the Tower of Babel to symbolize their unity and strength.

"And they said, 'Come, let us build ourselves a city, and a tower whose top is in the heavens; let us make a name for ourselves, lest we be scattered abroad over the face of the whole earth.'" – Genesis 11:4

In response, God exercised His divine sovereignty over the affairs of men by confusing their ability to communicate with one another in the same language.

> *"But the LORD came down to see the city and the tower which the sons of men had built. And the LORD said, 'Indeed the people are one and they all have one language, and this is what they begin to do; now nothing that they propose to do will be withheld from them. Come, let Us go down and there confuse their language, that they may not understand one another's speech.' So the LORD scattered them abroad from there over the face of all the earth, and they ceased building the city. Therefore its name is called Babel, because there the LORD confused the language of all the earth; and from there the LORD scattered them abroad over the face of all the earth."* – Genesis 11:5-9

This event is reminiscent of the world today (think "Jeddah Tower", referenced on page 133), a world where human knowledge is increasing exponentially. Buckminster Fuller, a 20th century inventor and visionary, noticed that human knowledge doubled every hundred years up to the 19th century, and then began doubling every 25 years by the end of World War II. In 1982, according to IBM, human knowledge was doubling every 13 months and was on the verge of doubling every 11-12 hours by 2020 (*Industry Tap News 2013* – "Knowledge Doubling Every 12 Months, Soon to be Every 12 hours", by David Russell Schilling).

Is the exponential growth of human knowledge being used for good or for evil? As an example, global IT connectivity provides unprecedented opportunity to improve life throughout the world and to share the gospel, but it also provides unprecedented opportunity for self-absorption and the rejection of God. The scales are in God's hands, but we are clearly on a path to deifying man—because human knowledge, untempered by God's word, leads to pride ("making a name for ourselves"), and Satan, the ruler of the world, is pride personified.

ONE OF THE WONDERS OF reading God's word or engaging in ocean sports is that I never know from day to day what to expect. Every time I open the Bible or immerse myself in the ocean is a unique experience. God uses both His word and the ocean to reveal Himself to me.

All ocean sports share one common distinction: they are all subject to a mixture of universal forces that create unique and variable ocean conditions. They are universal because, as we learned at the end of the last chapter, God has set every planet, moon, star, solar system, and galaxy in balance. He has perfectly harmonized and tuned them to flow in certain patterns. As human beings, we often take for granted that we can comfortably sit, stand, walk, run, surf, or do anything else on this planet, only because God has created the gravitational forces that allow us to do so, instead of simply letting us be whipped off the surface of the earth at a thousand miles per hour, the speed of the earth's rotation.

Ocean sports are always diverse due to the size, power, and direction of every storm or wind-generated swell released upon the coastlines of the world. They are also different: due to water temperatures that vary with every current and season; the distinctive contours of the ocean floor that shape incoming swells; and the diversity of sea life that inhabit various locales.

The main attraction of any ocean sport is the opportunity to adapt to, and become one with, these unique and ever-changing conditions. Following Jesus is very similar because we are constantly challenged to become one with His will, regardless of the special and erratic events of our lives.

Most people, when they think of ocean swimming, probably imagine changing into a swimsuit on a warm summer day, walking down to the water's edge, playfully wading through some small waves, and either treading water for a while or taking a few strokes back and forth in the shallows. That is a far cry from year-round open-ocean swimming, which requires years of familiarity with mercurial marine conditions, the right wetsuit, and a deep respect for the force and power of the sea displayed in all its manifestations.

Like any other sport, there are variations of open-ocean swimming that range from a swim across the English Channel to a short swim along the beach. The common denominator is a passion to be one with the most elemental feature of God's creation, the ocean.

Open-ocean swimming is now a year-round sport in Southern California, thanks to the advent of triathlon-inspired wetsuits that provide effortless shoulder rotation and seasonal variations for warmth. Slipping in and out of these skintight suits can be enhanced by applying a secret sauce I concocted—a few squirts of Neutrogena body oil in a plastic cycling bottle, add hot water, and shake (hot water warms the interior of the suit on a cold winter morning).

Unfortunately, great white sharks are now a consideration when open-ocean swimming in California. Before the state passed legislation outlawing commercial and public fishing for great whites in 1994, the danger of a great white attack was considerably less than today. As a direct result, great whites are now flourishing and they can't tell the difference between a seal, a sea lion, a swimmer, or a surfer—until they taste you, and occasionally, they like the taste.

Handmade open-ocean swimming goggles
– circa 1950s – a gift from a
La Jolla Cove, California old-timer [3]

According to the California Department of Fish and Wildlife:

- "There were 12 shark attacks in the 1950s and 50 attacks in the 2010s.

- "From 1950 to 2019 there have been 185 shark incidents, of which 164 involved great white sharks. Of those, 13 were fatal and all the fatalities involved great whites."

Great whites typically begin their attack of a large mammal with a vicious bite, let it bleed out, and then leisurely enjoy their meal. In the past, I never thought twice about swimming out beyond the break and heading up or down the coast.

Today, I very rarely venture out beyond the break unless I decide I need a challenge—like the time I celebrated my seventieth birthday by swimming from the southern border of Crystal Cove State Park in Corona del Mar, California, to the first publicly accessible cove in north Laguna Beach, Crescent Bay. I did this because I wanted to view two contiguous private ocean front residential communities from the ocean, Irvine Cove and Emerald Bay, that are otherwise inaccessible to the public.

Abalone Point (foreground) is located at the southern end of Crystal Cove State Park. To the south of Abalone Point are the two beaches that comprise Irvine Cove. Emerald Bay is the third and last beach visible to the south of Irvine Cove. Crescent Bay (not visible) is located to the south of Emerald Bay. – Photo: Courtesy – Dean Ledger, Real Estate Broker [4]

Crescent Bay, Laguna Beach, California, with grandson Jude –
the morning grandaughter Reese was born – January 21, 2022 [5]

Other than this swim around Abalone Point, I usually like to swim along the breaking wave-line. I do this for two reasons: one, I love to swim at the edge of waves just before they break, in order to feel the motion of the ocean in a way that can't be felt anywhere else; and two, because I feel I am better positioned to avoid an attack by a great white. If the surf is less that 2-3 feet, I am swimming over a shallow bottom. Great whites usually like to attack from the bottom up, so I feel I am slightly safer in the shallows, even though if they want to make a meal of me there is no way to prevent it.

The velocity of the learning curve for an ocean sport, or for understanding God's word, is greatly increased by others who can mentor us. As I reflect on my passion for both the ocean and His word, I can clearly remember the individuals who encouraged my interest and shepherded my path. However, unlike my ocean-sports mentors, many

of those who most impactfully mentored me in the study of God's word lived during the 18th, 19th, and 20th centuries. Although they have now passed into heaven, their words are timeless and their writings have helped illuminate and encourage my growth in the Lord (see "Mentors" at the end of this book).

Phillips Brooks, an American Episcopal clergyman and author of the 19th century, said:

"While it is good to walk among the living, it is also good to live with the wise, great and good dead. It keeps out of life the dreadful feeling of extemporaneousness, with its conceit and its despair. It makes us always know that God made other men before He made us. It furnishes a constant background for our living. It provides us with perpetual humility and inspiration."

WAVES OF GRACE

At this time in my life, surfing became a passion. In fact, it became an obsession. In retrospect, I think God was speaking His creative beauty into my life through the pulsing swells He sent my way. I believe every surfer is touched in this way and that is why God has blessed global surf ministry evangelism over the years.

14

CABO SAN LUCAS, MEXICO

22.8 °N, -109.9°W

In 1981, as a novice board surfer, I flew to Cabo San Lucas, Baja, Mexico, to surf for a week with some friends that had taught me the sport. The day we arrived, they took me to "Monuments", a surf spot with a large rock outcropping that juts out in the middle of the break. On a low tide, the wave begins to form over a very shallow reef in the takeoff zone, the best place to be positioned to catch and ride a wave.

"Monuments" surf break – Cabo San Lucas, Baja California Sur, Mexico –
Photo: Joe Tyson [1]

On average, the amount of time involved in catching and riding a wave to completion is five to ten seconds. Fifteen seconds or more is considered a fairly long ride, although there's a barreling wave in Namibia (southwest Africa) that can be ridden for up to two minutes.

The three steps that lead to catching a wave occur in a couple of seconds: step one, paddling into the wave on your stomach; step two, popping up to your feet; and step three, shifting your weight to begin a bottom-turn (the first turn a surfer makes, to the right or left, to begin the ride). These three steps are explosive and flow instantaneously.

Skeleton Coast, Namibia – Photo: Teddy Jones [2]

My friends had returned to the beach to wait out a higher tide and I decided to catch one more wave before joining them. As a wave approached, I turned my board and paddled in. At the same moment I popped to my feet, the face of the wave sucked up suddenly on the shallow reef and the front of my board dropped out from under me. It seemed like I was suspended in time, staring straight down at a shallow reef bottom with no room for forgiveness.

By the grace of God, I bottom-turned and avoided a face plant. I could hear my friends on the beach cheering that I had pulled this off as a novice surfer, but I was locked in the power-pocket (the central energy source of a breaking wave) and headed for an instant collision with the rock outcropping. In the next moment, I bailed out the back of the wave by turning my board up and over the crest, avoiding a collision. I paddled in and stayed on the beach the rest of the afternoon, thankful that I wasn't dead or seriously injured.

Shallow reef bottom with no room for forgiveness –
Photo: Vladimir Kudinov [3]

IN RETROSPECT

This was another event in my life where I can now look back and appreciate that God's loving hand was guiding my ways. Despite the fact that I had no interest in Him, He was interested in me. On numerous occasions, in varied circumstances, He has graciously protected me. He loved me before the foundation of the universe and He has always had a calling on my life.

I first learned to surf in 1980, at the age of thirty-three. That summer, a friend encouraged me to take his *longboard* out at 11th Street in Del Mar. I was hooked. The next day I drove to the nearest surf shop and bought my first board. Surfing added a totally new dimension to my love for the ocean. It enabled me to combine my love to ocean swim with my love to bodysurf with fins. Despite my passion for surfing, I have never reached the level of competence of friends who have grown up board surfing. Although I couldn't surf at their level, I was comfortable in most conditions. Regardless of the size or shape, I knew if I fell off my board and my leash snapped, I could handle the aftermath, which might mean a long swim to shore through powerful surf to retrieve it.

As mentioned earlier, I grew up playing golf and played competitively through high school and college. I share this because surfing and golf are very similar in one essential way: both require a tremendous amount of practice to attain proficiency, which is much easier to acquire when you're young and possess a limber agility to imprint patterns of behavior.

11th Street, Del Mar (San Diego County), California [4]

After years of surfing since childhood, when accomplished surfers drop into a five-foot barreling wave, they are not consciously thinking about next steps because their patterns of execution have been subconsciously fixed from years of practice and experience. Their focus is on the result—a perfect ride—not a step-by-step process. They have mentally imprinted the process through practice and they can subconsciously feel the flow and sense the outcome, and even capture the moment with a hand-held camera—like the image below—filmed by Hawaiian pro surfer Mikala Jones during a Bali, Indonesia, sunrise session in 2018.

As I discussed in the introductory "Essentials" section of this book, probably the best example of this occurred over 2,000 years ago. As Jesus hung on His cross, one of the two criminals that hung on crosses next to Him heard Him forgive those who crucified Him, believed He was God, and asked Jesus to remember him in His kingdom. Jesus didn't instruct him to climb off his cross, get baptized, and follow the ten commandments, He simply said, in love and grace:

"...today you will be with Me in Paradise." – Luke 23:43

Mikala Jones (1979-2023) – 5' barreling wave (Hawaiian) – Bali, Indonesia – Photo: Mikala Jones [5]

As opposed to surfing, knowing Jesus does not require a tremendous amount of practice or the physical agility of youth. Anyone can enter His kingdom, from a young child entering nursery school to an elderly person gasping their last breath. Simply hearing or reading His word and believing that a Holy God became a Holy Man, to suffer and die for the sins of all who would ever believe in Him, is sufficient.

WAVES OF GRACE

Regardless of who we are—and what we have done with our lives up to this moment in time—we can believe in Jesus, as this criminal did, and receive Him into our hearts as our personal Lord and Savior. All we need to do is to ask God to empower us with the seed of faith to turn away from our sins and to pray the following, silently or aloud, from our heart:

"Dear Lord Jesus, I know I am a sinner. I believe You died for my sins. Right now, I turn from my sins and open the door of my heart and life. I confess You as my personal Lord and Savior. Thank You for saving me. Amen."

15

BAJA MALIBU, MEXICO

32.4 °N, -117.0°W

In January 1983, before up-to-the-minute ocean swell forecasts on smartphones became as common as the hourly weather reports on the radio, a series of winter storms battered Northern Mexico and Southern California. Professional surfer Sam George called it "the last of the free-range swells"—swells that arrived unannounced from unknown origins—swells, that surfers would experience, not because they had glanced at their smartphones several days before but because they were dedicated to a daily "dawn patrol" to check conditions.

If you walk into Duke's restaurant on Prospect Street in La Jolla, California, turn left after you enter, and climb the stairs to the second floor, you will be greeted by an expansive photograph of La Jolla Cove being pounded by a 20-foot wave. Judy and I stood on the cliffs watching with hundreds of others as one of a series of epic winter swells wrapped into the cove forming perfect "peeling" waves that broke left all the way to La Jolla Shores.

"Dawn Patrol" [1]

"Peeling" Left [2]

Those of us on the cliff had the advantage of watching the sets build long before the handful of surfers in the lineup had a clue about what was happening. Later in the day, we sighted a huge clean up wave forming outside and the crowd went wild, shouting and screaming. The surfers got the message and began scratching (paddling) for the horizon to try and get over the back of the wave before it broke. They were too late; the twenty-foot-plus wave broke in front of them and totally wiped them all out.

The aftermath was pure bedlam. Lifeguards trained in cliff rescue had roped themselves off and desperately tried to assist surfers who had lost their boards and were being uncontrollably driven into the cliffs, as their broken boards were hurled about in the cove. The spectators were mesmerized by the sheer power, energy, and mayhem of the moment. To the best of my knowledge, no one was seriously hurt or injured due to the heroic efforts of the lifeguards.

These winter storms seriously damaged the coastline, from the Northern Baja peninsula to Southern California. To this day, The Marine Room, a high-end waterfront restaurant, located in La Jolla, California, promotes the fact that waves crash into its famous dining room windows on high tides. During one of these storms, their windows were smashed in by huge granite rocks.

An oceanfront homeowner in Del Mar, just north of La Jolla, arranged for massive granite boulders to be placed on the beach fronting his property in anticipation of high tides. The next evening, he left for the movies, only to return home and find the same boulders in his living room!

A friend of mine owned a trailer in Baja Malibu, a private oceanfront community just a short drive across the Mexican border from San Diego. Baja Malibu is known for producing North Shore-like surf on the West Coast. Deep ocean swells impact the nearshore and shallow coastal shelf generating powerful lefts, rights, and occasionally, perfect A-frames—waves that form a peak as they begin to break and provide the opportunity to ride the wave either right or left.

La Jolla's Marine Room Restaurant [3]

Baja Malibu – A-Frame – Northern Baja, Mexico [4]

I had surfed Baja Malibu several times but had never surfed it in epic conditions. I had no idea what it could do when fully turned on. I was also an inexperienced, foolhardy, but completely committed surfer. Watching the winter storm swells slamming La Jolla Cove convinced me that a drive south was in order and I persuaded Judy to go with me.

The next morning, as we pulled into Baja Malibu, I was mesmerized by the six- to eight-foot spitting tubes, formed when waves are breaking so hard, they form a barrel or tube and the air pressure on the spray, produced in the inside of the back of the barrel, is forced or spit out the open front.

"Spitting Tube" – Photo: TF [5]

No one was in sight. I slipped on my wetsuit, grabbed my board, and strode down to the beach with Judy. The only person around in either direction was a lady sitting in a beach chair reading her newspaper. Judy turned to say hello to her, and when she turned back to look for me, I was gone.

A super swift current was running north, and as soon as I began paddling out, swept me along. I never should have driven south, let alone paddled out. In an instant I was a quarter mile north of my entry point with no opportunity to paddle in. The combination of winter storm waves and record high tides had destroyed many of the coastal homes sitting on the cliffs, creating a shoreline littered with jagged cement and structural remnants.

As I desperately searched for a spot to safely paddle in, I was pounded by the firing surf. By God's grace, I spotted a narrow ribbon of sand, slightly north of my position, and angled in. In retrospect, I think I reached this spot, several miles from Baja Malibu, because God sent an angel to guide me to it. Walking back through private coastal communities, I finally reunited with a distraught Judy, who thought I had been lost at sea. God had once again intervened!

Entrance to the Baja Malibu private residential community [6]

IN RETROSPECT

Several years ago, on the television show *The West Wing*, the main character, President Bartlet was presented with a difficult choice. The script called for the telling of a story to help him make his choice, a story about a major storm that threatened central Texas and a farmer who ignored the threat. It went something like this:

"In the morning, as the storm began unleashing its fury, the Sheriff stopped by and warned the farmer to evacuate because the river was rising. The farmer replied that he had lived there all his life and wasn't worried.

"Later in the afternoon, a Texas State Trooper drove up and ordered the farmer to evacuate immediately because the river had overflowed and would quickly flood his house. The farmer replied that he wasn't worried; he knew the river and what it would do.

"As the State Trooper left, the water flooded his house, and the farmer climbed up on the roof. A helicopter was dispatched by emergency services to rescue him and the farmer replied that he'd be all right and refused their offer.

"Soon the farmer's house was swept away, and the farmer drowned. As he drowned, he cried to God, 'I don't understand. You're letting me drown.' God said, 'Now, let's take a look at My records. This morning I sent the Sheriff to warn you, this afternoon I directed a Texas State Trooper to order you to evacuate, and this evening I dispatched an emergency services helicopter to rescue you.'"

One evening in the mid-1970s, while I was working for Bechtel in San Francisco, I was riding home from work to Walnut Creek on a BART commuter train. I glanced up at an advertisement that promoted a Tibetan Buddhist meditation center in Berkeley. Intrigued, I dropped by one weekend to check it out and became immersed in Tibetan Buddhism. Like all of us, I had a deep inner longing to understand my existence and this seemed like a path. Over the next year, I read about a hundred books on the subject and spent a lot of time at this meditation center in the lotus position.

One weekend afternoon, on my way home after a meditation session, I was racing my ten-speed bicycle down a Berkeley hill—weaving back and forth. Unfortunately, on one of these weaves, my timing was slightly off, the pedal struck the pavement, the bicycle came to an abrupt standstill, and I was catapulted high in the air over the handlebars. While airborne, I somersaulted with a half-twist and landed on my feet—facing the bicycle. All forward momentum came to an immediate end at that moment—I did not continue falling over backwards or rolling downhill. My feet were firmly planted and I was leaning forward, knees bent, and arms outstretched like I was riding a wave.

Like many before me, and some reading this book, I have innumerable memories of the times God has rescued me, even though I didn't know or believe in Him. I now recognize these were all warning signs I had ignored, and I might have been killed or seriously injured but for His grace. Is God warning you?

Warped bicycle rim after a crash [7]

As I stood there looking at it, I noticed that the front rim had been warped into a perfect figure-eight by the force and torque of the crash. At the time, I thought I had been saved from death or serious injury by my own brilliant coordination and reactions. However, as I reflect on this experience now, I am certain that a guardian angel guided my path and landed me on my feet.

> *"For He shall give His angels charge over you, to keep you in all your ways. In their hands they shall bear you up, lest you dash your foot against a stone." – Psalm 91:11-12*

God was warning me again, but I was oblivious to His intervention. God warns each of us, in many unique ways, because He wants to rescue all of us, if He hasn't already.

> *"Him we preach, warning every man and teaching every man in all wisdom, that we may present every man perfect in Christ Jesus." – Colossians 1:28*

WAVES OF GRACE

From 1983-1986, I commuted back and forth from our home in San Diego to Washington, D.C. A friend of mine, Keith Thompson, the elder brother of Dan Thompson (my friend and dive partner in Saudi Arabia) and I had decided to resurrect a business enterprise his father, Darrow, had started in 1970: the development of a new commercial aircraft—an air pressure jet (APJ) helicopter. I had met Keith and Dan in college, attended graduate school with Keith, and had worked with Darrow on a consulting basis in 1972 during the development of the first experimental 1-seat, proof-of-concept, APJ prototype. Unbeknownst to me, this chapter in my life would end with the most important event of my life.

16

WASHINGTON, D.C.

38.9°N, -77.0°W

An air pressure jet (APJ) helicopter eliminates torque, the nemesis of the conventional helicopter. In a conventional helicopter, torque is created by a central drive shaft that connects to and turns the main rotor blades. Because of the attachment of the central drive shaft to the main rotor blades, the body of the helicopter turns in the opposite direction of the main rotor blades, necessitating a long extension boom and tail rotor to counteract the torque generated. This is a perfect example of Newton's third law of motion: for every action, there is an equal and opposite reaction.

The APJ helicopter removes torque by utilizing a turbine engine to drive an air compressor, that forces compressed air up a hollow shaft and out hollow rotor blades, where it exits curved nozzles at the tips. The pressurized air turns the main rotor blades from the tips rather than twisting them through a central drive shaft, thus eliminating torque. Placing a rudder in the exhaust stream of the turbine engine provides yaw control, thus allowing the pilot to turn the aircraft left or right as the rudder swivels from side to side.

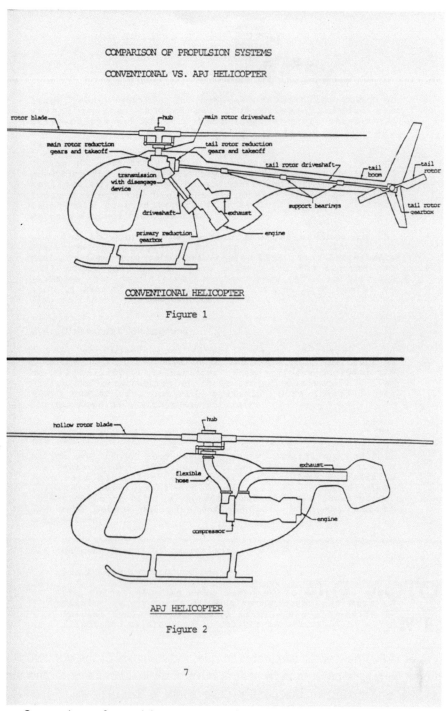

Comparison of propulsion systems – Conventional vs. APJ helicopter –
VOLJET™ R&D, Ltd., Business Plan, June 1985 [1]

Cross-section of the first APJ rotor blade [2]

Watching the first test flight of the 1-seat,
proof-of-concept APJ prototype –
November 1972 [3]

Darrow's chief aeronautical engineer, Bruno Nagler, a brilliant Austrian, had worked with the Germans during World War II to develop futuristic helicopter concepts. One of his passions was APJ technology, that eliminated ninety percent of the moving parts of the conventional helicopter. An APJ helicopter was not only simple and safe, it was easy to fly. If you had the psychomotor skills needed to drive a stick shift car, you could fly an APJ helicopter.

I had worked with Darrow as a consultant in 1972, at the inception of this effort, when the first 1-seat prototype was built and test-flown. In December of 1972, I flew to London with film of the first test flight and a directive from Darrow to introduce the APJ development program to commercial attachés attached to certain embassies and consulates (a commercial attaché is a diplomatic official attached to an embassy or legation, especially in a technical capacity).

My mom and dad were living in London at the time, and my dad cautioned me that bringing a new aircraft to market was much riskier than bringing a new automobile to market. I took my dad's advice and signed another contract with the Chapman College WCA program.

Chuck Tucker – Chief Test Pilot – 1973 –
demonstrating hands-free stability of the first 1-seat,
proof-of-concept – APJ helicopter prototype [4]

By 1981, the Thompson family had built three proof-of-concept aircraft—1-seat, 2-seat, and 4-seat prototypes—and flown over 300 successful test flights. Unfortunately, Darrow had then run out of funds and suffered a stroke. In 1983, Keith and I decided to pick up the pieces and raise the funds to develop an 8-seat pre-production prototype.

I share all of this to testify that I was extremely full of myself at this stage in my life—not atypical of someone who thinks he is on top of the world. By 1985, I was Chairman and CEO of the company and had a significant equity interest. We subleased office space in downtown Washington, D.C., from our law firm, Pillsbury, Madison, and Sutro.

Voljet Headquarters – Washington D.C. – 1985 [5]

1-seat, 2-seat, and 4-seat proof-of-concept, APJ helicopters
and rendering of the "Voljet 585" 8-seat, pre-production prototype [6]

One day our lead attorney, the former head of the U.S. Consumer Product Safety Commission, told me I was going to be a billionaire. I had visions of building a house with a heliport in San Diego, equipping one of our 8-seat helicopters with surfboard racks, and flying the Pacific coast of the Baja peninsula with friends searching for otherwise inaccessible waves. However, God had a better plan—He was about to transform the driveshaft of my life.

Cover of Popular Mechanics magazine – February 1987 [7]

SAN DIEGO, CALIFORNIA

32.7 °N, -117.2°W

In 1985 the cost of product liability insurance shot through the roof and completely cratered the general aviation manufacturing industry. Prior to this event, general aviation aircraft manufacturers had been selling thousands of aircraft per year. In 1986, that number dropped significantly and undermined our fundraising efforts, at a time when we were trying to raise fourteen million dollars to build our 8-seat pre-production prototype, the VOLJET 585, and certify it with the FAA and/or the CAA (British Civil Aviation Authority).

In the fall of 1985, as the helicopter business began to unravel, my sister Linda's husband suddenly died of a heart attack in Houston, Texas, leaving her with three young boys. I jumped on a flight from Washington, D.C. to Houston, thinking I would provide encouragement and support for Linda and the boys. Little did I know God had other plans; He was orchestrating a time in my life when I would meet Him through His church.

I was there for about a week before the memorial service and witnessed Linda's small church love her through this challenging time. An attorney provided legal counsel, a CPA helped with financial planning, church members donated funds to help her with certain cash flow issues, and the women of the church prepared food to fill her refrigerator and freezer with meals to feed her growing boys.

"Pure and undefiled religion before God and the Father is this: to visit orphans and widows in their trouble, and to keep oneself unspotted from the world." – James 1:27

From left to right: two of my nephews, Paul and Leith, Judy, me, and my sister, Linda – Houston, Texas – 1985 [8]

No one from Linda's church mentioned a word to me about God or invited me to church, they simply shared the love of Jesus working in and through their lives, as they ministered to my sister and her family in their hour of need. I now know that the love of God is most powerfully expressed when His followers display their love for one another to those around them. In so doing, they are answering the prayer of Jesus for His church:

"I do not pray for these alone, but also for those who will believe in Me through their word; that they all may be one, as You, Father, are in Me, and I in You; that they also may be one in Us, that the world may believe that You sent Me." – John 17:20-21

After the memorial service, when I boarded a plane to San Diego, I knew I wanted what they had, but I had only one idea about how to get it. As soon as the plane landed, I drove to a B. Dalton Bookstore, walked up to the cashier, and asked if he would recommend a Bible for me to buy. Little did I realize that he probably knew less about the Bible or God than I did. He sold me the most expensive, largest, and heaviest Bible in the store: a Roman Catholic family table Bible with the Apocrypha (early Christian writings not included in Protestant Bibles because they are not considered inspired by God).

For the next several months I lugged that giant Bible around the world. I knew it was a lifesaver, but I didn't have a clue how to study it or how it was going to save me. When I first began to read it, I felt the need for solitude, so I drove to the main library of the University of California San Diego campus, took an elevator up to the top floor, found a secluded desk, turned to the first page of the first chapter of the first book, Genesis, and began stumbling my way through.

It never occurred to me to begin reading anywhere other than the first chapter (book). By the time I got to the third chapter, Leviticus, I was totally confused. I didn't know that in order to understand the word of God, I needed to be born spiritually, a birth that occurs in a special moment of time, when the Holy Spirit empowers a person by faith to confess Jesus is Lord and believe in their heart that God raised Him from the dead. At this same moment, He also opens the spiritual eyes and minds of new believers, enabling them to understand His word.

It is in that special moment that God leads a person to repent of their sins, trust Jesus as their personal Lord and Savior, receive the indwelling presence of the Holy Spirit, and become a new creation in Christ Jesus.

"I have been crucified with Christ; it is no longer I who live, but Christ lives in me; and the life which I now live in the flesh I live by faith in the Son of God, who loved me and gave Himself for me." – Galatians: 2:20

We have nothing to do with the timing or the creation of this special moment. It is a moment foreordained by God before the creation of the universe, that occurs when He bestows His free gift of grace by faith on a believer. It is a moment that can occur in the heart of a child or someone on his deathbed. It is a moment that cannot be explained in worldly terms. It is a spiritual moment that followers of Jesus understand intuitively, when bonds of sin are broken and blind eyes are opened. It is a moment when the love, joy, and peace of God begin to flood the heart.

"The Lord opens the eyes of the blind; the Lord raises those who are bowed down; the Lord loves the righteous." – Psalm 146:8

SAN JUANICO, SCORPION BAY, SOUTHERN BAJA, MEXICO

26.2 °N, -112.4°W

In July of 1986, as I became perplexed with the Bible and as funding for Voljet began to dwindle, a friend of mine, Ron Taylor, and I decided to take a surf trip to Scorpion Bay, a famous right point surf break located on the Pacific coast of Southern Baja in San Juanico (about 700-900 miles south of the U.S./Mexican border, depending on whether you take the paved highway or an off-road shortcut).

Looking back now, I was probably seeking to escape the uncertainty of the pressure cooker I had been living in, but God was leading me to discover the certainty of what real life was all about.

A couple of hours before dawn, on a July morning, we loaded up my 4X4 Chevy S-10 Blazer for a ten-day *surfari*. We took two boards apiece (I had a 9' *longboard* for smaller waves and a 7'9" *gun* for larger ones), a two-man tent, fishing poles, and a hundred other things that are mandatory when you're off-road and hundreds of miles from civilization in the Baja wilderness.

We were headed for what is arguably one of the West Coast's best series of right point breaks, if and when the angle of a south swell connects them. Scorpion Bay has a series of points, or cliffs, that jut out into the Pacific. They are oriented in such a way that when an ocean swell from a southerly direction hits them perfectly, they form an extremely long wave that can connect, point to point, gradually diminishing in size to First Point.

Scorpion Bay, Baja California, Mexico – Photo: Fillipo Maffei [9]

The Baja peninsula is one of the earth's most consistently clear land masses when viewed by satellite. The scenery is bleak but spectacular in its bleakness. Heading south past the town of Ensenada, about 100 kilometers south of the border, the Trans Peninsular Highway becomes a two-lane ribbon of blacktop that stretches out over a thousand miles to the tip, Land's End.

The crystal-clear atmosphere, total lack of traffic, and beautifully formed cacti and rock formations combine to provide the perfect escape from Southern California and the material world. It is sensory deprivation in the best sense of the term, with nothing to think about but the south swell we hoped would arrive the same time we did.

About halfway down, we camped overnight at another right point, Santa Rosalillita, that breaks on a straight west swell. In the morning, after deflating the tires to cushion the ride, we took the shortcut and headed off-road. As we traversed sand tracks, rock creeks, and washboard roads, we monitored the coastal mountain range on the left and the Pacific Ocean on the right to help guide our way.

Baja California Sur pit stop – 1986 [10]

Off-road [11]

After several hundred miles, as the remaining light of day faded away, we pitched our tent in the middle of nowhere, hoping we were close to San Juanico. When we got up the next morning and scanned the crystal-clear horizon, we could see what looked like perfect rights peeling in the distance. Unfortunately, although they were perfect rights, when we approached the Second Point of Scorpion Bay, we discovered the waves were only a foot high!

During our one-week stay we never scored the south swell we hoped for, but we quickly adjusted to a daily ritual: waking up early in the morning to check the surf; brewing a pot of Arabian Mocha Java coffee as the sun came up; *longboarding* two- to three-foot perfect peelers; competing with one another for the longest ride;

feasting on ceviche lunches we had cooked in lemon juice the night before from fish we had caught the day before; and enjoying siestas after lunch when the wind came up. Dinner was usually fresh fish or lobster washed down with Corona's.

For the first three days we had Scorpion Bay all to ourselves. On the fourth morning, we watched from the lineup (the distance from the beach to where the waves are breaking) as a van pulled up with a lone surfer who waved from the cliff overlook. When we paddled in and climbed the cliff, we met Phil Vedder, a Southern California high school teacher, coach, and long-time member of the San Onofre Surfing Club. He had been making annual treks to the Baja Peninsula and Scorpion Bay since the early '60s and thought nothing of making the trek solo or with friends.

Second Point dawn patrol from our campsite [12]

Connecting with Phil was one of the highlights of our trip. We surfed and shared meals with him—and he regaled us with stories of his Baja adventures and taught us how to score lobster on a low tide. The trick, we learned, was using a three-foot long, half-inch wooden dowel, with a metal hook screwed into one end. At low tide, you walked the tide pools looking for lobster antennae. When you spotted one, you simply slipped the dowel underneath the lobster with the hook turned sideways—then flipped the hook up and pulled back. Voilà! Lobster dinner!

Phil Vedder holding one for dinner [13]

As I reflect on this chapter of my life, I see a parallel between the technology we were trying to introduce to the aerospace industry and my relationship to God. Eliminating the tail rotor of the conventional helicopter was a radical concept. I can remember two incidents where this was confirmed by executives of two prominent helicopter manufacturers of the time, Bell Helicopters and Westland Helicopters.

In 1972, when I worked as a consultant for Darrow Thompson, Bell Helicopters sent out one of their top manufacturing engineers, from their headquarters in Fort Worth, Texas, to our headquarters in Phoenix, Arizona, to view a test flight of our 1-seat APJ experimental prototype. He had planned an afternoon visit, but after watching the test flight, was so mesmerized by the technology that he decided to extend his stay another day to pursue discussions with our chief test pilot, Chuck Tucker, and various engineering personnel.

He shared with Darrow later, that when he returned to Ft. Worth, he reported his findings to his boss, one of Bell's "C-suite" manufacturing executives. Upon hearing about the flight of an aircraft that could revolutionize the helicopter industry, the executive walked him over to the large picture window in his office. As they looked out over a new multimillion-dollar manufacturing facility for the production of tail rotor mechanisms and driveshafts, the executive shared that what they were looking at was the reason why Bell would never consider eliminating the tail rotor.

In 1985, I traveled to London, England, for a meeting with the Vice Chairman of Westland Helicopters, a British helicopter manufacturer. When we met, I shared a ten-minute video of our 1-, 2-, and 4-seat APJ experimental prototypes in various flight envelopes (you can view this video by googling Voljet). The video concluded with renderings of our 8-seat Voljet 585 pre-production

prototype, the aircraft we were in the process of developing for certification. After we watched the video, he turned to me in amazement and marveled at what he had just witnessed. However, like the Bell executive thirteen years before, he was disturbed by the challenge APJ technology posed to conventional helicopter manufacturing and production.

THIRTY-FIVE YEARS LATER, I AM beginning to realize how radical my relationship is to God and the parallel it has to my experience developing a new helicopter. When Bruno Nagler designed a helicopter that eliminated the central drive shaft and replaced it with a flexible hose, he eliminated torque and thus the need for a tail rotor to counteract it. He also eliminated the complex transmission system and driveshaft needed to power the tail rotor. The genius of his design was the transformation of a complex aircraft into one that was simple, safe, and easy to fly.

One of the most dangerous aspects of the conventional helicopter is power loss. If the engine malfunctions or fails, the following sequence of events occurs: the main rotor blades stop turning, the body of the helicopter spins uncontrollably, and unless the main rotor blades can be immediately disengaged from the main driveshaft and rotate freely, the helicopter will be unable to glide to a safe landing.

In comparison, if the APJ helicopter loses power, the main rotor blades will continue to rotate freely and the high-inertia APJ rotor system provides a much slower rate of rotor RPM (revolutions per minute) decay, providing the APJ helicopter with the long glide slope needed to land safely. (This safety aspect of APJ helicopters is demonstrated in the video previously referenced.)

Replacing the vertical axis of the main rotor driveshaft with a flexible hose was a transformational development. At the time, in addition to passenger helicopters, we had plans to utilize APJ technology to develop large heavy-lift helicopters and drones. APJ aircraft were also capable of flying in the hot and high conditions common to desert and high-altitude environments, that often render conventional helicopters inoperable. The sky was the limit.

In much the same way, when I received Jesus into my heart, my life was transformed. He is now the vertical axis of my life, not me. In retrospect, although it might seem paradoxical, the surrendering of my life to Jesus empowered me to experience real life for the first time. Like an APJ helicopter pilot removing his hands from the controls without losing control, I am now able to trust Jesus with my life because He is in control.

Just as the elimination of the main rotor driveshaft allows the APJ helicopter's main rotor blades to rotate freely, I am now free to disengage from worldly lusts, even though I still sin and fail to disengage from time to time. Surrendering to God will always be a challenge in this temporal physical body and in a temporal world ruled by Satan.

Despite being continually tempted by the lust of my eyes, the lust of my flesh, and my pride of life, lusts that still sway my thoughts, words, and deeds, I am a new creation in Jesus, and I know that one day I will move into the perfect body God has created for me in heaven—not a nebulous undefined, spiritual vapor but a real, glorified, immortal, spiritual body, like the one Jesus received upon His resurrection.

"For we know that if our earthly house, this tent, is destroyed, we have a building from God, a house not made with hands, eternal in the heavens." – 2 Corinthians 5:1

God is now the power of my life; He has gifted me with the faith to trust in Him, lean not on my own understanding, and know that He will always direct my paths. When I stay close to Him—through His word, prayer, and fellowship with other believers—He is the vertical axis of the horizontal plane of my earthly existence. I no longer view success through my eyes, but His.

I am so thankful that the helicopter business failed because, if it hadn't, I might still be caught up in the claws of self-absorption which were rapidly consuming me. I was working long hours, seven days a week, laser focused on launching the helicopter company. Had it succeeded, I'm certain I would have been tempted, and probably succumbed, to every enticement the world has to offer. I was constantly on the road from San Diego to Washington, D.C., and back, and quite often traveled to London, where we kept a small office. I was also making side trips to Dallas, Seattle, San Francisco, Sydney, Hong Kong, Rome, Florence, and elsewhere, assembling a board of advisors, meeting with lawyers, and raising capital. I was doing all of this without a clear moral compass and knowledge of my eternal destiny.

After my salvation experience, I began to realize that success is no longer determined by the world around me, but by God within me. I am no longer defined by what others think about me, but by what Jesus is doing within me—to conform me into His image and make me holy as He is holy—otherwise known as sanctification, the life-long process of being conformed into the image of Jesus. No one will ever know perfection on earth. Only God is perfect. It is impossible for anyone to live up to God's sinless standard of perfect holiness and righteousness and He will not allow anyone to enter heaven that is not as holy and righteous as He is. That's why God, Jesus, became the Son of Man and died on the cross for the sins of all who would believe, thus imputing His holiness and righteousness to those who believe in Him.

WHAT DOES IT MEAN TO be saved? It means by God's gift of faith: we have believed Jesus is God; repented (or turned) from our sins; God has forgiven all of our sins (past, present, and future); God is eternally alive in us (Father, Son, and Holy Spirit); and we are eternally alive in God. Following is the prayer Jesus prayed for His disciples and all believers following the last supper, on the evening before His crucifixion:

"I do not pray for these alone, but also for those who will believe in Me through their word; that they all may be one, as You, Father, are in Me, and I in You; that they also may be one in Us, that the world may believe that You sent Me. And the glory which You gave Me I have given them, that they may be one just as We are one: I in them, and You in Me; that they may be made perfect in one, and that the world may know that You have sent Me, and have loved them as You have loved Me." – John 17:20-23

The world doesn't see a visible manifestation of our salvation experience because in this world we are alive in corrupt physical bodies. However, God's presence within us manifests our oneness with Him, that the world may know God sent Jesus and loves every believer as He loves Jesus. After the last supper and before His prayer quoted above, Jesus had the following conversation with His disciples:

"A little while longer and the world will see Me no more, but you will see Me. Because I live, you will live also. At that day you will know that I am in My Father, and you in Me, and I in you. He who has My commandments and keeps them, it is he who loves Me. And he who loves Me will be loved by My

Father, and I will love him and manifest Myself to him."

Judas (not Iscariot) said to Him, "Lord, how is it that You will manifest Yourself to us, and not to the world?"

Jesus answered and said to him, "If anyone loves Me, he will keep My word; and My Father will love him, and We will come to him and make Our home with him. He who does not love Me does not keep My words; and the word which you hear is not Mine but the Father's who sent Me." – John 14:19-24

How do I know if I'm saved? Assurance of salvation is not an uncommon concern for many believing Christians. As we backslide or fall back into previous patterns of sinful behavior, we often question or doubt our salvation experience and wonder if we're really saved. We stumble ourselves with our doubts and we end up looking in, rather than up, and that's not a good place to be.

We need to remember that we had nothing to do with our salvation experience; it was entirely a work of God—from the seed of faith He planted in our hearts, to the moment we confessed Jesus as Lord with our mouths and believed in our hearts that God raised Him from the dead. How do you know if you're saved? Pastor John MacArthur suggests asking yourself several questions:

- "Do you desire to honor and glorify Christ?"

- "Do you love God?"

- "Do you desire to worship God, obey God, rejoice in God, and praise God?"

- "Do you believe Scripture?

"If you do, then God has saved you by making your unwilling and corrupt heart willing. And that's the miracle of conversion—your old self didn't have those delights and desires."

WAVES OF GRACE

I didn't realize it at the time, but our surf trip to Scorpion Bay was my last surf trip as an unbeliever. As we began our drive back to San Diego through central Baja, I was beginning to feel what I now know was a God-inspired desire to abandon my self-absorbed ways and embrace His eternal love for me.

A physical analogy of a spiritual reality.

Monarch Butterfly Chrysalis [14]

"For we are His workmanship, created in Christ Jesus for good works, which God prepared beforehand that we should walk in them." Ephesians 2:10

Monarch Butterfly Adult Metamorphosis [15]

"Therefore, if anyone is in Christ, he is a new creation; old things have passed away; behold, all things have become new." – 2 Corinthians 5:17

CONNECTED

PART 3

17

SAN DIEGO, CALIFORNIA

32. 7 °N, -117.2°W

One weekend, about a month after my trip to Scorpion Bay, Judy and I were driving north in our van to visit my parents in the San Francisco Bay Area. This was a nine-hour trip, and when it was Judy's turn to drive, I pulled into a rest area so we could trade places. I hopped in the back looking for something to read that would put me to sleep and found a book Judy had checked out, from the church library she attended, on how to study the Bible. I figured that would do the trick. When I turned to the Preface, it read:

"The Bible is actually sixty-six different books inspired by God and written by forty people on three continents over several thousand years."

Suddenly, a flood of light illuminated my mind. I realized that the Bible was not necessarily a book that you begin to read from start to finish, but a series of books divinely inspired by God—God's own words! I began to appreciate that the wisdom of God was available on every page, and that every word, every verse, was a gift from God! Shortly thereafter, someone suggested I start reading the New Testament Gospel of John, and as I did, God began to prepare the soil of my heart to receive the Spiritual seed of faith that would soon serve to birth my new life in Jesus.

A few weeks after our drive to the San Francisco Bay Area, in the late summer of 1986, a Christian friend of mine, who knew I was searching for God, gave me a copy of Chuck Colson's book *Born Again*. I think I related to Chuck Colson's testimony because he had journeyed to the peak of success and power and down again.

At the time President Nixon appointed him Special Counsel to the President, he was one of the most highly paid attorneys in the United States. He had transitioned from the pinnacle of a private practice career to an unparalleled position of power and influence in the Executive Office of the President. In the eyes of the world, he was a success in every definition of the word—before transitioning to federal prison following his involvement in the Watergate scandal, that toppled the Nixon administration.

As I was reading Chuck's book, I came to the turning point in his life. One day, shortly before his imprisonment, he had an encounter with one of God's ambassadors, Tom Phillips, a follower of Jesus and president of Raytheon, a Fortune 500 company. Tom shared his personal testimony and conversion experience with Chuck. As Chuck listened to him, he couldn't figure out why Tom needed religion, after all, he was president of a huge electronics company. Nevertheless, Chuck could sense Tom's inner peace, something Chuck longed for.

A few months later, in August of 1973, just before entering prison, Chuck returned to Tom's home. As they were sharing tea, Tom read some passages from C.S. Lewis' book, *Mere Christianity*, and encouraged Chuck to pray and receive Jesus as his Lord and Savior. Chuck shared that he wasn't ready yet. Tom then read some passages from the Old Testament book of Psalms and the words seemed to come alive to Chuck. Tom asked Chuck if he could pray with him and Chuck agreed.

As Tom prayed, Chuck felt the power of the Holy Spirit sweep over him and he had to fight back the tears. Later that evening, on his drive home, Chuck pulled his car over to the side of the road and invited Jesus into his heart. Then, after serving his prison term, he went on to establish the largest prison ministry in the world, Prison Fellowship, and became an accomplished author of numerous faith-based books.

Late one night, as I was reading this passage in Chuck's book, God began to reveal His presence and eternal love for me. As I continued reading, I rose from our dining room table, walked into the living room, dropped to my knees at the coffee table, and prayed to receive Jesus into my heart as my personal Lord and Savior. I didn't hear a hallelujah chorus or see a bolt of lightning, I simply walked upstairs, went to bed, and shared my newfound faith with Judy the following morning. Despite Judy living out the love and faithfulness of Jesus to me throughout our marriage, it had taken fifteen years for God to open my blind eyes.

Later that day, I called my dad and shared my conversion experience with him, and several days later, he gave his life to the Lord as well. I was 36 and he was 66. Not only could he hear the sincerity and commitment in my voice, he could feel in his heart that I was a new creation. Although I never had a conversation with my mom about this moment in the same way, I'm certain she was impacted by my testimony as well. Many years later, after my dad had passed into heaven and she was living in an assisted living facility in Fresno, California, one of her favorite pastimes was to have me read the Bible to her when we visited.

My dad and I – Christmas 1986 – brothers in Jesus [1]

Shortly after my conversion, I felt prompted to announce my good news to Desmond Bittinger, the dean of the ship my first semester with the World Campus Afloat program, and the minister who married Judy and me. Desmond and his wife, Irene, had moved to a senior community for retired pastors built by the Church of the Brethren, located in La Verne, California.

The Bittinger's were now in their 80's and invited us over for afternoon tea. When we arrived at their modest home and rang the doorbell, Desmond greeted us at the door and gave each of us a big hug. I then looked him in the eyes and shared that I had invited Jesus into my life as my personal Lord and Savior. As I spoke these words, Desmond, who was shorter than me, reached up, cupped his hands around my face, drew my face down to his, and kissed me on the lips!

"Greet all the brethren with a holy kiss." – 1 Thessalonians 5:26

One of the most important questions for an unbeliever to understand is the question about how one is born again. It was an important question 2,000 years ago, when Nicodemus came to Jesus by night; it is no less so today.

"There was a man of the Pharisees named Nicodemus, a ruler of the Jews. This man came to Jesus by night and said to Him, 'Rabbi, we know that You are a teacher come from God; for no one can do these signs that You do unless God is with him. Jesus answered and said to him, 'Most assuredly, I say to you, unless one is born again, he cannot see the kingdom of God.' Nicodemus said to Him, 'How can a man be born when he is old? Can he enter a second time into his mother's womb and be born?' Jesus answered, 'Most assuredly, I say to you, unless one is born of water and the Spirit, he cannot enter the kingdom of God. That which is born of the flesh is flesh, and that which is born of the Spirit is spirit.'" – John 3:1-6

Although the answer is quite simple, it is also the essence of salvation, freedom, and eternal life: God is a Spiritual Being and the only way to connect to God eternally is through spiritual birth, often referred to as being born again.

Unfortunately, when virtuous Adam and Eve sinned and broke spiritual fellowship with God, every human being born thereafter inherited their carnal, fleshly nature, incapable of connecting to God. When God gave the Jews His law, the Ten Commandments, they added several hundred other rules and regulations, the *Talmud*, and attempted to obey the *Talmud* by outward displays of self-righteous works.

God's purpose in giving the Jews His law was to demonstrate man's inability to fulfill His law, because only perfect Spiritual love and holiness can fulfill His law. Not only did the Jews fail to fulfill His law in their fallen carnal state of being, they compounded their failure by formulating their own laws. In response, God mercifully fulfilled His law by sacrificing His Son on the cross for the sins of all who would believe in Him. In so doing, God imputed (or accounted) the righteousness of Jesus to mankind by grace alone, through faith alone, in Christ alone. Grace and self-righteousness are mutually exclusive, as are spiritual life and carnal life.

"There is therefore now no condemnation to those who are in Christ Jesus, who do not walk according to the flesh, but according to the Spirit. For the law of the Spirit of life in Christ Jesus has made me free from the law of sin and death. For what the law could not do in that it was weak through the flesh, God did by sending His own Son in the likeness of sinful flesh, on account of sin: He condemned sin in the flesh, that the righteous requirement of the law might be fulfilled in us who do not walk according to the flesh but according to the Spirit." – Romans 8:1-4

Pastor Chuck Smith compares God, a superior trinity (Father, Son, and Holy Spirit) to man, an inferior trinity (body, soul, and spirit). Life without Jesus features the body on top, the mind in the middle, and the dead or dormant spirit on the bottom. Our carnal body appetites drive our mental, emotional, and behavioral patterns. Depending on our proclivity to practice certain sins, we can be sexually immoral, covetous, malicious, envious, violent, proud, unforgiving, and the list goes on. The root cause of our sinfulness is the corruption of our carnal body.

Conversely, after we are born again, our spirit flips to the top and our body is on the bottom. We now have a spiritual connection to God by the imputed righteousness of Jesus, and through the indwelling power of the Holy Spirit, we are empowered to turn from the same sins that used to trip us up. Nevertheless, we still live in a corrupt carnal body, that is constantly at war with our spirit for the dominance of our mind. It is a war that will never end until we pass from earth to heaven. Thus, we trip up from time to time.

> *"I find then a law, that evil is present with me, the one who wills to do good. For I delight in the law of God according to the inward man. But I see another law in my members, warring against the law of my mind, and bringing me into captivity to the law of sin which is in my members. O wretched man that I am! Who will deliver me from this body of death? I thank God—through Jesus Christ our Lord!" – Romans 7:21-25*

If we know and follow Jesus, Satan has no power over us. However, as long as we live on earth, he will tempt us to sin. He will sometimes succeed, but if we confess our sins, God is faithful and just to forgive us our sins and to cleanse us from all unrighteousness. Prayerfully confessing our sins serves to draw us back to the eternal reality of God's saving grace and unchanging love. God, like any loving father on earth, forgives His children when they misbehave. Confessing our sins is simply a family matter; it is no longer a matter of eternal life or death.

> *"Blessed be the God and Father of our Lord Jesus Christ, who has blessed us with every spiritual blessing in the heavenly places in Christ, just as He chose us in Him before the foundation of the world, that we should be holy and without blame before Him in love, having predestined us to adoption as sons by Jesus Christ to Himself, according to the good pleasure of His will, to the praise of the glory of His grace, by which He made us accepted in the Beloved." – Ephesians 1:3-6*

Being born again does not mean that believers are perfect and will never sin again. It means that we've been delivered from death to life, all of our sins have been forgiven, and we have embarked on a journey, through our remaining days on earth, of sanctification. As mentioned before, sanctification is the life-long process of being conformed into the image of Jesus and being made holy as He is holy. Our journey will end when we breath our last breath, are instantaneously transformed into His image, and live eternally in the heavenly light of His presence.

Being born again also means that God who now dwells within us is greater than Satan who is in the world. Never equate Satan with God, there is no comparison. Satan was created by God and is subject to God. As previously mentioned in the "Essentials" introduction to this book, God is omnipotent (all-powerful), omniscient (all-knowing), and omnipresent (everywhere all the time). Satan is none of these things, but in God's divine plan for the universe Satan is currently the ruler of the world. Why? Only God knows. But we know that God's ways are always perfect.

AS PREVIOUSLY DISCUSSED IN CHAPTER 6, Saul—a Jew, Pharisee, and Hebrew of the Hebrews—thought he was righteous before God because he was religious and obeyed all of God's law. Nearly two thousand years ago, when he met Jesus on the road to Damascus, he came to the realization that it is not by carnal works of obedience that one becomes virtuous, but by belief in Jesus.

Saul went on to become the apostle to the Gentiles (non-Jews), was renamed Paul, and was empowered by God to write much of the New Testament, based on his comprehensive understanding of Old Testament prophecies, including the following prophetic words of God about Jesus, written by Isaiah over 600 years before Jesus was born:

> *"Thus says God the Lord, Who created the heavens and stretched them out, Who spread forth the earth and that which comes from it, Who gives breath to the people on it, and spirit to those who walk on it: 'I, the Lord, have called You in righteousness, and will hold Your hand; I will keep You and give You as a covenant to the people, as a light to the Gentiles, to open blind eyes, to bring out prisoners from the prison, those who sit in darkness from the prison house. I am the Lord, that is My name; and My glory I will not give to another, nor My praise to carved images. Behold, the former things have come to pass, and new things I declare; before they spring forth I tell you of them.'" – Isaiah 42:5-10*

Although Paul remained deeply devoted to sharing the gospel with his Jewish brethren, his main mission was to share the gospel with the Gentile or heathen world. God's church knows no racial or cultural barriers—all are one in Jesus.

> *"...if you confess with your mouth the Lord Jesus and believe in your heart that God has raised Him from the dead, you will be saved. For with the heart one believes unto righteousness, and with the mouth confession is made unto salvation. For the Scripture says, "Whoever believes on Him will not be put to shame." For there is no distinction between Jew and Greek, for the same Lord over all is rich to all who call upon Him. For "whoever calls on the name of the Lord shall be saved." – Romans 10:9-13*

WAVES OF GRACE

In September of 1986, shortly after my conversion, I began pursuing a career in commercial real estate brokerage. There was still a possibility we might be able to resurrect the helicopter company and I figured commercial real estate would be a good place to invest some of the profits if we were successful. I joined one of the largest investment brokerage companies in the nation and began to learn the ropes of the commercial real estate business. I also felt drawn to walk closer to God and learn more about Him. In retrospect, this was because His plan was to use me in ways I could never ask, think, or imagine.

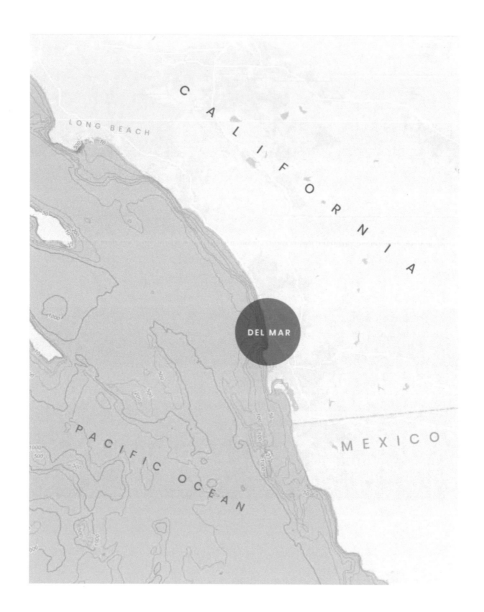

18

DEL MAR, CALIFORNIA

32.9 °N, -117.2°W

Shortly after I began my commercial real estate career, Judy and I woke up early one morning so she could take a pregnancy test. It was positive and we were both elated. I decided to call my dad to share the news. I knew he was an early riser and that he and my mom had been waiting fifteen years for Judy and me to have a baby.

When the phone rang, my dad picked it up and the conversation went something like this:

"Dad, guess what?"

"What?"

"Judy's pregnant!"

"Leith, guess what?"

"What?"

.

"When the phone rang, I was on my knees praying for a baby for you!"

The helicopter company eventually ran out of money and was dissolved, but I had entered God's eternal kingdom, and in answer to prayer, God blessed Judy and me with our one and only child, Allison.

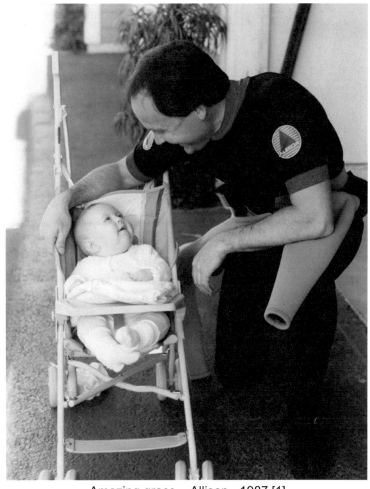

Amazing grace – Allison - 1987 [1]

In 1995, one of my commercial real estate clients, who was headquartered in San Diego, helped me start my own brokerage company, Prime Net Realty Advisors. He provided office space close to our home and near the beach. That winter, in January 1996, on a brisk, clear San Diego day, I called the lifeguard tower at 17th Street in Del Mar for a recorded report. I was informed that the air temperature was 62°F and the ocean water temperature was a chilly 57°F.

I had started work at 5 a.m. to accommodate my East Coast clients, and by noon I was ready to change gears and head down to the beach for a mid-day ocean swim. Surfing and open-ocean swimming were my mental and physical release; however, I had no idea I was about to have my own West Wing experience, like the farmer in Texas who had ignored God's warning signs about an impending flood.

Cresting Del Mar Heights Road and descending to the Coast Highway in Del Mar, I was mesmerized by the beauty of the Pacific Ocean panorama. From a distance, it resembled "victory at sea" conditions, a term often used by surfers to describe crazy, mixed-up, ocean surface conditions (probably a reference to the *Victory at Sea* title screen of the World War II *Battle of the Atlantic* episode on the high seas). But the sky was bright blue, the sun was brilliant, and the atmosphere crystalline from the powerful winds that had blown through. This was my first warning sign of dangerous ocean conditions.

Approaching the train station parking lot across the street from Power House Park, I noticed several things: one, the train station parking lot was empty; two, there were no cars parked on the street; three, no one was in the ocean; and four, the "victory at sea" conditions were much worse than I had anticipated (second warning sign).

Del Mar, California – Train station
and Powerhouse Park [3]

"Victory at sea" conditions [2]

I pulled into the train station parking lot and began changing into my uniform: wetsuit shorts, rash guard, and sleeveless tank top. I also grabbed my O'Neill Squid Lid, a neoprene hat with the visor cut off. Prior to the introduction of triathlon wetsuits, I had gradually developed my own way to maximize shoulder rotation, provide warmth for my vital arteries, and prevent heat loss from my head.

Crossing the street and heading down to the beach, I noticed the lifeguards had placed yellow warning tape across the entire beach frontage, in hopes of preventing anyone from descending to the beach, let alone entering the ocean (third warning sign). Ducking under the tape, I walked down to the beach and waded into the ocean thinking I would swim out beyond the break, check my bearings (line-of-sight markers, like a palm tree or a house, familiar to me and situated along the coast relative to my position in the ocean), and then decide whether to head back to the beach or continue my workout.

I should mention at this point, that swimming beyond the break in Southern California almost always involves dealing with currents flowing north to south or south to north. Summer currents typically run north and winter currents south, but you never know for sure. If you are swimming parallel to the shore, it is often difficult to gauge the distance you want to swim utilizing line-of-sight shore markers due to the currents, so I have developed a reflexive, subconscious ability to count my strokes and still enjoy the workout. Also, as mentioned before, when open-ocean swimming through heavy surf or storm waves, I do not wear goggles because they are more nuisance than asset, as they can be easily ripped off or fill with water.

When I'm swimming out beyond the break in large swells, I duck dive under incoming waves. Have you ever watched a surfer submerge their board under an incoming wave as they paddle out to the lineup? They lift their butt and one leg up in the air while simultaneously dipping the front of their board and their head underwater. This displaces non-buoyant weight to their upper body, providing velocity to facilitate submerging the board. I do the same thing using both legs. Then, when I hear and feel the suction of the wave breaking behind me, I surface through the trough in front of the next oncoming wave and grab a breath. I should also mention that I never use fins when ocean swimming.

Surfer duck diving a wave [4]

When I had swum out beyond the break, I checked the coastline to determine where the current had carried me. I was about a hundred yards offshore and about two hundred yards north of where I had entered (fourth warning sign). I decided to do one more test to sample the strength of the current by freestyling two hundred strokes north and then gauging my position again. When I finished and looked to shore, I was about a mile offshore in leftover storm waves that were cresting at five to seven feet. I could barely see the tops of the hills above the coast of Del Mar.

Unknowingly, I had connected to a major ocean current sweeping west and out to sea. To the best of my knowledge, no one had watched me enter the ocean. I was on my own. Regardless of my open-ocean swimming ability, I realized I had made a succession of wrong choices and God had provided a series of warning signs. It might take me an hour to swim parallel to the coast and out of the current before trying to swim back to shore. My make-shift wetsuit would not provide the degree of warmth I would need to accomplish that. In addition, I probably wouldn't have the strength and energy to pull it off.

After ten years of following Jesus, I knew instinctively it was time to pray, "Lord, please guide me back to shore in Jesus' name." I put my head down, aimed for shore, and began swimming. Although I had every reason to panic, He blessed me with His peace that surpasses all understanding and guided me back to the exact spot I had entered the ocean. Rescued again!

ON ANOTHER OCCASION, EARLY ONE morning, as I drove to the same beach for a swim, the coast was blanketed in a thick fog. I wasn't concerned about not being able to see the shore from beyond the break, because I can usually feel the force and direction of the swell as it surges toward the beach.

To my surprise, at the same moment I duck dived a wave on my way out, and began surfacing in the following trough to catch a breath, a pod of about ten pelicans decided to swoop down and glide through the air foil created by the face of the next wave. When I broke the ocean surface, my peripheral vision caught the lead pelican only a few feet away, wildly back-flapping his wings to avoid colliding with my head, as those following went into a complete panic mode trying to avoid crashing into each other!

Once again, God used this occasion to remind me that every moment of my existence is in His loving hands. Had I surfaced a split second later, my head would have collided with the pelican's beak and I might have been seriously injured, blinded, or even killed. As it was, it was a moment of hilarity, not a moment of trauma.

All of us have close calls: some we are aware of; most we are not.

A pod of pelicans gliding through the air foil created by an incoming wave [5]

IN RETROSPECT

Everyone is connected to something and it is a good idea to reflect on what we are connected to. Are we connected to God or are we adrift at sea, absorbed in our self? Whatever we are connected to is either building us up to spend an eternity in heaven with our Creator or it is destroying us to the point that we will spend an eternity in hell without Him.

Pastor Chuck Smith once shared (Chuck Smith, Through the Bible, C2000 Series Bible Studies, Audio, Genesis Through Revelation, 1979-1986, Ephesians 1.):

"About those who believe—our life on this earth is all of the hell we are ever going to know. And about those who don't believe—their life on this earth is all of the heaven they're ever going to know."

The global entertainment, social media, and *news* industries occasionally create a product that is wholesome and inspiring, but for the most part, they are flooding the earth with a mind-numbing outpouring of filth, carnal corruption, lies, and wickedness.

> *"The wicked plots against the just, and gnashes at him with his teeth. The Lord laughs at him, for He sees that his day is coming." –*
> *Psalm 37:12-13*

If we are addicted to movies, television, the internet, and/or our smartphone, we are probably being unconsciously indoctrinated to accept as normal the moral depravity created by people who are knowingly and unknowingly channels of pure evil. It can ensnare and destroy us, as it has ensnared and destroyed others, including many of the actors, actresses, musicians, talking heads, and business moguls who are acting it out and/or creating it. Just look at or listen to today's headlines to read or hear about the latest casualty.

> *"The lamp of the body is the eye. If therefore your eye is good, your whole body will be full of light. But if your eye is bad, your whole body will be full of darkness. If therefore the light that is in you is darkness, how great is that darkness!" –*
> *Matthew 6:22-23*

The only way to ensure that we wouldn't be separated from Him eternally was for God to provide a sinless sacrifice: Jesus. His sacrificial death on the cross for the sins of all who would believe in Him, opened the door to eternal life—if we will simply confess with our mouths that Jesus is Lord and believe in our hearts that God raised Him from the dead. If we do, our sins are forgiven and we will spend an eternity in heaven. It's as simple as asking God for the faith to pray and take this step. We can't conjure up faith, but God can provide it.

> *"So then faith comes by hearing, and hearing by the word of God." –*
> *Romans 10:17*

We cannot earn our way into heaven. Faith in Jesus is not based on rituals, traditions, rules, or regulations. These might help direct our way, but usually only obscure the truth that we are saved by grace alone, through faith alone, in Christ alone. We are not saved by baptism, church attendance, church membership, tithing, the way we dress, whom we hang with, or who our parents are.

What is your faith in Jesus premised on?

There is nothing we can do to add to what Jesus has already done for us. Believing that Jesus died for our sins is the only way. Not only did Jesus die for our sins, once God raised Him from the dead and Jesus returned to heaven, God sent the Holy Spirit to dwell in the hearts of those who freely accept His gift of grace and choose to believe in Jesus. The Holy Spirit is the believer's comforter and guide into all truth and every believer is His temple. The Spirit is our guarantee of eternal life.

"Now He who establishes us with you in Christ and has anointed us is God, who also has sealed us and given us the Spirit in our hearts as a guarantee." – 2 Corinthians 1:21-22

God knew each of us before He created us. He gave each of us life, and one day, He will take our earthly life to live with Him eternally in heaven or to die and suffer eternally in hell. There is not a moment in our existence that He is not intimately familiar with, and if we trust that Jesus died for our sins, He will never forsake us. We will continue to sin and make wrong choices, from time to time, but we won't practice sin.

Without Jesus, we are chained to our sinful life eternally because we are powerless; however, if we believe He died for our sins, God will set us free eternally and the Holy Spirit who resides in us will comfort us and guide us in all our ways.

"For the wages of sin is death, but the gift of God is eternal life in Christ Jesus our Lord." – Romans 6:23

Being saved doesn't mean all our cares and worries will vanish. On the contrary, we will still experience trials, tribulations, and persecutions. There will be consequences for wrong choices, but we know that we are always in His hands. We will experience His peace that surpasses all understanding, regardless of what we've done or what we're going through.

"And we know that all things work together for good to those who love God, to those who are the called according to His purpose." – Romans 8:28

We measure our lives in years, but eternity is forever. Comparing eternity to a life span is like comparing the expanse of the universe to the smallest particle visible through an electron microscope. There's no comparison. Our life is a vapor. We each need to ask ourselves, where do we want to spend eternity—in the heavenly love, light, and joy of God, or in the darkness and loneliness of hell?

WAVES OF GRACE

In 2001, Bryan Jennings, ex-pro surfer and founder of Walking on Water ministries, and I flew to Sydney, Australia, to introduce the new Walking on Water surf film, "Changes", to the Christian Surfers International organization. Bryan and I had become close friends during the production of "Changes", and he asked me to join the Walking on Water Board of Directors in 1998. God was beginning to show me that His ways are always higher than our ways and that He always answers prayer perfectly— according to His will.

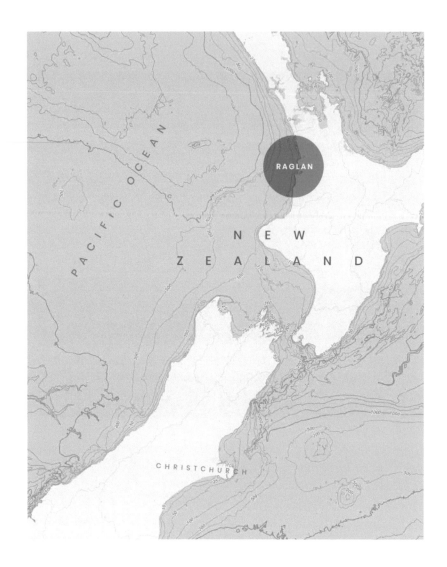

19

RAGLAN, NEW ZEALAND

-37.8°S, 174.8°E

My lifelong friendship with Bryan Jennings began during the summer of 1997, when he called me to discuss a documentary film, *Changes,* he was planning to produce with another surfer, Ed Feuer, a talented videographer and director. Bryan and I had first met over the phone earlier that year when I had called to ask permission to use his first surf film, *Beyond the Break*, for an outreach event we were organizing for San Diego North County surfers.

Bryan Jennings, Ex-Pro Surfer and Founder, Walking on Water –
Photo: Tim McCaig [1]

Bryan and I agreed to meet the next day for breakfast in La Jolla. As we broke bread, Bryan began to describe *Changes*—a film that would begin with several Christian professional surfers sharing their faith and surfing world class waves—before ending with the Chris O'Rourke story—a story Ed had a passion to film and direct.

Chris O'Rourke was one of the most well-known and talented surfers in California during the 1970s. He was also one of many La Jolla, California, Windansea Beach locals, who practiced an extreme form of territorial ownership. They didn't tolerate anyone they didn't know surfing their break, even to the point of turning over a VW bus and burning it while the occupants were out surfing.

I had never heard of Chris O'Rourke, but as Bryan began to share his story over breakfast I was mesmerized. At the beginning of what promised to be a stellar surfing career, when he was only seventeen, Chris was diagnosed with cancer and shortly thereafter met and began to follow Jesus. From that point on, despite his cancer and suffering, God used Chris to share his faith until he passed into heaven at the age of twenty-three.

Bryan asked if I would consider helping produce this film and I agreed under one condition—he and Ed would come to our house, once a week, to pray. Bryan, Ed, Judy, and I met and prayed for about a year, and God answered our prayers. The last half of *Changes*, the Chris O'Rourke story, turned out to be one of the most Holy Spirit-anointed segments of any of the twelve subsequent documentary films produced by Walking on Water over the last 25 years. After Chris passed, God used *Changes* to share his faith journey with the world (you can view *Changes* for free on YouTube by googling: Changes Surf Movie).

Chris O'Rourke – Photo: Warren Bolster [2]

Windansea Beach, La Jolla, California – Photo: (peasap) [3]

As *Changes* grew in popularity, Bryan and I felt called to travel to Australia and New Zealand, and introduce it to the Christian Surfers International organization. After a whirlwind visit, where we met with key Christian Surfers leadership in Australia, including Brett Davis, the founder, we flew to Auckland, New Zealand, to meet up with the Christian Surfers International leadership in that country.

Changes – video jacket – 1998 [4]

We also connected with Brian Hughes, founding pastor of Calvary Chapel Auckland. In his day, Brian was an accomplished surf photographer and waterman. Brian shared that the forecast for Manu Bay, Ragland, a world-class wave, on the west coast of the north island, looked perfect and invited Bryan and me to drive up and surf it, as well as to meet up with Brendan Hull, the Christian Surfers National Coordinator in Mt. Maunganui.

We picked up Brendan and—as we crested the hill overlooking the Ragland coast—it was *corduroy to the horizon* (surf speak for perfect conditions). We parked, pulled on our wetsuits, grabbed our boards, and headed to a rocky outcropping to shorten our paddle out to the lineup.

I was 53 at the time and had undergone two shoulder surgeries that year—rotator cuff of one and scope (clean up) of the other. I was still in recovery mode, besides the fact that I had never timed a jump from a rock with my board—high above large breaking surf. When my turn came, I landed on my board with my chest, knocking the breath out of me! In hindsight, I should have jumped and landed to the side of my board while holding on to it.

Have you ever been sucker punched in the gut or had the wind knocked out playing football? That's what it felt like. I couldn't catch my breath, and an eight-foot set was about to sweep me into the rocks. Again, by God's grace, Brendan turned, saw my predicament, paddled back, offered his leash, and towed me out beyond the break.

Manu Bay – Ragland, New Zealand – *corduroy to the horizon* [5]

Brendan's rescue of my life at that critical moment reminds me of several things:

- We can't escape the presence of God and without Him we can do nothing. In essence, it was God that empowered Brendan with the sensitivity to turn, see my predicament, and risk his life to save mine.

- Nature reveals God to man, but there is no testimony to the gospel of God's saving grace in nature. Nature testifies to a God of law, a God of justice, a God of power, a God of wisdom, a God of beauty, and a God of orderliness, but God saves men and women by grace alone, through faith alone, in Christ alone.

- The most awesome manifestation of His grace occurred two thousand years ago through His one and only Son, Jesus. Since that time, He has used millions of men and women to manifest His grace throughout the world, as they believed in Jesus and became His followers and ambassadors. My sister's church testified to His grace by loving her through a difficult time—and in so doing—expressing His love to me.

- Lastly, we need to recognize God in the everyday circumstances of life. He doesn't just reveal Himself in supernatural ways, although He can and sometimes does. If you are reading this book, He has manifested Himself to you through the Scripture passages I have shared. He can also reveal Himself through believers, unbelievers, nature, circumstances, prayer, angels, and in many other ways.

There is no limit to the ways He can touch our lives and draw us to Himself, but He will always use the Holy Spirit, who, as previously mentioned, is our comforter and guide into all truth. The Holy Spirit moves like the wind: invisible, sometimes gentle and comforting, but always with latent power.

He moved in a special way when He connected me to Bryan Jennings. God gifted Bryan with an amazing heart to share God's love with the world and an incredible assortment of spiritual gifts and natural talents to do it. I have been privileged to know and work with him.

> *"The wind blows where it wishes, and you hear the sound of it, but cannot tell where it comes from and where it goes. So is everyone who is born of the Spirit." – John 3:8*

As Pastor Chuck Smith once said:

"Someone might say God resides in this church or that building, but God is just as present in the bar down the street as He is anywhere else in the universe. He is everywhere, all the time. He doesn't dwell in temples made with men's hands, nor is He glorified with ornate altars, as though He needed material goods."

> *"Heaven is My throne, and earth is My footstool. Where is the house that you will build Me? And where is the place of My rest? For all those things My hand has made, and all those things exist," says the Lord. "But on this one will I look: on him who is poor and of a contrite spirit, and who trembles at My word." – Isaiah 66:1-2*

WAVES OF GRACE

In the early 1990s, a young couple moved in next door to us. The husband was from Peru and was a skilled surfer and freediver. We began surfing together and one day he offered to teach me how to freedive and hunt fish using a speargun—without scuba gear. As with surfing, I got hooked. Freediving was a perfect complement to surfing along the California coast—because when the ocean was calm and the surf nonexistent, the visibility underwater to hunt fish was the best. God was blessing me with the opportunity to explore the ocean in a way I had never explored it before.

20

DEL MAR, CALIFORNIA

32.9°N, -117.2°W

Have you heard the story about the frog that was placed in a pan of cool water on a stove? He was in his element. He could have jumped out if he wanted to, but he was perfectly content to lounge in the refreshing water. Little did he realize that the burner had been turned to low. As the water gradually heated up, he remained totally unaware of the temperature change, until it was too late. His energy to jump out was ever so slowly sapped away and he boiled to death.

Similarly, if we ignore the gospel of the grace of God and choose to reject Him—when we die—we will be eternally separated from Him. There can also be a time when God releases us to our own devices. He no longer touches us through those who know and follow Him, through circumstances, or even through a book like this. Once that happens, we are a hair's breadth from eternal separation from Him.

I experienced a reminder of this one day when I was freediving off the coast of Del Mar, California. One of my favorite go-to spots for lobster hunting was a ten-minute drive from our house, a reef off 10th Street, where I always seemed to find a couple of bugs (lobsters) for dinner.

That day the viz was remarkably good for Southern California (SoCal), and sure enough, while scouting the bottom at a depth of about twenty feet, I spotted what looked like a two-pounder tucked under a reef ledge in a crevice. I surfaced, took another breath, and dove back down to check out how he might escape if I spooked him.

Lobsters are cagey and can easily slide back into an escape hole or tunnel in the reef, especially mature, big guys—like this one—who know their way around. Sure enough, when I dove down, I could see a hole in the ledge above his hiding spot—so I wedged my speargun in to it, to block it off.

I surfaced for another breath, dove back down, positioned myself in front of him and—as quickly as I could—snatched him with both hands. The snatch must be executed with split-second timing—and in such a way that you are close enough to grab him but not close enough to disturb his long, outstretched antennae and spook him (in California it is illegal to shoot a lobster with a speargun).

With my hands clenched on the lobster like a vice, I was unaware that the small dive light attached to my left wrist had also penetrated the opening of his reef hide-a-way. I couldn't pull the lobster or my hands out. Although I had blocked his escape, he had locked his tail firmly to the back of the crevice. I couldn't budge him, but I was determined to have him for dinner. Little did I know I was also tempting death.

A California Spiny Lobster (bug)
tucked inside a reef crevice on the ocean floor –
Photo: Kirk Wester [1]

One of the most dangerous aspects of freediving is shallow water blackout—caused by holding your breath too long underwater which results in a loss of consciousness. Shallow water blackout occurs due to lack of oxygen to the brain. There are no warning signs—and unless resuscitated immediately by a diving companion you will die. It usually happens to younger, more aggressive freedivers, prone to push their limits, or older people, like myself, that prefer to dive solo.

Like the frog in the pan, I was oblivious to my circumstances, when all I had to do was release the lobster and pull my hands out one by one. I was so intent on capturing the lobster the thought of releasing him never entered my mind. By God's grace, I broke the lobster free, released my left hand and pulled it out with the flashlight, pulled the lobster out with my right hand, surfaced in the nick of time for a breath, and enjoyed a lobster dinner with Judy. Are you holding on to something that could kill you?

"The fear of the LORD is the beginning of knowledge, but fools despise wisdom and instruction." – Proverbs 1:7

IN RETROSPECT

There are different variations of freediving. The common denominator is that no one wears a scuba tank. Whether you dive to seven or seven hundred feet, you do so with one breath of air. For some, it is a sport that focuses on how deep you can dive or how long you can hold your breath; for others it is a sport that focuses on hunting fish. These two aspects of the sport are as disparate as the people who practice them. I don't think I have ever met anyone who loves to dive to test their breath or depth threshold, who is equally passionate about hunting fish. Nothing wrong with either sport; they are simply distinct cultures.

The freediving I'm about to introduce focuses on hunting game fish, otherwise known as bluewater hunting. Bluewater hunting involves diving in open-ocean waters for large pelagic species. Pelagic fish live in the pelagic zone of the ocean—an offshore zone where water depths are measured in hundreds or thousands of feet—in contrast with demersal fish, which live close to shore and near the bottom, or reef fish, which are associated with coral reefs. Bluewater hunting involves hunting for large species like marlin, tuna, or yellowtail (kingfish).

Why would someone freedive to hunt fish when they could put on a scuba tank and not worry about holding their breath? The answer is that hunting fish is like hunting deer: they are wary of foreign sounds and movement. Stealth is key. Minimizing your presence will increase your success in killing your quarry. Scuba tanks produce bubbles underwater that frighten fish, particularly large game fish that are very sensitive and skittish.

Freediving requires an ability to hold your breath underwater for an extended period. For the average freediver, this might mean a minute or two. Try it; a minute is a long time. Some champion bluewater hunters can hold their breath for five or six minutes. My max is a little over two minutes.

When bluewater hunting, a freediver floats on the surface with a loaded speargun before his descent. The spear is attached to the gun by about 25 feet of coiled line that releases with the trigger pull. The butt of the gun is attached to 100 feet of rubberized cord, that in turn is attached to a buoy or series of buoys on the surface, each about three times the size of a football. Additional buoys are connected to each other by 100 feet of coiled line, each wrapped by a rubber band that will break and release when needed, providing additional play for a large game fish fighting for its life.

Bluewater speargun and fins
(fins are 3', gun is 6'6") [2]

Riffe freediving float buoy [3]

A hundred-pound kingfish that has been speared but not stoned (killed) can easily dive several hundred feet down or out. The buoys create drag that tires the fish. Sometimes it takes hours to exhaust a large fish, pull it to the surface, and kill it with a properly placed knife thrust, like a toreador with a bull. Occasionally, if the fish remains lively and another speargun is available from a following boat or dive buddy, the fish is shot a second time at close range to kill it.

IN THE SPIRITUAL REALM, SATAN and his fallen angels (demons) are hunting down every person on earth, wounding many and going for the kill shot (eternal separation from God). Satan may wound or kill believers in Jesus, but he can never separate believers from God, nor can he ever possess them.

Satan may ignore certain unbelievers because he can see they are on a self-destructive path and he doesn't feel the need to bother with them. Conversely, he may scheme to seriously wound or kill them because he is a murderer by nature. Satan and his demonic army can also possess unbelievers and cause them to do unspeakable things. Many of the most horrible atrocities we hear or read about are carried out by demon-possessed people, but they are very rarely recognized and reported as such.

"You are of your father the devil, and the desires of your father you want to do. He was a murderer from the beginning, and does not stand in the truth, because there is no truth in him. When he speaks a lie, he speaks from his own resources, for he is a liar and the father of it." – John 8:44

Make no mistake, there is spiritual warfare occurring all around us — 24/7 — that is beyond our imagination. There is a hierarchy of demon angels over every nation on earth—intent on the destruction of souls—and they are engaged in an all-out battle with God's angel host. Followers of Jesus know that victory is assured, but the battle is fierce, and in my opinion, and the opinion of many others, is reaching a fevered pitch in world history.

God gives us a glimpse of this spiritual battle in the book of Daniel. In the context of the following verses, written 2,500 years ago, the prophet Daniel has been fasting, praying, and mourning—in order to learn more about the last times of his brethren the Jews—when he is awakened from a deep sleep by an angel sent from God. The angel informs him that God heard his prayers and dispatched him twenty-ones days before, but he was withstood by the demonic angel in charge of Persia, and was unable to prevail against Satan's demonic forces until one of the most powerful angels in God's kingdom, the archangel Michael, came to help him.

"Then he said to me, 'Do not fear, Daniel, for from the first day that you set your heart to understand, and to humble yourself before your God, your words were heard; and I have come because of your words. But the prince of the kingdom of Persia withstood me twenty-one days; and behold, Michael, one of the chief princes, came to help me, for I had been left alone there with the kings of Persia. Now I have come to make you understand what will happen to your people in the latter days, for the vision refers to many days yet to come.'" – Daniel 10:12-14

Although Satan is currently the ruler of the world, God is sovereign over all creation. God alone installs and removes every world leader and governing body for blessing or for judgment. He did so in Daniel's day and He is doing so now. But, as in Daniel's day, so as today, when world leaders and governing bodies don't acknowledge God, honor God, and thank God, they become fools and provoke God's judgment and wrath (see Romans 1:18-28). Again, as in Noah's day, so as today, believers are in the ark of God's grace and unbelievers are on the precipice of God's judgment and wrath.

WAVES OF GRACE

In 2005, I had the opportunity to join an eight-day bluewater freediving charter to New Zealand's uninhabited Three Kings Islands, led by seven-time Australian Open Spearfishing Champion, Rob Torelli, and his good friend, six-time Australian Open Spearfishing Champion, Ian Puckeridge. Although this was a freediving trip of a lifetime, it was also an opportunity for me to make new friends and share the gospel through some of the Walking on Water films we watched together during evenings at sea.

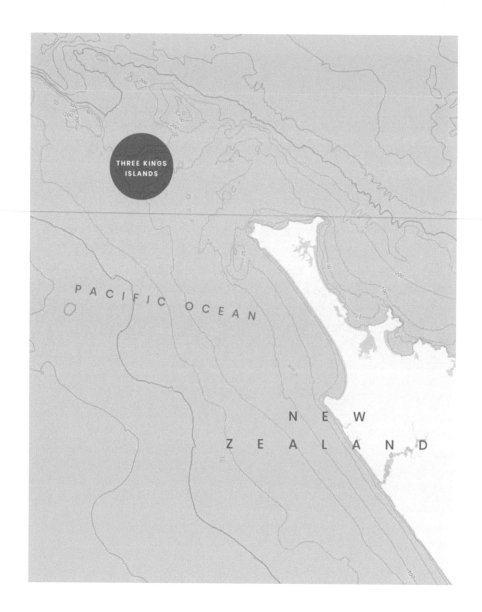

21

THREE KINGS ISLANDS, NEW ZEALAND

-34.1°S, 172.1°E

The Three Kings Islands are uninhabited rock outcroppings that reach up to the surface of the ocean from about 3,000 feet below sea level. They are located about a hundred miles northwest of the northern tip of the north island of New Zealand, where the Tasman Sea and the Pacific Ocean meet.

Our sportfishing boat traveled a full night and a day to reach these famed hunting grounds for hundred-pound kingfish or yellowtail, as they are known in San Diego. One morning, as we cruised alongside one of these islands, the sixty-foot sport fishing boat slowed to about five knots. One of the deck hands opened a gate on the port side and we took turns dropping into the clear Tasman Sea, heels down and fins up, with spearguns, buoys, and lines in hand.

As I hit the water and began stretching and loading the five half-inch rubbers of my gun, I noticed that a swift current was sweeping us past the shoreline of the rock outcropping, where another current, flowing perpendicular to the first and much stronger, swept us out into the open ocean. At that point, we were at the mercy of the current, but the captain of the mother boat had watched this develop and dispatched two rescue launches that picked us up, one by one, with the reassuring admonition from the Kiwi crew, "No dramas, mate!"

Three Kings Islands – New Zealand [1]

My first (and only) New Zealand kingfish – 2005 [2]

The pinnacle of bluewater hunting is to land a thousand-pound black marlin, which can reach speeds up to 80mph and weigh up to 1700 pounds. We trolled for them not far from the Three Kings over the top of a ridge that rose from several thousand feet below sea level to four hundred feet below the ocean surface. Huge black marlins search this ridge for food.

The captain monitored the ridge by radar and two deckhands kept their eyes on each of the two lines that trailed behind us from sport fishing poles. Each line was baited with a colorful, hookless lure. We planned to attract a marlin up from depth with the lures and then tease him to the stern by slowly reeling them in.

My friend, Terry Coombes, sat on the stern transom diving platform with Rob Torelli. Terry is a Marine Pilot for super tankers and Rob leads blue-water hunting trips, and publishes an Australian spearfishing magazine. Terry sat on the platform with his gun locked and loaded, while Rob sat next to him with an underwater camera ready to film the action. When hunted like this, marlins are known to retaliate and try to impale the hunter with their bill. It is a very dangerous undertaking (no pun intended).

Black Marlin (Makaira indica) leaping out of the sea off Australia – Photo: Georgette Douwma [3]

Terry – locked and loaded [4]

After an hour or so, the dorsal fin of a marlin broke the surface. The captain spotted him from the bridge and shouted out. The deck hands slowly reeled in the lures and the marlin followed. The captain gradually slowed the boat to a crawl. When the marlin maneuvered within a hundred yards of the stern, the captain cut the engine, and Terry and Rob dropped off the transom into a wake of bubbles, hoping their timing was perfect for a shot. Unfortunately, it was not to be—the marlin skidded away before he was in range.

After Terry missed this opportunity, Rob asked me if I would like to take a turn. By God's grace, even though I was tempted and felt a bit of pressure to measure up to some of the more accomplished freedivers on the trip, I declined. This was my first bluewater hunting trip, and up to this point in time, I had only speared smaller fish off the coast of Southern California. God gave me the presence of mind to decline the opportunity to shoot a marlin, which was well beyond my skill level. I had nothing to prove. I was and am complete in Jesus.

Rob Torelli –

Ian Puckeridge –
Three Kings Island, New Zealand – 2005 [5]

After we had completed our eight-day trip out to the Three Kings, Terry and I stayed overnight at our Manganui hotel before boarding our respective flights home. We decided to stroll around the village and shop for our loved ones. One of our first stops consisted of a government-run tourist information office with a small gift shop featuring traditional handicrafts made by indigenous Māori craftsmen.

As we examined the crafts, the sweet little old lady who ran the shop took in our sunburned, salty, and unshaven appearance, before asking us, "Where have you boys been?" Terry replied, "We've been fishing the Three Kings." She immediately inquired, "Did you see the 20-foot great white? He's legendary for following the sport fishing boats around!" Terry and I quietly smiled at each other. Little did she know that we had been freediving, and at times, wrestling with bloody kingfish. By God's grace we had not been shark bait.

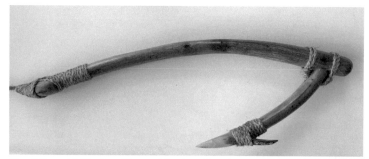

Traditional Māori gaff used for landing large fish into a boat [6]

Great white shark – Photo: Elias Levy [7]

DEL MAR, CALIFORNIA

32.9 °N, -117.2°W

In the summer of 2008, on a small surf day, I was sitting on my board waiting for a wave and realized that I wasn't getting any exercise. I needed a challenge and the idea surfaced that I should try to bodysurf without fins, through an entire year, in all conditions. A year later, I was hooked and never looked back.

Bodysurfing without fins, like any open-ocean sport, is an ever-changing experience. You are totally one with the ocean and immersed and connected with it in a way radically different from bodysurfing with fins or board surfing. In my opinion, it is the most organic form of surfing. You develop a special awareness of the ocean because you are constantly swimming with your eyes closed to protect them from the saltwater. Over time, you develop a sixth sense for the ocean's moods. For me, it became another opportunity to become one with God and His creation.

One of the most unique aspects of bodysurfing without fins is the incomparable sensation of flipping out of a wave and positioning your body underwater to adapt to the power release of the wave as it closes out. It's sort of like a front flip with a half twist from a diving board, which instantaneously results in your body being underwater, in a prone position, parallel to the bottom, fully elongated—with arms, hands, fingers, legs, feet, and toes fully stretched out.

In the shallowness of the water, the forces at work beneath the ocean surface—at the moment a wave closes out and curls under itself—cause your body to spin like a top from the tips of your fingers to the tips of your toes. Picture the position of a diver, just after entering a pool, but in a horizontal position, fingers pointed to the horizon and toes pointed to the beach. With practice, in swells generating 3-5' wave faces, the aftermath leads to landing on your feet facing back out to sea, positioned for awareness of a following wave, that you might need to duckdive.

In 2015, on a gloomy, overcast winter morning, the waves were three to five feet and very mixed-up from a passing storm. There was zero viz. The water was frigid for SoCal, about 56°F, and there was not a soul in sight. No problem, regardless of conditions, there's always a corner to glide in to (a corner is basically a sliver of a wave face, that opens up for a moment before closing out).

Midway into this session I flipped out of a wave, penetrated the surface, and slammed into a body! I knew I had smashed into something big and spongy—and—when I surfaced, a full-grown California sea lion surfaced five feet away, stared at me with fear and surprise in his eyes, and immediately turned and dived for his life.

California sea lion at rest – La Jolla, California –
Photo: fon thachakul [8]

In 2016, on another cold winter day, I arrived at the beach at daybreak and once again found crazy mixed-up storm surf. As I observed the conditions, I noticed that the best corners were the inside reforms in the shallow water close to shore. Reforms occur when larger waves break outside, then reform and break inside. I decided to go for it despite the meagre offerings.

Every wave was completely unique and unpredictable. Unfortunately, I was foolishly stretching the boundaries of safety and caution by exiting waves that not only broke in extremely shallow water, but were closing out on a normally smooth ocean bottom—now full of potholes and buildups caused by a series of winter storms.

Just before I was ready to end this session, I took off on a powerful wave face and was immediately spun out of control. I instinctively covered my head with my arms and hands and was drilled down into the cement-like bottom, hitting a build-up. By God's grace, my left shoulder took the brunt of the impact, had it been otherwise, I might be dead or paralyzed for life. As it was, it took several months of care and healing before I could rotate my left arm.

This was the same shoulder I had injured surfing in 1997, that had resulted in rotator cuff surgery and six months of rehab. There are costs associated with ocean sports, just as there are costs associated with driving on Southern California freeways, crossing the street, and following Jesus. It all goes with the territory.

AS I REFLECT ON THIS special gift God has allowed me to enjoy for so many years, there was one moment that provided the opportunity for me to utilize all of the skills and training I had developed bodysurfing without fins over the years. It happened in August 2014, when a mega swell generated by Hurricane Marie slammed the coast of Southern California for several days.

The focal point for the swell's impact were the Orange County beaches, but the surf throughout Southern California was epic. On the biggest day, with Orange County surf in the 15- to 20-foot range, I decided to drive up to the Wedge in Newport Beach to watch the action, but first had to sample the energy myself in Del Mar.

Unknown bodysurfer at the Wedge – Newport Beach, California –
Photo: Snoty Pimpin [9]

A few minutes before sunrise, I entered the ocean at 14th Street in Del Mar, a couple of blocks south of my usual entry point. Due to the strong current sweeping north, I knew I would need ample shoreline to go with the flow. The reef bottom in Del Mar ends at 15th Street, followed by a sandy bottom for several miles north. The wave faces reached six to ten feet on the sets and I was swept up the coast past intermittent groups of surfers.

I cruised north to 29th Street, occasionally catching a short corner of a wave. When I reached 29th, I swam to shore and walked back down to 14th to start over again. On this second reentry, I was carried by the current about halfway down to 29th when a huge, beautifully formed, and glassy (mirror-like surface) set began pumping through. By God's grace, I was perfectly positioned to tuck into the best wave of my life. I was so powerfully thrust across the face of the wave that I was airborne one moment and freefalling the next.

Bodysurfing without fins in six- to ten-foot surf is very tricky. Everything must line up perfectly in terms of the form of the wave and your position to it. It is critical to be in the right place at the right time, with very little you can do to maneuver into that place in a strong current and powerful swell. God created that wave and connected me to it.

In much the same way, by His waves of grace, He connected me to Jesus. Only He could have delivered me to a point in time when, by His gift of faith, I dropped to my knees and invited Jesus into my heart as my personal Lord and Savior. However, when that occurred, I didn't realize that to whom much is given, much is expected. I have been learning that lesson ever since.

"...For everyone to whom much is given, from him much will be required; and to whom much has been committed, of him they will ask the more." – Luke 12:48

IN RETROSPECT

The Bible is chock-full of those who have suffered and sacrificed their lives for their faith, from Abel to Zechariah in the Old Testament and from John the Baptist to Stephen in the New Testament. Many followers of Jesus are suffering and dying for their faith throughout the world as you read this. Our lives of faith are not measured by how deeply we are loved by those around us, but by how deeply we love them through the One who led the way.

> *"If the world hates you, you know that it hated Me before it hated you. If you were of the world, the world would love its own. Yet because you are not of the world, but I chose you out of the world, therefore the world hates you." – John 15:18-19*

When God gave me eternal life, He also gave me the precious gift of understanding His word by the power of the Holy Spirit. And as He did, I began to appreciate that one of the most foundational truths to following Jesus is counting the cost. In the Gospel of Luke, Jesus, on His way to Jerusalem to be crucified, turned to His disciples and the multitudes following Him, and said:

> *"If anyone comes to Me and does not hate his father and mother, wife and children, brothers and sisters, yes, and his own life also, he cannot be My disciple. And whoever does not bear his cross and come after Me cannot be My disciple. For which of you, intending to build a tower, does not sit down first and count the cost, whether he has enough to finish it—lest, after he has laid the foundation, and is not able to finish, all who see it begin to mock him, saying, 'This man began to build and was not able to finish'"?* *– Luke 14:25-30*

Jesus didn't mince words. Although these are tough words to hear, hear them we must, because if we don't hear them, we will have laid the foundation of our faith on the shifting sands of our worldly self. Jesus is not commanding those who seek to follow Him to literally hate their father, mother, wife, children, brothers, sisters, and their own life, for such a commandment would be antithetical to the truth that God is love. To the contrary, He is defining discipleship as a Christ-centered life, a life encompassing self-denial, obedience to God's commandments, worshiping God, praying to God, loving one another, fellowshipping with one another, serving one another, suffering, and even dying for His sake.

One of those who counted the cost was Mary, the virgin mother of Jesus. When the angel Gabriel appeared to her as a young teenager and announced that she had been chosen to give birth to the Son of God, she was engaged to Joseph. Mary understood that she would be carrying the baby Jesus in her womb before she was legally married. According to Jewish law, she could be accused of adultery, an offense punishable by stoning. Mary chose to believe the word of God and bless the world.

> *"Then Mary said, 'Behold the maidservant of the Lord! Let it be to me according to your word.'" – Luke 1:38*

WAVES OF GRACE

Throughout the Bible, God recounts the lives of men and women of faith that trusted Him and were directed by Him to glorify Him. None of them were perfect. All of them were flawed in one way or another. Their stories are told to remind us that God can use anyone to do anything. Nothing is impossible for God. J. Hudson Taylor once said: "Our work is to rest in Him." In the following chapters, I share some spiritual insights into God's ways that I am only now beginning to better understand.

J. Hudson Taylor, 1832-1905 –
British missionary and Founder,
China Inland Mission [10]

"Single bunch of Shiraz grapes on a vine" [11]

"I am the vine, you are the branches. He who abides in Me, and I in him, bears much fruit; for without Me you can do nothing." – John 15:5

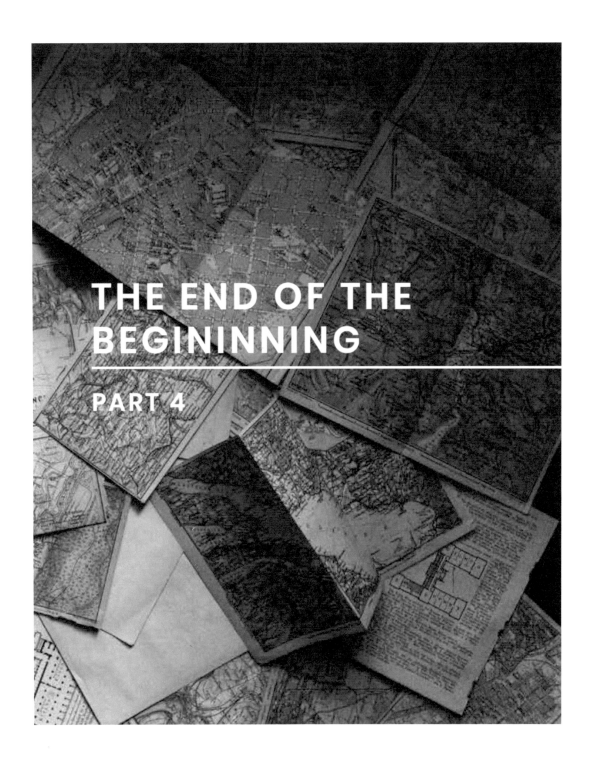

THE END OF THE BEGININNING

PART 4

22

SPIRITUAL GROWTH

"Many of us have need to ask for enlarged capacities. If we had more room for the Lord's gifts we should receive more. Pray to Him, 'Lord, enlarge my heart, expand my soul, and give me a nobler mind, more free from selfishness, less cramped with ideas of my own consequence; make me less important, more loving, more careful for the souls of others, more ambitious for thy glory, more intensely consecrated to thy word and will.'" – Charles Spurgeon

Once we know Jesus, there are three foundational principles to spiritual growth that will serve to draw us closer to Him; enable us to joyfully worship Him; and empower us to glorify Him by expressing the amazing natural talents and spiritual gifts He has bestowed upon us. They are God's word, prayer, and Christian fellowship. Think of them as three legs of a stool, underpinned by our triune God, that we can always rest upon to build us up spiritually and empower us to glorify Him in every endeavor He calls us to.

Three-legged stool [1]

If we neglect any of these principles, we will totter and occasionally fall. On the other hand, as we begin to embrace these principles, we will be filled with His love and joy, and experience His peace that surpasses all understanding. He will use us in ways we could never ask, think, or imagine. There will never be a time on earth when these three principles are not foundational to spiritual growth and ministry callings.

Before my conversion, if anyone had suggested that I would be involved in church ministry, such as helping to guide a nonprofit that produced evangelistic surf films, facilitating a men's prayer group, or any of the other ministry activities God has called me to, I would have thought they were out of their mind. Nothing is impossible for God and success in our callings is not defined by the world's perception of the outcomes of the ministries He calls us to, but by our faithfulness to pray and obey.

Also, because His ways are not our ways, we may not always understand or observe the outcome of what He has called us to do. We are to simply take the steps He leads us to take, not knowing what's next, but understanding that He alone knows the end from the beginning. He will reward us for the work He calls us to do, not the results of that work. The results are totally in His hands. Our work is to rest in Jesus, everything else will follow. We can do nothing without Him. This is a lifelong lesson. As pastor-teacher John MacArthur once said:

"We're just slaves. We're nothing more than that. We're slaves who have been given the responsibility to deliver the truth; God does the saving."

The ministries we are called to undertake will not be a cakewalk. In fact, it may be that God will call us to accomplish a task for His kingdom that is extremely difficult. Jeremiah, one of the major prophets of the Old Testament, was called to deliver a message of judgment to Israel at a time when Israel had become so carnally corrupt that God decided to destroy it. Jeremiah's calling was one of the most difficult because it was not a message Israel's corrupt leadership was willing to hear. The outcome was that Jeremiah suffered extreme persecution.

"So they took Jeremiah and cast him into the dungeon of Malchiah the king's son, which was in the court of the prison, and they let Jeremiah down with ropes. And in the dungeon there was no water, but mire. So Jeremiah sank in the mire." – Jeremiah 38:6

Perhaps Jeremiah was emboldened to deliver God's message because it also included God's promise to restore Israel in the last days—after the rapture of the church—by putting His law in their minds and writing it on their hearts. God has wonderful plans to bless Israel in the future because they are His covenant people, who will never be cast away. The rapture of the church is a future moment in time when Jesus returns for His church and all believers, dead and living, will join Him in heaven—prior to the tribulation (see Chapter 27).

"But this is the covenant that I will make with the house of Israel after those days, says the Lord: I will put My law in their minds, and write it on their hearts; and I will be their God, and they shall be My people." – Jeremiah 31:33

Throughout the New Testament and throughout church history, God reveals that the persecution of those who believe in Him never impedes the growth of the church, but serves as a catalyst for it to thrive. Jesus, the head of the church, is the supreme testimony to this truth.

GOD'S WORD

God's words are our most precious possession on earth. Never place anything else before them. They are our rock and foundation, and God will use them to conform us into His image and make us holy as He is holy. It is when we forget to feed on God's word that we begin to drift away from Him, embrace the world, disturb His peace that surpasses all understanding, and lose His joy.

"Heaven and earth will pass away, but My words will by no means pass away." – Mark 13:31

The Bible is the most miraculous book ever written. Think about it. Every word in the Bible was inspired by God. He used various men to write the words, but these men were simply His instruments, expressing His heart, through their personality, by the power of the Holy Spirit.

Following are a few of my favorite quotations about God's word, shared by men over the last several centuries, who God anointed and used in a special way. My prayer is that their words will encourage you, as they have encouraged me, to stay close to God through His word:

- "Some think that sinners can only be reached when a definite Gospel message is preached, but the Holy Spirit can reach the lost through any portion of the written Word of which He is the author." – Arno Gaebelein (1861-1945)

- "My business is sowing the seed, the word of God. It is the business of the Spirit of God to touch the hearts of those who hear." – Vernon McGee (1904-1988)

- "Scripture completely disables our nature." – Alexander Whyte (1836-1921)

- "There are hundreds of texts in the Bible which remain like virgin summits, whereon the foot of the preacher has never stood. I might almost say that the major part of the Word of God is in that condition: it is still an Eldorado unexplored, a land whose dust is gold. After thirty-five years I find that the quarry of Holy Scripture is inexhaustible, I seem hardly to have begun to labor in it!" – Charles Spurgeon (1834-1892)

- "They sit in the seat of pestilence, who fill the church with the opinions of philosophers, with the traditions of men, and with the counsels of their own brain, and oppress miserable consciences, setting aside, all the while the word of God, by which alone the soul is fed, lives, and is preserved." – Martin Luther (1483-1546)

- "Those that have been healed by Christ's word should be ruled by his word, whatever it costs them." – Matthew Henry (1662-1714)

- "Let the Word of God dwell richly in you, and never attempt to study it without asking for the Holy Ghost to teach you." – Marcus Rainsford (1820-1897)

PRAYER

Prayer is inspired by the word of God and subject to the will of God. Jesus centered His life on earth in prayer and He is now our prayer intercessor in heaven. He is also the greatest example we have of the power and importance of prayer during our pilgrimage on earth. If God, Jesus, based His life on earth on the power of prayer, how can we do any less?

There are numerous stories of the power of prayer contained in the Bible and countless examples believers have shared throughout history. Let's take a look at a contemporary example involving a young woman named Bethany Hamilton.

While surfing in Kauai, Hawaii, in 2003, at the age of thirteen, Bethany was attacked by a 14-foot tiger shark that tore off her left arm. Today, sixteen years later, Bethany is a living testimony of God's faithfulness to answer prayer. What happened? When Bethany was attacked, almost instantaneously, a grapevine of believers was alerted by Bethany's family and friends, and prayers began to be lifted up. It is my belief that a core theme to these Holy Spirit-inspired prayers went something like this:

"Heavenly Father, we lift up Bethany and her family to You and pray that You would take this horrific life-threatening injury, as well as all the suffering and anguish Bethany and her family are experiencing, and turn it all around in such a way that You would be glorified and the world would know Your love and grace in ways we could never ask, think, or imagine. In Jesus' name we pray. Amen."

This is not an uncommon prayer in a tragic situation and one God always answers perfectly.

In the years following this attack, Bethany has served as God's ambassador by helping others overcome their physical and mental challenges throughout the world. She also committed herself to an intense physical and mental regimen to become a competitive professional surfer, and in a 2016 World Surf League competition in Tavarua, Fiji, beat six-time world surfing champion, Stephanie Gilmore, and the top-ranked surfer in the world, Tyler Wright, to reach the semifinals. In 2017, she was inducted into the Surfer's Hall of Fame.

Most importantly, during these intervening years, God is using Bethany, now a happily married mother of two, to inspire people throughout the world with her message of faith in God and God's faithfulness to her. In 2014, President Barack Obama invited her to speak at the National Prayer Breakfast in Washington D.C. Following are two excerpts from her remarks:

"Because of where Jesus brought me, I have no regrets of the adversities God has allowed me to go through. As you look at me, you could think, 'Wow, have pity on her, she lost her arm to a shark.' But I look at it as something beautiful. God has taken something awful and turned it into something incredibly amazing.

"I felt as though I had lost more than just my arm. I thought that my hopes and dreams to become a pro-surfer and adventure the world were stripped away, but the faith I had in Jesus Christ gave me the strength to comprehend and lean on Him for understanding, even as a young girl."

A few months after the National Prayer Breakfast, in an interview with Fox News, she shared:

"I remember after I lost my arm, I just had this sense of peace that God was in control and that's kind of weird for a 13-year-old to be like, 'Hey, God, you're in control, like I just lost my arm.'"

Bethany is a living testimony to the power of prayer to overcome life's challenges with resilience and fearlessness.

WE DON'T NEED TO SPEAK to God as if we have a doctoral degree in our native tongue. God is not interested in whether we articulate the right word or form the perfect grammatical sentence. Jesus is listening to our hearts and perfectly translating everything the Holy Spirit prompts our hearts to express. Also, God is not timing how long our prayers are. He is not interested in the amount of time we spend in prayer but the quality of the time expended.

When Jesus instructs us to pray in His name, He is not implying that we need to ask Him to ask the Father. To the contrary, His death on the cross and the gift of the Holy Spirit have provided us with direct access to the Father, through the Son, by the power of the Holy Spirit. We pray in the name of Jesus because we are alive in Him and our prayers are based on His resurrected life. We pray in His name to glorify Him and build His kingdom based on His merit.

"In that day you will ask in My name, and I do not say to you that I shall pray the Father for you; for the Father Himself loves you, because you have loved Me, and have believed that I came forth from God." – John 16:26-27

The first Sunday I attended church as a new believer, I was sitting in a pew looking over the church bulletin before the service started. I noticed an announcement regarding a Men's Prayer Group that met on Saturday at 7:00 a.m. I thought to myself, "I started this journey with a prayer, inviting Jesus into my heart, I should check this out." The next Saturday, I arrived a few minutes before seven and walked around the church grounds trying to find the meeting room.

Bethany Hamilton – September 8, 2016 – Photo: Troy Williams [2]

Eventually, I quietly began to open the door to a classroom, and as I looked in, noticed ten men seated in a circle, all of whom were seventy years of age or older. I was thirty-six. I thought this might be a senior citizens group meeting, but as I opened the door a little wider, they noticed me and all of them stood up, greeted me, pulled up a chair, and welcomed me into their circle.

I spent the next five years with these amazing brothers in Jesus every Saturday morning. One of them, Bob Theetge, along with his wife Lorraine, helped Loren Cunningham start Youth with a Mission (YWAM). Bob took me under his wing and began to mentor me. He encouraged me by example and instruction to grow in Christ, as Jesus did with His disciples. I learned a lot about prayer from these veteran warriors.

Prayer is often one of the most difficult of God's gifts to exercise, because it defeats Satan at every one of life's turns, and Satan will always try to divert our attention to something else. As we think about entering into God's presence, Satan will tempt us with every imaginable excuse not to pray. We can defeat these enticements by remembering the following equation: The more we are tempted not to pray the greater our need for prayer. Failure to pray is often the root cause of life's most difficult circumstances.

Years ago, Judy and I attended a married couple's weekend retreat. On Friday evening, some of the participants performed a skit on stage that involved a husband and wife planning a date night. As the couple talked with eager anticipation about the fun, they were going to have that night, they agreed that the husband would call the wife later in the day to confirm the time and place where they would meet.

Shortly after the husband left the house, a lady dressed as the Wicked Witch of the West (Satan) appeared onstage at the wife's ear and began whispering that her husband would forget to call her because he would be too busy with his job, as he usually was. Then the witch appeared at the husband's ear and began whispering that his wife was being selfish because she should have taken care of the time and place to meet, leaving him more time to do his job.

The witch's whispers continued throughout the day to the point that when they met that evening they were at each other's throats. The last thing either of them wanted to do was to spend time together. At this point in the skit, while the witch was jumping up and down and rejoicing in the background, the husband turned to his wife and declared, "We need to pray!" They dropped to their knees, and as they began to pray in the name of Jesus the witch screeched, began crumbling up, and vanished into her black hat.

Wicked Witch's Hat from the "Wizard of Oz" – [3]

Another important point to remember about prayer is how we pray in a group setting. If we feel prompted by the Spirit to participate, we must always direct our prayers to God and not to the other people. Group prayer is a powerful expression of the Holy Spirit directing us to pray God's will be done—not a speech.

> *"Again I say to you that if two of you agree on earth concerning anything that they ask, it will be done for them by My Father in heaven. For where two or three are gathered together in My name, I am there in the midst of them." –*
> *Matthew 18:19-20*

Bob and these other mature believers helped me to realize that when we pray in a group, Jesus is in the midst of us. As they prayed, I noticed that they prayed from the heart. I also realized that it was important for me to focus on their prayers, rather than thinking about what I was going to pray about next.

It is a common temptation in a group prayer setting to be thinking about whether or not we should join in with our own prayer, rather than concentrating completely on the prayer that is being expressed. When we focus on the prayer that is being spoken, we lose ourselves in the moment and are led to participate as the Holy Spirit prompts us, not as we prompt ourselves.

Prayer is seeking the will of God, not imposing our will upon His. It is a two-way street, which is why His word and prayer are so integral to spiritual growth. By listening to Him as He shares with us through His word, he empowers us by the Spirit to share with Him. He speaks His will into our hearts through His word, as we pray His will be done. In essence, prayer is the harmonizing of our will with the will of God.

Billy Graham, one of the greatest evangelists that God has ever used, habitually read five *chapters* of Psalms and one *chapter* of Proverbs each day. He was empowered to pray to God as he read the Psalms and to hear God's will as he read the Proverbs. Every month, he cycled through both the Psalms (150—5 *chapters* a day) and the Proverbs (31—1 *chapter* a day).

That's a lot of Bible reading and prayer. It is a wonderful practice, but one that requires a lifetime of surrender. A good starting point might be to read a few verses of a Proverb and a few verses of a Psalm each day.

Connecting to God always begins with prayer. When we first believed in Him, we began by inviting Him into our heart with a prayer. From that point on, prayer becomes our most important lifeline to Him. The Old and New Testaments highlight the lives of many great men who were in love with prayer, including David, Daniel, and Paul. But the greatest prayer warrior of all was Jesus. He totally depended upon God the Father in prayer.

Arno Gaebelein shared that:

> "It should be said of every child of God that he is in love with prayer."

AS MENTIONED ABOVE, OUR NEW lives in Jesus are born in prayer. What breathing is to our bodies, prayer is to the maintenance and growth of our new life.

When Bob Theetge began to mentor me, he shared some words of wisdom I have never forgotten. He asked me to pinpoint the best part of my day. I mentioned that I loved the early morning because I was wide awake and alert. It was a time when I could go to the office and work through complicated tasks with clarity of mind and without telephone or interpersonal distractions.

Bob responded that I should give God the best part of my day in prayer. Wow! That would be a major change! I couldn't imagine forfeiting that precious time just to pray. Now, over thirty-six years later, it has become a habit, and I can't imagine not spending that time in prayer. Habits, good or bad, are ways of life that begin to develop over time. We don't just decide one day to have this or that habit. It is a progression of commitment that develops as we make a conscious decision to follow a lifestyle.

The biggest mistake we can make is to aim for a change and then give up when we fail in our effort the next day. We shouldn't beat ourselves up, but realize that all good habits take time. As we transition from a conscious decision to pursue a goal, to a more disciplined effort to achieve it, an unconscious habit starts to form. I occasionally neglect to pray in the morning, especially when I'm traveling, but I have never forgotten those words of wisdom.

The best habit I would encourage someone to develop to improve their prayer life is the study of Christian biography. Many years ago, Warren Wiersbe, an internationally known Bible teacher and the former pastor of The Moody Church in Chicago, ignited my interest in Christian literature through his book *Walking with the Giants: A Minister's Guide to Good Reading and Great Teaching*, featuring short biographies of famous preachers throughout church history.

Fortunately, I lived close to the Bethel Seminary library in San Diego, a treasure trove of Christian literature. On one of my first visits to this library, I checked out a book by Charles Spurgeon titled *Sermons on Prayer*. Spurgeon was a great evangelist and Bible expositor who lived during the 19th century in England. As I read Spurgeon's gifted insights on prayer, I began journaling in notebooks certain nuggets I found compelling. I can now look back and point to Spurgeon's book as one of the most important catalysts leading to the development of my prayer life.

Many years and many books later, I had compiled several journals and felt led to transcribe these nuggets to my computer. Rather than simply performing a transcription, I shared each nugget daily by email, with a Scriptural reference, to family and friends. This transcription became my first book, *Words of Wisdom*. Approximately twenty-five percent of the quotes featured in *Words of Wisdom* focus on prayer, and many of them are derived from Spurgeon's *Sermons on Prayer*.

Charles H. Spurgeon, "Prince of Preachers" – [4]

Charles Spurgeon once declared:

"You that have Christ's words abiding in you are equipped with those things which the Lord regards with attention. If the word of God abideth in you, you are the man that can pray, because you meet the great God with His own words, and thus overcome omnipotence with omnipotence. You put your finger down upon the very lines, and say, 'Do as thou hast said'. This is the best praying in all the world."

Entering God's throne room is an awesome privilege available 24/7. Sometimes there is only a moment to lift up an arrow prayer, like when we are in the middle of a conversation, but developing the habit of setting aside a quiet time during the best part of our day is more than worth the effort.

Count on the reality that going to prayer will almost always be a battle, because it is the last thing Satan, the world, and our flesh, wants us to do. Following are four ways that help me to enter into His presence and begin my quiet time:

1. Spending time in God's word. As I read His word, He speaks His will into my heart, prompting me to pray and blessing me with His peace that surpasses all understanding.

2. Beginning my prayer time with thanksgiving. Offering thanks helps me to recognize His goodness and majesty, and my total dependence upon Him.

3. Meditating upon the truth that God is the Creator and Sustainer of the universe. There is nothing out of His control.

4. Acknowledging the certainty that God is intimately familiar with every circumstance I might find myself in. His love for me is all-encompassing and never-ending.

I would also encourage all of us to step up the amount of time we spend listening to God versus the time we spend talking to Him. As previously mentioned, a springboard for developing this habit is reading God's word because, as we do, He will impress His will upon our hearts and empower us to pray His will be done— not ours. After all, only He knows everything about everything.

"All Scripture is given by inspiration of God, and is profitable for doctrine, for reproof, for correction, for instruction in righteousness, that the man of God may be complete, thoroughly equipped for every good work." – 2 Timothy 3:16-17

Lastly, God Himself, through the Holy Spirit inspired words of His servant, King David, declares that His word is above all His name:

"I will praise You with my whole heart; before the gods I will sing praises to You. I will worship toward Your holy temple, and praise Your name. For Your lovingkindness and Your truth; for You have magnified Your word above all Your name." – Psalm 138:1-2

FELLOWSHIP

Fellowship, gathering together with other believers, is essential to Christian growth and is often thought of as attending church. Attending church is a very important and wonderful practice, but it is only one component of fellowship.

Shortly after I prayed and asked Jesus into my heart, I called my sister to share what had happened. I knew she had been praying for me and I wanted her to be one of the first to know. She encouraged me to attend a five-year Bible study called "Bible Study Fellowship" (BSF), an international, interdenominational program founded by A. Wetherell Johnson.

Wetherell Johnson was a young lady of high society who was born in England during the early 20th century. She was raised in a Christian home, but during her late teens her missionary father brought her to Paris and placed her under the tutelage of a cosmopolitan lady of high intellect. While her father traveled through France, pursuing ministry work, her tutor introduced Wetherell to noteworthy intellectuals who frequently gathered at someone's home to discuss various secular philosophies of life.

Wetherell gradually drifted away from Christianity before returning home to England and recommitting her life to Jesus. She became a missionary to China, never married, and ministered to the Chinese in a remote northern village for many years. During World War II she was captured by the Japanese, imprisoned, and suffered cruelly under their heartless discipline. At the end of the war she was released, returned to England to recuperate, traveled back to China to pursue missionary work, and then traveled back to England through Southern California.

While in Los Angeles, she met a group of women who asked her to lead them in a Bible study. She agreed—on the condition, that these ladies would in turn study the passage of the Bible she assigned. She would then lead them in a study of that passage, and afterwards, provide them with commentary notes she had previously prepared. This approach formed the pattern for what was to become the BSF program, which is now one of the largest international, interdenominational Bible studies in the world.

My initial reaction to my sister's suggestion mirrored my reaction to Bob Theetge's suggestion—that I give God my best time: shock. Attend a five-year Bible study? No way! I didn't have time for something like that. However, I mentioned Linda's suggestion to Judy and she started attending the BSF woman's study.

When Judy wasn't looking, I would sneak a peek at the study notes she brought home afterwards. I was so intrigued by these awe-inspiring notes, written by Wetherell Johnson, that I started attending the local BSF men's group on Thursday evenings.

What made these notes so awe-inspiring? They were written by a brilliant woman who had completely surrendered her life to Christ and was gifted by Him to express His love, and exposit His word, in a profound way. She possessed a God-given talent to take the eternal truths of God's word down from heaven and present them in an easily understandable way, like taking a cookie jar down from a high shelf so a child can reach it.

There were about two hundred of us, who gathered weekly to worship the Lord, share His word together in small groups, and listen to an exposition of the Bible passages we were studying each week at home. We then closed in prayer and returned home with a copy of Wetherell Johnson's notes. We ranged in age from eighteen to eighty and represented a cross-section of every ethnic, socio-economic, and denominational demographic in San Diego.

A few weeks after Judy and I started attending BSF, my dad caught the bug and started attending a BSF men's group close to their home in the San Francisco Bay Area! Five years later, Dad, Judy, and I all completed the five-year BSF program. The three of us also served our last three years in BSF leadership positions.

Looking back now, over thirty years later, I realize that this was one of the best things I could have done when I first began following Jesus. BSF firmly grounded me in the essentials of prayer, Bible study, and fellowship. The goal of BSF is not to absorb you into a BSF culture, but to prepare you to live out your faith in service to your local church and the world.

WHEN JUDY AND I BEGAN attending church, we also met with others at the home of a married couple who were mature believers and facilitated our gathering. We met once a week in the evening to study the Bible, pray, and fellowship with one another. Occasionally, we participated in a potluck dinner. Looking back now, I can see that we were simply modeling the response of the new believers in Jerusalem, following the Day of Pentecost:

"And they continued steadfastly in the apostles' doctrine and fellowship, in the breaking of bread, and in prayers." – Acts 2:42

We can get lost in a large church. It's easy to drift in and out without connecting with anyone. Home fellowships are an integral part of many churches because they provide the opportunity to interact with other believers in a more intimate setting. We get to know and pray for each other in ways not easily replicated by simply attending a church service.

About twenty-five years ago, one of the greatest blessings of my life occurred, shortly after I was asked to lead a Home Fellowship group. One of the men in our group, which consisted mostly of couples, suggested we also start a Bible study for the men. We loved the idea because we could be transparent with one another without sharing personal issues that might cause discomfort in mixed company.

We began to rendezvous at a coffee shop on Tuesday mornings before work. We would study the Bible, have breakfast, share, and pray together. As we continued to meet, we realized we could share more freely in a private setting, so we moved to the office of one of the men who is a physical therapist. As our bond with one another deepened, we realized that one of the most precious elements of our time together was the time we spent sharing and praying for one another.

Gradually, our Bible study began to morph into a prayer meeting. We still started our gathering with a short devotional from the Bible, but then we would take turns sharing prayer requests and praise reports. One of the men became our scribe, documenting all of our requests and praises in a journal. When we were finished sharing, we knelt and prayed for one another. We now have nearly three decades of journals that reflect God's faithfulness to us.

All of our sharing is confidential. Occasionally, someone shares something that is deeply troubling, perhaps a work- or family-related issue. As the Spirit leads, we drop to our knees and pray for that person—or we ask him to kneel and we lay hands on him as we pray. Laying on hands is a symbolic gesture. God doesn't command that we pray in a specific physical position or dictate how we use our hands.

Annual prayer group retreat – Las Gaviotas, Baja, California – 2003
Photo: Eddie Hillard [3]

23

SPIRITUAL GIFTS

"When God raises up a man for special service, He first works in that man the principles which later on are, through his labors and influence, to be the means of widespread blessing to the church and to the world. Before God works through a man, He works in a man, because the work that we do is the outgrowth of the life that we live. Jesus spent thirty years preparing for three years of ministry! God prepares us for what He is preparing for us." – J. Hudson Taylor

God has gifted each of us in different ways. Even the faith He bestows upon us is allocated in different measure. There are several passages in the Bible that specifically list various spiritual gifts God has distributed among believers. In my opinion, they are only a broad outline of the infinite ways God has gifted His church.

Some believers are called to become great evangelists, like Billy Graham, while others are called to be great teachers, like John MacArthur and Chuck Smith, but everyone is equal in God's sight. Some are multi-gifted; some are not. No formula exists to determine how we are gifted. We will discover our gifts as we pray, read the Bible, and fellowship with other believers. God has a unique call on our lives and will use all of us—but never covet another's gifts, God created you to be you! I'm a good example.

About twenty-five years ago, God impressed upon my heart a desire to share the gospel with surfers through surf film outreach. A close friend of mine, Morgan Miller, had hosted a surf film outreach event in Ocean Beach (San Diego) at a grammar school. A local surfer turned Calvary Chapel pastor, Ricky Ryan, gave an evangelistic message and I saw the potential.

A group of us gathered to pray about next steps and Larry Gordon, co-founder of Gordon & Smith surfboards, provided previously unscreened surf film footage from Bruce Brown, producer of *The Endless Summer*. Ed Wright, a gifted North County San Diego board builder, follower of Jesus, and owner of Sunset Surfboards, agreed to be our featured speaker. During the next major winter swell we plastered flyers on the windshields of surfer's cars, parked at the North San Diego County beaches, and over 500 people showed up to see a free surf movie and hear the gospel.

At our next event, in answer to prayer, God directed us to: Larry Gordon who served as master of ceremonies; Joey Buran, a former Pipeline Masters Champion, to share the gospel; *The Surfaris*, the band who created the 1960s hit song "Wipe Out," to entertain us; well-known San Diego board builder, Dan Van Zanten, to donate a high-performance *longboard* for a free raffle; and professional surfer Bryan Jennings, who provided his first surf film, *Beyond the Break*. God also surprised us when Tom Curren, a three-time World Champion, showed up unexpectedly!

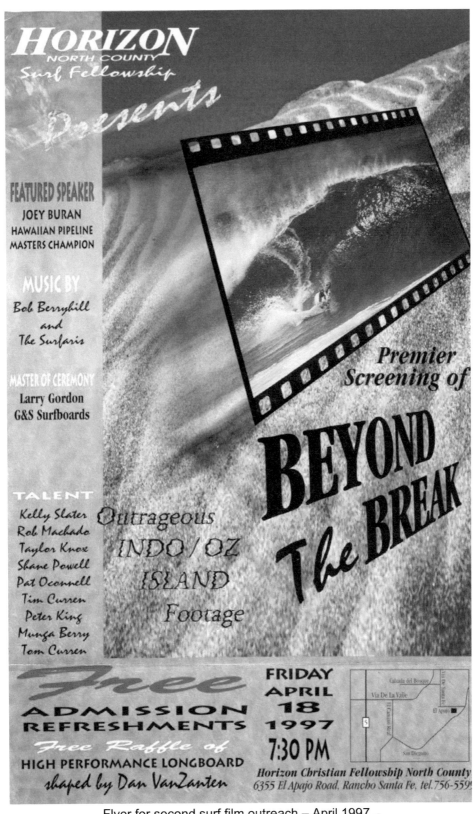

Flyer for second surf film outreach – April 1997
Poster designed by Joe Hall – Visions Unlimited [1]

Two champions following Jesus: Tom Curren (left), three-time World Champion and Joey Buran (right), Pipeline Masters Champion – Hollister Ranch, California – 1997 [2]

In 1998, God blessed me with the opportunity to serve on the Board of Directors of Walking on Water for over 20 years (the ministry I introduced in Chapter 19 and which recently came to an end). By God's grace and answered prayer, from 1995-2018, Walking on Water: produced 12 faith-based surf movies and translated these movies into over a dozen languages; hosted 24 consecutive summer surf camps for over 2,500 students; and sponsored over 100 mission trips to 40 countries. Approximately 500,000 people attended live global screenings of Walking on Water movies and millions heard the gospel through movies, outreach events, surf camps, and mission trips!

IN 2004, I FELT CALLED to create a Christ-centered version of the World Campus Afloat Program (Chapters 6-10) and founded the non-profit Global Oceanic Foundation (GO). The mission of GO is to provide an accredited, Christ-centered, global shipboard university program, empowering students and alumni to become effective change agents for God's Kingdom in the 21st century and beyond.

The vision undergirding GO is for students and alumni to not only circumnavigate the world as one body physically, from every country in the world, but to become so spiritually unified at sea and in port, that they go forth generation to generation as one in Jesus—working together as His hands and as His feet—that the world may believe and know that God sent Him—based on the prayer of Jesus for his church found in the Gospel of John 17:20-23.

This was a massive undertaking, both in time and financial resources, but by God's grace and the encouragement of many we stepped out in faith. After several years developing the implementation of Global Oceanic (GO), working alongside several Christian universities and colleges for accreditation, and Cru (Campus Crusade for Christ) for spiritual formation, we recently decided to put it on the shelf due to the Covid pandemic and the current demise of the international cruise ship industry. Should Jesus tarry and God resurrect the cruise ship industry, perhaps God will resurrect GO in the future.

Global Ocean Academic Consultative Group – featuring current and former Chief Academic Officers, faculty, and other leaders in Christian higher education from Christian colleges, universities, and organizations, including: Azusa Pacific, Bethel, Biola, Handong Global, Indiana Wesleyan, Nyack, Pepperdine, Taylor, Westmount, the South African College of Applied Psychology, the International Council for Higher Education, and the Council for Christian Colleges and Universities (CCCU) – Washington D.C. – 2008 [3]

Global Oceanic – All Board Member Retreat – San Diego, California – 2010 [4]

WHEN WE BEGIN TO FOLLOW Jesus, God will probably not call us to move to Africa to minister to lepers. Instead, He will call us to express our spiritual gifts and natural talents in a ministry we currently are, or will become, passionate about. He may take His time. Matthew Henry, another of my favorite Bible commentators, said:

"Sometimes it is long before God calls his servants out to that work which of old he designed them for and has been graciously preparing them for. Moses was born to be Israel's deliverer, and yet not a word is said of it to him till he is eighty years of age."

After Saul was converted on the Damascus Road, he spent three years in the Arabian desert learning about God. He then spent eight years in Tarsus, his hometown, before Barnabas sought him out and brought him to Antioch to teach for a year. God prepared Saul for twelve years, before the Holy Spirit anointed Saul and Barnabas for the work to which He had called them. During their first missionary trip, Saul adopted his Roman name Paul and became an evangelist, teacher, apostle to the Gentiles, and one of the principal Holy Spirit-inspired authors of the New Testament.

Another case in point is that of Pastor Chuck Smith. What a lot of people don't know about Chuck is that he served for over seventeen years in a large denominational church trying to exercise a spiritual gift he didn't have—evangelism. After striving to perform his pastoral duties to please the church hierarchy and express a spiritual gift he didn't have, Chuck finally resigned. Shortly thereafter he was called to a small church, discovered his gifts as a pastor-teacher, and God birthed Calvary Chapel; a ministry God has used to birth thousands of other churches throughout the world and to grow His kingdom in countless other ways.

24

WHY DO BAD THINGS HAPPEN TO GOOD PEOPLE?

"For My thoughts are not your thoughts, nor are your ways My ways," says the Lord. "For as the heavens are higher than the earth, so are My ways higher than your ways, and My thoughts than your thoughts." – Isaiah 55:8-9

Every day we are challenged to understand why something happened. When I first wrote this, people throughout the world were straining to make sense of why a man in Las Vegas murdered nearly sixty people and horribly wounded over five hundred others during a concert. Years later, with all the resources in the world available, the authorities still cannot uncover a motive.

Why do good people suffer? We don't know. If we believe in God, we know that He is in control. We don't need to understand why because we trust and have faith in the truth that He is a loving, good, fair, and just God all the time. His thoughts towards each of us are more than the sands of the sea, and they are for good, not evil. I have read a lot of books about wonderful men and women who have been used by God in powerful ways, and not one of them had an easy time of it. All of them were persecuted, suffered grievously, or both.

Although no one can explain why this tragedy occurred, if we are following Jesus, we know that God allowed it to occur. He knew it was going to occur, He was there, and He had the power to prevent it. So why didn't He? Your guess is as good as mine. We can shine the light of our temporal human perspective on this question, but our explanation would be as inadequate as our interpretations as to why a Holy God loved us enough to send His only begotten Son to suffer and die for the sins of all who would believe In Him.

It would amount to lunacy to think we can figure out why God did this or that with our very limited human wisdom and understanding. We simply don't know why good people suffer and evil people prosper, but we do know that Satan is the ruler of the world and that explains a lot. "Wait a minute!", someone might say, "That's a very strange statement to make. If the Bible teaches that God created the universe and Jesus has all power and authority over heaven and earth, how could Satan be the ruler of the world? I don't understand." Neither do I, exactly, but Jesus explicitly refers to Satan as the ruler of the world:

"Now is the judgment of this world; now the ruler of this world will be cast out. And I, if I am lifted up from the earth, will draw all peoples to Myself." – John 12:31-32

At some point in eternity past, around the time God created Adam and Eve, He created a heavenly host of spiritual beings and ranked them according to a hierarchy of spiritual principalities and powers (cherubim, seraphim, archangels, angels, etc.). He also created them as free moral agents with self-determination to choose whom they would serve.

Satan, who was one of the most beautiful and powerful angels created by God, decided to challenge God's supreme authority and led about a third of the heavenly host in rebellion against God. When this occurred, God cast Satan and his demonic angels from unrestricted access to His presence. For the time being, God allows Satan to rule the world utilizing his demonic counterpart to God's heavenly host.

"For we do not wrestle against flesh and blood, but against principalities, against powers, against the rulers of the darkness of this age, against spiritual hosts of wickedness in the heavenly places." – Ephesians 6:12

We also know from the Scriptures that Satan has access to God and that God, at times, directs Satan's ways to accomplish His purposes. One of the ways God uses Satan is to test our faith. We see numerous examples of this in the Bible. In the book of Genesis, Satan used Joseph's brothers to betray him and sell him into slavery, but Joseph remained faithful to God despite suffering severe trials and persecutions. God's plan was for Pharaoh to set Joseph over all of Egypt and use him to save the Israelites from famine, which he did.

On another occasion, in the book of Esther, Satan used Haman, the highest-ranking prince in the Persian empire under King Ahasuerus, to create a plan to exterminate the Jews, but Esther, the Queen, faithfully shared Haman's plan with the King, even though the King might have had her executed for speaking out of turn. God's plan was to use Esther to save the Jews from extermination, which she did. In each of these examples, there were other ways for God to achieve the same outcome, but He wanted to test their faith.

If someone doesn't believe in Jesus, Satan and his host of demonic angels can corrupt, possess, and destroy them—like he corrupted, possessed, and destroyed Judas, the betrayer of Jesus. If we believe in Jesus, we are also prone to demonic attacks, however, we can never be possessed because we are a temple of God (Father, Son, and Holy Spirit) and He who is in us is greater than he who is in the world.

Also, never forget the reality that Satan is one of the most beautiful angels created by God, despite his attempts to lead us to believe he is the grotesque beast he is often depicted to be—like a creature with a forked tail, two horns, carrying a pitchfork, and wearing a red leotard. The truth of the matter is that Satan cloaks himself in beauty in order to deceive both believers and unbelievers.

"...For Satan himself transforms himself into an angel of light." – 2 Corinthians 11:14

THE DEATH AND RESURRECTION OF Jesus and the sending of the Holy Spirit marked the beginning of the Church Age, sometimes referred to as the Age of Grace. The Church Age is an undefined period of time that began with the coming of the Holy Spirit on the Day of Pentecost, the day on which the Holy Spirit descended upon His apostles and disciples, which occurred fifty days after Jesus ascended to heaven after His resurrection. The Church Age will end with the rapture of the church (see Chapter 27).

The Church Age is an age when everyone is free to believe in Jesus, an age that had a beginning and will have an end. When will it end? Only God knows, but we know we are in the last days. Those who receive Jesus as their personal Lord and Savior before the rapture will be saved, those who reject Jesus will be left behind and experience a seven-year tribulation period (again, see Chapter 27). During the tribulation period the Antichrist (the lawless one) will be revealed. The Apostle Paul prophesies, in his second letter to the Thessalonians, how Satan will embody the Antichrist with his power to deceive:

> *"The coming of the lawless one is according to the working of Satan, with all power, signs, and lying wonders, and with all unrighteous deception among those who perish, because they did not receive the love of the truth, that they might be saved." – 2 Thessalonians 2: 9-10*

The only reason there is a modicum of sanity during the Church Age is the restraining power of the Holy Spirit operative through God's church. This doesn't mean the Holy Spirit departs the world when the church is raptured—simply that one of God's primary means of sharing the gospel has departed. He will use other means during and after the tribulation (see Chapter 27). As previously mentioned, the Holy Spirit, like God the Father and God the Son, is omnipresent—He is everywhere all the time. He is the agent by which God converts sinners. He was present from the beginning of creation—

> *"In the beginning God created the heavens and the earth. The earth was without form, and void; and darkness was on the face of the deep. And the Spirit of God was hovering over the face of the waters." Genesis 1:1-2*

—and He will be present at the end of the age.

> *"And the Spirit and the bride say, "Come!" And let him who hears say, "Come!" And let him who thirsts come. Whoever desires, let him take the water of life freely." – Revelation 22:17*

IF SOMEONE IS WONDERING WHY so many children are starving throughout the world, why millions of Jews were exterminated during the Holocaust, why slavery and human trafficking still exist, or why some of the vilest people on this planet live and prosper, don't blame it on God, blame it on Satan.

Many are unaware of the reality that we live in both a temporal, physical world and in an eternal, spiritual world. God wants us to understand that we live in two distinct spheres of existence simultaneously, one seen and the other unseen. Although God is fully in control of both, He currently allows Satan to rule the world.

In the New Testament, the Apostle Paul provides another glimpse into the hidden world of spiritual eternity, when he is caught up to heaven. In the book of 2 Corinthians, Paul shares that what he heard in heaven was so wonderful it was inexpressible, because human language is totally inadequate to explain heavenly reality. We can only imagine what it will be like to join the chorus of the heavenly host worshipping God.

"It is doubtless not profitable for me to boast. I will come to visions and revelations of the Lord: I know a man in Christ who fourteen years ago—whether in the body I do not know, or whether out of the body I do not know, God knows— such a one was caught up to the third heaven. And I know such a man—whether in the body or out of the body I do not know, God knows— how he was caught up into Paradise and heard inexpressible words, which it is not lawful for a man to utter." – 2 Corinthians 12:1-4

Also, God sometimes allows Satan to challenge our comfort in order to sanctify us. He used a thorn in Paul's flesh to keep him humble on earth. Paul doesn't share the exact source of his discomfort, but some speculate it was a disease associated with his eyes. Whatever it was, God knew how to sanctify Paul, as He knows how to sanctify each of us.

The Bible is very clear about the truth that those who reject Jesus, and die rejecting Him, will spend eternity in hell separated from God. Life does not end when we breathe our last breath; we simply move to a spiritual dimension—heaven or hell. Scripture teaches that hell is a place without God and thus without light, because God is light.

"Then Jesus spoke to them again, saying, "I am the light of the world. He who follows Me shall not walk in darkness, but have the light of life." – John 8:12

Several years ago, Judy, Allison, and I visited the volcanic Lava River Cave near Bend, Oregon. Thousands of years ago, a volcano erupted. As a river of lava flowed down the sides of the mountain to the valley below, it began to fold over itself and gradually formed a tube, that over the years eventually hardened and was covered by soil. We joined a guided tour and entered this tube through a wide opening at the surface.

Entrance to Lava River Cave near Bend, Oregon –
Photo: Ryan Harvey [1]

The lava tube runs below and perpendicular to the valley floor for about a quarter of a mile before narrowing to a point you can barely squeeze into. Each of us had a lantern. When we reached the end of the tube the guide asked us to extinguish our lanterns and be quiet.

The silence of blackness was pure and terrifying, never before had I felt so isolated. It was like being totally blind and imprisoned in solitary confinement with no hope of escape. We couldn't wait to relight our lanterns, talk with one another, and quickly walk back out to the opening.

As followers of Jesus, we are always in the hands of our loving God who will lead, guide, and protect us until our appointed time to join Him in heaven. As evangelist George Whitefield once said:

"A man of God, in the will of God, is immortal until his work is done on earth."

God will deploy His holy angels to minister to us and protect us. We are eternally alive in Jesus. We have nothing to fear!

"For He shall give His angels charge over you, to keep you in all your ways." – Psalm 91:11

If we are following Jesus, when we breathe our last breath we will experience a spiritual metamorphosis, analogous to the physical metamorphosis of the butterfly pictured on page 173. In the twinkling of an eye, we will move out of our earthly bodies into spiritual bodies from God, not made with hands, but eternal in the heavens. Followers of Jesus never die, they simply move from a carnally corrupt temporal body into an incorrupt spiritual body.

We can choose to spend the rest of our lives wondering why God does this or that, or we can choose to trust in the certainty that He has a perfect plan for each of us.

"Oh, the depth of the riches both of the wisdom and knowledge of God! How unsearchable are His judgments and His ways past finding out!" – Romans 11:33

25

FAMILY PLANNING - AN ETERNAL PERSPECTIVE

"Human nature may be polished up, educated and made very amiable, but God cannot accept such products of self-improvement, for it is written, 'They that are in the flesh cannot please God.' Behind all these efforts of the natural man to do right and live right lurks the same corrupt nature, and 'that which is born of the flesh is flesh' still holds good. Those whom God can accept are they who have believed in His Son, who are washed in His blood and saved by Grace." – Arno Gaebelein

When I meet a married couple who love Jesus, I like to ask them how they met because I know it was a divine appointment. Everything they had experienced up to that moment in time played a part in their meeting one another. It is a moment they will always remember and a juncture in time God orchestrated.

"Known to God from eternity are all His works." – Acts 15:18

If you search Amazon for books on marriage, you will find over 70,000 titles. It seems as though everyone is an expert on marriage. I am not, but I know that marriage, as defined by God, is between a man and a woman. Unfortunately, the corrupt temporal world we are journeying through gravitates to moral relativism. It embraces a philosophy that truth changes with the times and morality must be made to conform with modernity. It is a philosophy of life devoid of an eternal moral compass premised on the word of God.

I've been engaged twice in my life: the first occurred when Judy and I were engaged during the summer of 1972, and the second occurred during the fall of 1986, when I invited Jesus into my heart. My marriage to Judy was consummated in November of 1972. My marriage to Jesus will be consummated when God creates a new heaven and a new earth, at the end of the age, when the marriage supper of the Lamb occurs (see Chapter 27).

"Now I saw a new heaven and a new earth, for the first heaven and the first earth had passed away. Also there was no more sea. Then I, John, saw the holy city, New Jerusalem, coming down out of heaven from God, prepared as a bride adorned for her husband." – Revelation 21:1-2

From the time God created Adam and Eve the sanctity of marriage has been integral to God's master plan for humanity. Sanctity implies an inviolability and security from profanation. In other words, marriage, according to God, is a sacred covenant or promise made by both the husband and wife to be faithful to one another until they are separated by death.

> *"Therefore a man shall leave his father and mother and be joined to his wife, and they shall become one flesh." – Genesis 2:24*

I believe Satan is as intent on destroying the sanctity of marriage as God is in preserving it. Satan will do anything he can to corrupt and distort a society's belief in the sanctity of marriage. He has done so from the beginning of time. His victims include one of the most prominent men of the Bible, King David, who broke several of the ten commandments in one fell swoop. He coveted his neighbor's wife, committed adultery with her, and arranged for the murder of her husband. But he confessed his sins, God forgave him, and he suffered the consequences.

God has revealed to us through David and other believers in the Old and New Testaments, that those who trust in Him are not perfect. All followers of Jesus still sin on a daily basis, but we don't practice sin. We don't consciously and continually choose to repeat the same sin, over and over, without remorse and a repentant heart.

> *"For everyone practicing evil hates the light and does not come to the light, lest his deeds should be exposed." – John 3:20*

God knows that all of us have a sinful nature constantly at war with the Holy Spirit who dwells within us. He also recognizes that when we confess our sins, we are opening ourselves to His work of sanctification. We don't confess our sins because we might lose our salvation; we confess our sins in order to more fully experience His presence, His peace, and His joy—things Satan wants to deprive us of.

There are thousands of sins a follower of Jesus can be tempted to commit and some of the most common are the sins we practiced before we were saved. But God, who dwells within us, is greater than he who rules the world. One of the differences between believers and unbelievers is that when believers sin the Holy Spirit pricks their spirit—prompting them to confess and repent like David. When unbelievers sin, they will often repeat or "practice" the sin because their minds are ruled by their bodily appetites: the lust of the flesh; the lust of the eyes; and the pride of life.

> *"For he who sows to his flesh will of the flesh reap corruption, but he who sows to the Spirit will of the Spirit reap everlasting life." – Galatians 6:8*

In 1987, in answer to prayer, God gifted Judy and me with the most precious gift in the world, our daughter, Allison. As any parent will share, the birth of a child is such a wonderful and life-changing moment that it's difficult to explain the feeling to anyone other than another parent. Allison is a blessing in every sense of the word.

While Judy was pregnant and after Allison was born, we prayed regularly that God would introduce her to a husband who loved Jesus. Once again, God was faithful, and seven years ago she met and married Bobby. We were not only blessed to receive Bobby into our family, we received a double-blessing in the form of Bobby's family. In fact, his folks had been praying that God would introduce Bobby to a wife who loved Jesus as well. We were quadruple blessed in March 2020 when our grandson, Jude, was born and then again in January 2022 when our granddaughter, Reese, was born.

Allison, Reese (2 months), Bobby, and Jude (2 years) – children's dedication service – Rockharbor Church, Costa Mesa, California – Sunday, March 20, 2022 [1]

Our most important treasures on earth are children. God expressed this truth to us through the birth of His only begotten Son. After all, God is God and nothing is impossible for Him. If He simply wanted to save us from ourselves, He could have come up with an infinite number of ways to do so, but He chose the birth of a child because children are His treasure and marriage, between a man and a woman, is at the heart of His love for the universe He created.

UNFORTUNATELY, BECAUSE ADAM AND EVE chose death rather than life by eating from the tree of the knowledge of good and evil (the tree of death), the church is not alive in the perfect universe God originally created but is alive in Jesus on a dying planet ruled by Satan. We are pilgrims on a journey through an alien world.

Look around. The United States is on the same downward spiral and path to extinction as every other world power throughout history.

Leading the way—and often working hand-in-hand—are: corrupt politicians; unelected and *woke* government officials and military leaders; deceitful *news* and social media conglomerates; politically correct CEOs of mega corporations; Marxist-leaning secular institutions of higher education; and a wide variety of apostate *churches*. These individuals and organizations reject the God of the Bible and are intent on destroying the essence of God's creation, the sanctity of marriage. Their byword is hypocrisy, their need is Jesus.

Young children are being systematically desensitized to traditional family values and gender distinctiveness by humanistic, socialist-driven public education systems and policies. The unborn and newly born are considered a disposable by-product of sexual promiscuity, and the bedrock foundations of our country—faith, family, freedom, and justice—are rapidly evaporating before our eyes.

God is calling His church to prayer.

"...if My people who are called by My name will humble themselves, and pray and seek My face, and turn from their wicked ways, then I will hear from heaven, and will forgive their sin and heal their land." – 2 Chronicles 7:14

Evil and carnal corruption are so deeply embedded in the sinful nature of unbelievers, that nothing is sacred in our contemporary society except dead-end secular idols such as sex, wealth, fame, and self-fulfillment. The resultant emptiness has led to a dramatic increase in the incidence of suicide throughout the world. According to a June 8, 2018 report by the CDC (Center for Disease Control), "suicide rates in the United States have risen nearly 30% since 1999, and mental health conditions are one of several factors contributing to suicide."

Over 200 years ago, a Scottish historian, who served as Professor of Universal History, and Greek and Roman Antiquities, at the University of Edinburgh, Alexander Fraser Tyler (1747-1813), wrote the following:

"A democracy is always temporary in nature; it simply cannot exist as a permanent form of government. A democracy will continue to exist up until the time that voters discover that they can vote themselves generous gifts from the public treasury. From that moment on, the majority always votes for the candidates who promise the most benefits from the public treasury, with the result that every democracy will finally collapse due to loose fiscal policy, which is always followed by dictatorship.

"The average age of the world's greatest civilizations from the beginning of history has been about 200 years. During those 200 years, these nations always progressed through the following sequence: from bondage to spiritual faith; from spiritual faith to great courage; from great courage to liberty; from liberty to abundance; from abundance to selfishness; from selfishness to complacency; from complacency to apathy; from apathy to dependence; from dependence back into bondage."

Let's take a snapshot of the world our children are being born into. It is a picture that can be illuminated by the light of history and is based upon my opinion, that the intersection of technological development and innate human depravity, during the late 20th and early 21st centuries, has brought the world to the precipice of God's intervention and judgment. If God did not hesitate to judge and disperse His chosen people, the nation of Israel, for rejecting Him, how can the nations of the world reject Him now and expect anything less?

"The instant I speak concerning a nation and concerning a kingdom, to pluck up, to pull down, and to destroy it, if that nation against whom I have spoken turns from its evil, I will relent of the disaster that I thought to bring upon it. And the instant I speak concerning a nation and concerning a kingdom, to build and to plant it, if it does evil in My sight so that it does not obey My voice, then I will relent concerning the good with which I said I would benefit it." – Jeremiah 18:7-10

Thousands of years ago, at a similar junction in time to the present, when Noah was alive and life spans were measured in hundreds rather than tens of years, mankind lived on a planet that was still encapsulated in the pristine atmosphere and global climate God created for Adam and Eve.

Consider for a moment: if the intellect of 20th century mankind, developed over a lifespan of less than a hundred years, led to the landing of a man on the moon and the unraveling of the human genome, what the intellect of mankind, developed over a lifespan exceeding nine hundred years, might have accomplished in the days of Noah.

God doesn't share with us the technological advances made by man prior to the flood, but they must have been formidable if Noah could build an ark and load it with every living creature that moved on the earth. Although the purity of the earth's atmosphere in Noah's day resulted in longer life spans and the corresponding development of the intellect, it did not result in the purification of the human soul.

We don't know exactly how men and women behaved in this Shangri La environment, but we know that they behaved so wickedly that God caused a flood to destroy every living creature on earth, except for Noah, his family, and an ark full of animals, birds, and creeping things.

"Then the Lord saw that the wickedness of man was great in the earth, and that every intent of the thoughts of his heart was only evil continually. And the Lord was sorry that He had made man on the earth, and He was grieved in His heart. So the Lord said, 'I will destroy man whom I have created from the face of the earth, both man and beast, creeping thing and birds of the air, for I am sorry that I have made them.' But Noah found grace in the eyes of the Lord." – Noah 6:5-8

History is now repeating itself. Man's sinful nature and proclivity for depravity have begun to blossom into a worldwide pandemic of wickedness and godless humanism fueled by technology.

When I first looked at the CDC image of the coronavirus, the first thought that came to mind was: "This must be how God sees the earth today"—not the NASA image of the earth from space featured on page 15 of this book.

Despite the fact that we are the beneficiaries of amazing God-given scientific and technological advances, such as state-of-the-art computers, medicine, and aerospace, we are also the recipients of a flood of information on our computers and smartphones that incites the lust of the eyes, the lust of the flesh, and the pride of life—all of the base sins that serve to turn us from the God who loves us to a world that doesn't.

It seems like everyone has a smartphone. I can remember visiting a pub in London about twenty-five years ago when cell phones were the rage. As Judy, Allison, and I sat at our table, I was fascinated by a group of young people gathered around another table ignoring each other and talking on their cell phones. In retrospect, I was witnessing the seeds of where we are today, where families can often be seen in a restaurant—supposedly enjoying a meal together—all staring at their smartphones.

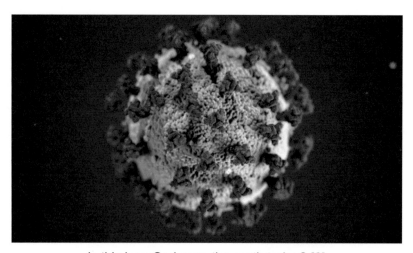

Is this how God sees the earth today? [2]

Although the smartphone provides us with innumerable benefits, it has also served to propel us down the slippery slope of human degradation by normalizing behaviors like cohabitation, abortion on demand, sexual orientation, pornography, etc. What the confluence of the internet, social media, the entertainment industry, secular "higher" education, and the smartphone have accomplished is the blurring or erasure of many God-given moral imperatives foundational to marriage, family, and civilization.

The smartphone is emblematic of other technologies that seduce the user to embrace a counterfeit reality totally devoid of spiritual truth, such as artificial intelligence and virtual reality. The advent of child sex robots and face-swapped pornography (a desktop app that allows people to scan the face of another person and upload it to a pornographic video) are just two of the most recent examples of how wicked things have become, not to mention ChatGPT—and state-of-the-art GPT-4 with capabilities far exceeding ChatGPT.

Molech, the ancient pagan god of child sacrifice [3]

"For if we sin willfully after we have received the knowledge of the truth, there no longer remains a sacrifice for sins, but a certain fearful expectation of judgment, and fiery indignation which will devour the adversaries. Anyone who has rejected Moses' law dies without mercy on the testimony of two or three witnesses. Of how much worse punishment, do you suppose, will he be thought worthy who has trampled the Son of God underfoot, counted the blood of the covenant by which he was sanctified a common thing, and insulted the Spirit of grace? For we know Him who said, 'Vengeance is Mine, I will repay,' says the Lord. And again, 'The Lord will judge His people.' It is a fearful thing to fall into the hands of the living God.'" – Hebrews 10:26-31

A quick look back at history will help shed light on what is happening around us. When God judged and destroyed the nation of Israel, using the armies of Nebuchadnezzar, King of Babylon (circa 600 B.C.), the Israelites, from the top down, had transitioned from the worship of God to the worship of idols. Two of their most cherished idols were Molech and Ashtoreth, both associated with the pagan worship of Baal, the supreme god worshipped in ancient Canaan and Phoenicia. Molech was a brass idol of a bull-headed man. When it was heated by fire to several hundred degrees, Israelite parents worshipped it by placing their firstborn children on its outstretched arms as a sacrificial burnt offering. Ashtoreth, Molech's female counterpart, was worshipped through ritual prostitution, divination, and fortune-telling.

"And you shall not let any of your descendants pass through the fire to Molech, nor shall you profane the name of your God: I am the Lord. You shall not lie with a male as with a woman. It is an abomination. Nor shall you mate with any animal, to defile yourself with it. Nor shall any woman stand before an animal to mate with it. It is perversion." – Leviticus 18:21-23

IT DOESN'T TAKE A ROCKET scientist to understand that societal acceptance of cohabitation, abortion on demand, pornography, and the deviant sexual practices prevalent on much of the earth today are simply history repeating itself. The smartphone is at the center of this outcome, as it is providing the means to stream a new reality of moral imperatives to a generation of children who have been permitted to use their smartphones unchecked, because they have inadequate or nonexistent parental supervision.

Technology is commandeering the minds of our children by enabling them to become addicted to instant gratification and self-absorption. They are being manipulated by companies led by men and women who, for the most part, are spiritually clueless.

In the United States, as young people graduate from grade schools and high schools governed by regulations bereft of God and enter the morally bankrupt culture of most secular institutions of higher education, the outcome is predictable: lost souls worshipping at the alters of political correctness and humanism they have been programmed to believe (evolution, globalism, manmade climate change, gender neutrality, identity politics, critical race theory, etc.).

What we are witnessing is the Satanic destruction of the family unit. Satan is referred to in the Bible by many names—one of them is Apollyon, which is Greek for destroyer. His grand plan is to destroy lives and his strategy is to destroy the family. If loneliness characterizes hell, Satan is doing a masterful job of shifting the focus of humanity from family love to self-absorption.

Over the last century, we can see this transition through the evolution of the broadcast and print media—from radio to movies, from movies to television, from television to the internet, and from the internet to smartphones; from a magazine titled LIFE, to magazines titled LOOK, PEOPLE, SELF, and I; from a time when families would gather together in the mornings and evenings to break bread and fellowship together, to broken homes and broken hearts.

Child on a smartphone [4]

The beauty and symbolism of the rainbow is another example of how political correctness and humanism are permeating global culture and corrupting the family unit. God's covenant sign of promise to Noah, that He would never again destroy the earth by flood, has been co-opted by carnal mankind to symbolize sexual sin and promote the tolerance of it.

> *"Thus I establish My covenant with you: Never again shall all flesh be cut off by the waters of the flood; never again shall there be a flood to destroy the earth." And God said: "This is the sign of the covenant which I make between Me and you, and every living creature that is with you, for perpetual generations: I set My rainbow in the cloud, and it shall be for the sign of the covenant between Me and the earth." – Genesis 9:11-13*

Anyone raising children in this culture of self-absorption and depravity has their work cut out for them. There is no simple solution to curb the temptation of young people to use their smartphone, other than proactive parental supervision.

In the February 18, 2018, edition of Business Insider, Chris Weller wrote an article titled, "Silicon Valley parents are raising their kid's tech-free—and it should be a red flag." Following is an excerpt:

"Silicon Valley's low-and anti-tech parents may seem overly cautious, but they actually follow longstanding practices of former and current tech giants like Bill Gates, Steve Jobs, and Tim Cook.

"In 2007, Gates, the former CEO of Microsoft, implemented a cap on screen time when his daughter started developing an unhealthy attachment to a video game. Later it became family policy not to allow kids to have their own phones until they turned 14. Today, the average American child get their first phone around age 10.

"Jobs, the CEO of Apple until his death in 2012, revealed in a 2011 New York Times interview that he prohibited his kids from using the newly released iPad. 'We limit how much technology our kids use at home,' Jobs told reporter Nick Bilton.

"Even Cook, the current Apple CEO, said in January that he doesn't allow his nephew to join online social networks. The comment followed those of other tech luminaries, who have condemned social media as detrimental to society. Cook later conceded Apple products aren't meant for constant use. 'I'm not a person that says we've achieved success if you're using it all the time,' he said. I don't subscribe to that at all."

Coastline Rainbow [5]

When Judy and I were raising Allison thirty years ago, we enrolled her in the public-school system to begin kindergarten. This wasn't our first choice, but the Christian school we had applied to was full. A few weeks after she entered kindergarten, we received a call from the Christian school that a space had opened up. We pulled her out of the public school and entered her into the Christian school—thinking everything had worked out.

While Allison progressed from first, to second, to third grade, Judy had the opportunity to become a teaching assistant at the same school and was able to more fully inspect the school environment. One of the things she observed was that many of the children were not receiving quality parental supervision at home, as manifested by the language and behavior their children exhibited at school. As a result, some of Allison's friends were introducing her to words and behaviors that weren't conducive to what we were trying to instill in her heart.

We prayed about it and decided to homeschool her. This was a major decision for us at the time because Judy had not had any formal training as a teacher. It also dried up a source of income we were counting on. Long story short, Judy homeschooled Allison from fourth grade through high school. She would often stay up late at night preparing lesson plans and then spend quality time with Allison during the day taking field trips, reading books, drawing, painting, and loving on her.

As opposed to public and private school children, most homeschool children spend very little time sitting at a desk. We belonged to an organized Christian homeschool community that included hundreds of other homeschool families, so there was always ample opportunity for social interaction.

When Allison graduated from high school, we had no idea how she would perform in college. She had never taken lecture notes or been regularly tested, but she graduated from college with honors and was involved in numerous on-campus social organizations. After graduation, she and some of her close college friends started a business in Uganda providing indigenous women with dignified job opportunities making jewelry, while simultaneously educating them to start their own businesses.

Judy and I had no idea how any of this would unfold. We simply prayed, took a step of faith, and by God's grace, it all worked out. In the interest of full disclosure, I didn't help teach a single class; Judy did it all, including two years of Latin in high school. When course requirements surpassed Judy's level of competence in a subject, such as high school math or biology, there were homeschool curricula she could purchase to help her through, and we occasionally hired a tutor for private lessons.

I'm not suggesting homeschooling as a panacea for the spectrum of challenges parents face raising their children, but it does provide certain families with an alternative. I also understand that a case can be made for public and private school education. It all depends on a variety of factors unique to each family and child, including financial and career considerations. Whatever path is followed, parents must be proactively involved in monitoring what their children see, hear, and do. In addition, they must possess a heightened sensitivity to the friends their children interact with.

As parents, we must also understand that all children are God's children. He treasures them, and He has entrusted them to us to love and nurture. Nevertheless, regardless of all we do to care for them, we cannot control whether they will follow Jesus or turn from Him and embrace the world. A prodigal child can be the fruit of loving parents following Jesus or the fruit of godless parents without a moral compass. God gifts all of us with our own free will, but He also gifts us with a promise:

"Train up a child in the way he should go, and when he is old he will not depart from it." – Proverbs 22:6

26

HEAVEN AND HELL

"God is the God of love, as much as He is the God of wrath. He must be that or He would not be the God of Light and Holiness. He cannot afford to let evil go on forever. He is the Lord slow to anger. His patience is great, but He will not acquit the guilty, who continue to sin and do evil." – Arno Gaebelein

God has gifted each of us with the ability to think. We can look back at something that happened or look forward to something we expect to happen. Our response to these thoughts is predicated on our relationship to Jesus. If we know Him, we know that He is our life, we are complete in Him eternally, and He will be faithful to complete the work He started in us. He is our anchor in a sea of worldly confusion and the lens through which our thoughts are filtered.

"This hope we have as an anchor of the soul, both sure and steadfast, …" – Hebrews 6:19

If we don't know Jesus, our thoughts are filtered by the lust of the flesh, the lust of the eyes, and the pride of life. These thoughts trigger other feelings to evolve and career from one emotion to another: one moment struggling with guilt or shame about something we've said or done, the next moment trying to quench a thirst for happiness, an emotional state of mind premised on outward circumstances that are enjoyable but short-lived. We are like ships adrift at sea without an anchor.

"For all that is in the world—the lust of the flesh, the lust of the eyes, and the pride of life—is not of the Father but is of the world." – 1 John 2:16

Bottom-line, our minds and our lives are defined by our perception of time and eternity. If we are not in relationship with Jesus, we are glued to the clock. A clock is one of the first things we see when we wake up, and one of the last things we see when we go to sleep. During our waking hours, we are constantly glancing at the time in our car, on our phone, or on our watch.

The passage of time, without an anchor for our souls, drives our lives. We live on a treadmill of activities that alienate us from the reality of aging and death. Look around, many people are driving themselves crazy trying to forestall or cloud the certainty of their end. For some, it's an extreme addiction to fitness or plastic surgery; for others, it's an addiction to work, food, drugs, alcohol, sex, money, cults, etc. Pick your poison.

God, heaven, and hell exist outside of time and space; they are spiritual and eternal. The absolute truth of eternity is woven in and out of the Old and New Testaments, because knowing we are eternal beings is essential to our salvation. To deny eternity is to deny the existence of God, heaven, and hell. It is a prideful response to an eternal reality.

"For thus says the High and Lofty One Who inhabits eternity, whose name is Holy: 'I dwell in the high and holy place, with him who has a contrite and humble spirit, to revive the spirit of the humble, and to revive the heart of the contrite ones.'" – Isaiah 57:15

Although heaven is God's realm, He graphically describes hell throughout the Scriptures in order to impress upon humanity the unbridgeable gulf between a Holy God and corrupt mankind—a gulf He bridged when, by His amazing grace, His only begotten Son sacrificed His life on the cross for the sin of mankind.

If we believe in God, we live in the light of His presence by the power of the Holy Spirit and we know, that when we pass from earth to heaven, we will never again experience darkness. Conversely, if we don't believe in God, we are currently alive in the darkness of our souls and we will pass from earth to hell to live eternally in darkness without Him.

"For you were once darkness, but now you are light in the Lord." – Ephesians 5:8

If the hope of our life is premised on self-fulfillment, we are traveling down a dead-end street. We are living in a body over which we have marginal control, a body which can crash and burn at any moment. Many who strive to achieve fame, fortune, or power on earth become distraught when they achieve their goals only to discover an unbearable emptiness.

A life of barrenness, characterized by self-absorption and hopelessness, often leads to despair, and in the extreme, to suicide. Check your favorite news feed to hear or read about the latest victim.

"Beware lest anyone cheat you through philosophy and empty deceit, according to the tradition of men, according to the basic principles of the world, and not according to Christ." – Colossians 2:8

Followers of Jesus are the temple of God (Father, Son, and Holy Spirit). We live for the hope of God's calling to be fully conformed into the image of Jesus when we pass from our earthly body, designed for an earthly environment, to our heavenly body, designed for a heavenly environment. Our mission on earth is to glorify God utilizing every spiritual gift and natural talent He has endowed us with.

Our heart's desire is for everyone to experience the same hope we have. We live to be His light in a temporal, dark world—that is on an accelerating path to extinction. We are alive in this world, but we are not of this world. We know with certainty that our time on earth is only an ambassadorial pilgrimage and that our eternal home is in heaven.

There are many people, both in and out of the church, who question the reality of hell. There are some who have read the Scriptures and don't believe that all of God's words are divinely inspired. There are others who have never read the Scriptures and don't believe in God, let alone a God that divinely inspired men to write the Bible. God, however, is crystal clear about the pure truth of His word and the reality of hell.

"The entirety of Your word is truth, and every one of Your righteous judgments endures forever." – Psalm 119:160

According to Billy Graham, Jesus spent more time discussing the reality of hell than any other person in the Bible. Graham said (Billy Graham Evangelistic Association, Answers by Billy Graham, January 11, 2012, Topics: Hell):

"The reality of hell should frighten us, because not one word in the Bible about hell would ever make you want to go there—not if you take it seriously. The Bible speaks of hell as a place of absolute loneliness and despair and hopelessness. It calls it a place of 'darkness, where there will be weeping and gnashing of teeth.' (Matthew 22:13). But Jesus didn't talk about hell just to scare us. He talked about it instead because He wanted us to know that God has provided a way of escape!'"

"And a servant of the Lord must not quarrel but be gentle to all, able to teach, patient, in humility correcting those who are in opposition, if God perhaps will grant them repentance, so that they may know the truth, and that they may come to their senses and escape the snare of the devil, having been taken captive by him to do his will." – 2 Timothy 2:24-26

There are many verses in the Bible that speak of hell. As Billy Graham shared, we know enough about hell to know we never want to go there. Hell is unspeakably horrible because it is the opposite of heaven, which is indescribably wonderful. In the last book of the Bible, Revelation, the Apostle John was given an epiphany of heaven and hell that is full of amazing promises for followers of Jesus and a sober warning for those who reject Him:

"And I heard a loud voice from heaven saying, 'Behold, the tabernacle of God is with men, and He will dwell with them, and they shall be His people. God Himself will be with them and be their God. And God will wipe away every tear from their eyes; there shall be no more death, nor sorrow, nor crying. There shall be no more pain, for the former things have passed away. Then He who sat on the throne said, 'Behold, I make all things new.' And He said to me, 'Write, for these words are true and faithful.' And He said to me, 'It is done! I am the Alpha and the Omega, the Beginning and the End. I will give of the fountain of the water of life freely to him who thirsts. He who overcomes shall inherit all things, and I will be his God and he shall be My son. But the cowardly, unbelieving, abominable, murderers, sexually immoral, sorcerers, idolaters, and all liars shall have their part in the lake which burns with fire and brimstone, which is the second death.'" – Revelation 21:3-8

Rev. Billy Graham preaches at his crusade –
June 25, 2005 – Flushing, New York – Photo: Anthony – Correia [1]

IT IS IMPORTANT TO UNDERSTAND that God's first humans, Adam and Eve, were created by God to love and to freely love Him in pure fellowship. He created them in His image and gave them a free will, but they believed the lies of Satan and chose to sin in disobedience to God's command, thus breaking their perfect fellowship with Him and passing along their carnal sin nature to us. God's response to the human condition, following Adam and Eve's sin, was to send His only begotten Son, Jesus, from heaven to earth to become the perfect Man in the flesh and to freely sacrifice His life for the sins of all who would believe in Him. Everyone who has faith in this truth, repents of their sin, confesses Jesus is Lord, and believes in his heart that God raised Him from the dead, will be saved and experience eternal life in heaven.

> *"He who overcomes shall be clothed in white garments, and I will not blot out his name from the Book of Life; but I will confess his name before My Father and before His angels." – Revelation 3:5*

We know from the Bible that God has created a final dwelling place for Satan and his army of fallen demonic angels, as well as anyone whose name has been blotted out of the Book of Life (the book that contains the names of those who have been spiritually converted and have dedicated their lives to the service of God). This final dwelling place is referred to in the book of Revelation as the "lake of fire". At the end of the age, when God burns up the heavens, the earth, and all the works that are in it, Satan and his demonic host, and those not written in the Book of Life, will spend eternity in the "lake of fire". Heaven and hell are real and eternal.

> *"The day of the Lord will come as a robber comes. The heavens will pass away with a loud noise. The sun and moon and stars will burn up. The earth and all that is in it will be burned up." – 2 Peter 3:10*

The "lake of fire", otherwise known as hell, is eternal condemnation and torment in the blackness of loneliness without hope—and without God. Heaven and hell are eternally separate from one another because a Holy God cannot abide unholiness. Followers of Jesus are holy in God's eyes because we are in Jesus. God does not see us; He sees Jesus and He loves us as He loves Jesus. Remember, God is always good, always just, always fair, always faithful, and He always honors His word. As Pastor Chuck Smith once said:

> **"We must realize that God does not send anyone to hell. He did not create a race of robots to love Him. People go to hell by their own free will. In fact, God has done everything possible to keep people out of hell, even to the point of sending His Son to suffer and die for them on the cross. Rather than ask how a loving God can send someone to hell, ask how someone can choose to go to hell when God has done everything possible to keep them out."**

> *"Do you not know that the unrighteous will not inherit the kingdom of God? Do not be deceived. Neither fornicators, nor idolaters, nor adulterers, nor homosexuals, nor sodomites, nor thieves, nor covetous, nor drunkards, nor revilers, nor extortioners will inherit the kingdom of God." – 1 Corinthians 6:9-10*

LASTLY, WE MUST ALSO UNDERSTAND that God is a judge of nations as well as individuals. We know from the Bible that God sovereignly controls the rise and fall of nations, and establishes national boundaries. We also know that there is only one nation He promises to restore in the last days—Israel. Although the Jewish people have been experiencing God's temporal judgment for thousands of years—due to their rejection of God (Father, Son, and Holy Spirit), God's law, God's prophets, and God's Messiah—the Scriptures are clear that God will eternally restore and glorify the nation of Israel at the end of the age.

Through the lens of state-of-the-art communication technology, we are now witnessing God's sovereign judgment of nations in real time. Countries throughout the world—including the United Kingdom and the United States—are self-destructing. Globalist elites—guided by Satanic forces of evil—are orchestrating mass migration of people groups and restructuring global financial systems. As a result, cultural norms are being radically transformed and nations are imploding. The United Kingdom, once a bastion of gifted Christian pastors and missionaries, has been spiritually eviscerated and the United States is not far behind.

Although the Christ-centered founders of the United States envisioned one nation under God, many contemporary national, regional, and local leaders—across a wide spectrum of influential institutions—have rejected God and exposed America to the unbridled wickedness of Satan and his demonic host. They oversee: branches and agencies of federal, state, and local governments; Fortune 500 companies; private mega corporations; social media conglomerates; secular institutions of "higher" education; public and private school systems; the national health care system; apostate churches; and the list goes on. "Sanctuary cities" have blossomed into "sanctuary states"—and now a "sanctuary country". Bankrupt cities have blossomed into bankrupt states—and now a bankrupt country. The United States currently has $31 trillion dollars of national debt and $6 trillion of assets (*Truth in Accounting*, Glencoe, Illinois).

Leaders across the country have forsaken God's laws and are enacting laws, regulations, and policies designed to destroy the bedrock foundations of the government our forefathers created in answer to prayer. As a result, in my opinion, God has lifted His hand of grace from the United States. As pastor-teacher John MacArthur expressed in a Sunday sermon he preached September 13, 2020, titled, "A Nation Under God?":

"**When you turn from God's law—reverence for God is gone, morality is gone, fear is gone, virtue is gone, and God is gone.**"

Pastor John MacArthur – Shepherd's Conference –
Grace Community Church – Sun Valley, California – March 7, 2014
Photo: Grace Community Church [2]

27

THE END OF THE AGE

"God's love and patience now are incomprehensible; His wrath and judgment will be so likewise. That day of wrath is rapidly approaching. The heavens will be silent no longer. The Lord will arise and shake the earth." – Arno Gaebelein

God has organized time according to dispensations or time periods that feature important events in church history. These events are recorded and/or prophesied in the Bible. The most important future event in church history, the end of the age, is known only to God. It is an event prophesied throughout the Old and New Testaments, but is perhaps most clearly revealed by a vision God gave to the Apostle John, which he recorded in the 21st chapter of Revelation:

"Now I saw a new heaven and a new earth, for the first heaven and the first earth had passed away. Also there was no more sea. Then I, John, saw the holy city, New Jerusalem, coming down out of heaven from God, prepared as a bride adorned for her husband." – Revelation 21:1-2

In the same chapter, John goes on to describe the holy city, New Jerusalem (the church), in greater detail, concluding:

"But I saw no temple in it, for the Lord God Almighty and the Lamb are its temple. The city had no need of the sun or of the moon to shine in it, for the glory of God illuminated it. The Lamb is its light. And the nations of those who are saved shall walk in its light, and the kings of the earth bring their glory and honor into it. Its gates shall not be shut at all by day (there shall be no night there). And they shall bring the glory and the honor of the nations into it. But there shall by no means enter it anything that defiles, or causes an abomination or a lie, but only those who are written in the Lamb's Book of Life." – Revelation 21:22-27

The names of everyone born into the world are written in the "Book of Life". The names of those who reject God are blotted out of the "Book of Life". The names of those who confess with their mouth that Jesus is Lord and believe in their heart that God raised Him from the dead are written in the "Lamb's Book of Life". All who reject God will be judged by their works. Remember, God knows every thought, word and deed that we have thought, said, or done. If we end up standing before Him in our own righteousness we will spend eternity in hell—because all have sinned and fallen short of the glory of God.

"And anyone not found written in the Book of Life was cast into the lake of fire." – Revelation 20:15

THE BEST VERIFICATION OF THE authenticity of the Bible is fulfilled prophecy. Charles P. McIlvaine (1799-1873), an Episcopal Bishop, author, educator, and twice Chaplain of the U.S. Senate, defined prophesy as:

"Prophecy is a declaration of future events such as no human wisdom or forecast is sufficient to make. It depends on a knowledge of the innumerable contingencies of human affairs which belong exclusively to the omniscience of God so that, from its very nature, prophecy must be divine revelation."

The probability of a dozen Bible prophecies occurring, exactly as predicted, is difficult to calculate. The probability of hundreds of historically-fulfilled Bible prophecies occurring is beyond measure. John MacArthur, pastor-teacher, Grace Community Church, Sun Valley, California, in a sermon series delivered from 1979 to 1980 on the book of Daniel, shed light on Bible prophecy with a focus on the first and second comings of Christ:

- "…prophecy occupies approximately one-fifth of Scripture and second coming prophecies occupy approximately one-third…

- "…there are 660 general prophecies and 333 of them are about Christ…

- "…of the 333 that are about Christ, 109 were fulfilled in His first coming and 224 are yet to be fulfilled in His second coming…

- "…for every time His first coming is mentioned, His second coming is mentioned eight times…"

THE FOLLOWING OVERVIEW OF THE events leading to the end of the age is based on my understanding of the Scriptures, coupled with my study of various commentaries. I would encourage the reader to search the Scriptures to find out whether these things are so, because the best commentary on the Bible is the Bible itself, comparing Scripture with Scripture.

Throughout history, Old Testament saints, those who believed in God for a salvation yet to be fully revealed, and New Testament saints, those who have believed in the revealed Messiah, have looked forward to the end of the age, a time when all believers will dwell eternally in the presence of God. There are several major events that lead chronologically to the end of the age:

- the birth of the church and the beginning of the Church Age on the Day of Pentecost, circa 32 A.D.;

- the dispersion of the nation of Israel when the Roman army invaded Jerusalem and destroyed the Temple, circa 70 A.D.;

- the end of the Church Age, a future moment of time when Jesus returns and removes His church (dead and living) from earth to heaven, known as the rapture;

- the seven-year tribulation period;

- the great tribulation, which begins three-and-a-half years after the tribulation period begins;

- the battle of Armageddon which occurs three-and-a-half years after the beginning of the great tribulation;

- the millennium, a period of one thousand years beginning at the conclusion of the battle of Armageddon, when Jesus returns to earth with His church and the nation of Israel is restored;

- and the "great white throne" judgment, the day of the Lord, and the marriage supper of the Lamb, which all occur at the end of the millennium.

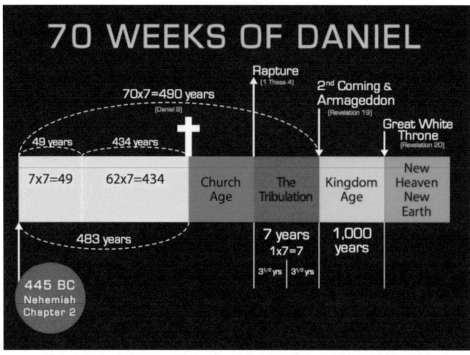

Timeline depicting the 70 weeks of Daniel – Image: Ilyas Mughal [1]

In the Old Testament book of Daniel, Chapter 9:24-27, written circa 600 B.C., Daniel is given an amazing prophecy and vision of the future—by God, through His messenger, the archangel Gabriel—that outlines the time periods during which the events mentioned above will occur. Sir Isaac Newton, one of the most brilliant Bible-believing scholars and scientists of the ages, said:

"We could stake the truth of Christianity on this prophecy alone, made five centuries before Christ."

Daniel's vision frames these events within a time span of seventy weeks. The Hebrew word week means a week of years or seven years. Seventy sevens equals 490 years, a time frame within which there are three consecutive periods, with a pause of indeterminate length between the end of the second and the beginning of the third periods:

- the first period of seven weeks (49 years) began when the Persian King Artaxerxes commanded the rebuilding of Jerusalem, circa 445 B.C., and ended when the book of Malachi (the last book of the Old Testament) was written, circa 400 B.C.;

- the second period of sixty-two weeks (434 years) began circa 400 B.C. and ended when Jesus triumphantly entered Jerusalem as the Messiah, was crucified, buried, raised from the dead, ascended into heaven, and sent the Holy Spirit to birth the church on The Day of Pentecost, circa 32 A.D.;

- PAUSE – The Church Age of indeterminate length;

- and the third period of one week (7 years) will begin with the rapture of the church, a future point in time known only to God, and will end when Jesus returns with His church to rule the world for a thousand years, otherwise known as the millennium.

There are hundreds of Old Testament prophecies that have been fulfilled in the lead-up to the rapture of the church. All of them were prophesied thousands of years ago. Many of them pointed to the birth, death, resurrection, and ascension of Jesus. In fact, the resurrection of Jesus is foretold in oldest book of the Bible, the book of Job, which was written circa 600 B.C.:

"For I know that my Redeemer lives, and He shall stand at last on the earth; and after my skin is destroyed, this I know, that in my flesh I shall see God, whom I shall see for myself, and my eyes shall behold, and not another. How my heart yearns within me!" – Job 19:25-27

Jesus speaks of the fulfillment of Job's prophecy in the Gospel of John:

"Most assuredly, I say to you, the hour is coming, and now is, when the dead will hear the voice of the Son of God; and those who hear will live. For as the Father has life in Himself, so He has granted the Son to have life in Himself, and has given Him authority to execute judgment also, because He is the Son of Man. Do not marvel at this; for the hour is coming in which all who are in the graves will hear His voice and come forth—those who have done good, to the resurrection of life, and those who have done evil, to the resurrection of condemnation." – John 5:25-29

As I write this, the Church Age has lasted about two thousand years. The Apostle Paul predicted the rapture of the church in his first letter to the Thessalonians:

"For the Lord Himself will descend from heaven with a shout, with the voice of an archangel, and with the trumpet of God. And the dead in Christ will rise first. Then we who are alive and remain shall be caught up together with them in the clouds to meet the Lord in the air. And thus we shall always be with the Lord. Therefore comfort one another with these words." – 1 Thessalonians 4:16-18

After the rapture occurs, a seven-year tribulation period begins that encompasses two halves. During the first half, Satan, through his human instrument the Antichrist, will introduce a three-and-a-half-year period of peace and prosperity on earth. He will also enter into a covenant with the nation of Israel to protect it from its enemies and to rebuild the temple.

When this period of peace and prosperity ends, the Antichrist will proclaim himself God, cause an image of himself (the Abomination of Desolation) to be placed in the temple in Jerusalem, and will command all who are alive on earth to worship his likeness or die.

The second half, referred to in the Bible as the great tribulation, features God's judgments, which will be super-natural and devastating, and will end with the battle of Armageddon, a battle where Satan and the armies of earth are defeated by Jesus and the armies of heaven.

At the end of the great tribulation, Jesus will return to earth with His church, bind Satan and imprison him in a bottomless pit, and reign with His church for a thousand-year period known as the millennium.

"Then I saw an angel coming down from heaven, having the key to the bottomless pit and a great chain in his hand. He laid hold of the dragon, that serpent of old, who is the Devil and Satan, and bound him for a thousand years; and he cast him into the bottomless pit, and shut him up, and set a seal on him, so that he should deceive the nations no more till the thousand years were finished. But after these things he must be released for a little while." – Revelation 20:1-3

During the millennium: Jesus will establish His kingdom on earth; the nation of Israel will enjoy all of the blessings promised by the prophets; God will protect the Jews and Gentiles who believe and are converted; and the earth will be characterized by peace, righteousness, and justice.

At the end of the millennium, Satan will be released from the bottom-less pit and be allowed to deceive the nations again. Although it's hard to believe that people living in the kingdom of God will be deceived, multitudes will rise up and attempt to destroy Jesus and all who follow Him, at which time God will devour Satan and his armies by fire.

"Now when the thousand years have expired, Satan will be released from his prison and will go out to deceive the nations which are in the four corners of the earth, Gog and Magog, to gather them together to battle, whose number is as the sand of the sea. They went up on the breadth of the earth and surrounded the camp of the saints and the beloved city. And fire came down from God out of heaven and devoured them. The devil, who deceived them, was cast into the lake of fire and brimstone where the beast and the false prophet are. And they will be tormented day and night forever and ever." – Revelation 20:7-10

This is the end of the age, a time when those who rejected Jesus will stand before God at the "great white throne" judgment.

"Then I saw a great white throne and Him who sat on it, from whose face the earth and the heaven fled away. And there was found no place for them. And I saw the dead, small and great, standing before God, and books were opened. And another book was opened, which is the Book of Life. And the dead were judged according to their works, by the things which were written in the books. The sea gave up the dead who were in it, and Death and Hades delivered up the dead who were in them. And they were judged, each one according to his works. Then Death and Hades were cast into the lake of fire. This is the second death. And anyone not found written in the Book of Life was cast into the lake of fire." – Revelation 20:11-15

It is also a time referred to in 2 Peter as the day of the Lord, or God's judgment in human affairs. Peter declares it a period when the heavens and the earth will pass away. God spoke the universe into existence, He holds it in His hands, and in a future moment of time, He will release it and it will burn up.

"But the day of the Lord will come as a thief in the night, in which the heavens will pass away with a great noise, and the elements will melt with fervent heat; both the earth and the works that are in it will be burned up. Therefore, since all these things will be dissolved, what manner of persons ought you to be in holy conduct and godliness, looking for and hastening the coming of the day of God, because of which the heavens will be dissolved, being on fire, and the elements will melt with fervent heat? Nevertheless we, according to His promise, look for new heavens and a new earth in which righteousness dwells." – 2 Peter 3:10-13

As mentioned at the beginning of this chapter (see Revelation 21:1-2), following the day of the Lord, the marriage supper of the Lamb occurs, which is the consummation of the engagement of Jesus to His church. God will then dwell with His people and death, sorrow, crying, and pain will pass away.

In the last chapter of Revelation, we are warned three times that Jesus is coming quickly to emphasize the urgency of this impending moment. We who are alive in Jesus should live accordingly. Our lives should reflect a holy reverence for, and joyful expectation of, the reality of His quick return.

All believers should also remember that in the first and last chapters of the book of Revelation God promises a blessing to anyone that reads, hears, and keeps the words of this book:

- *"Blessed is he who reads and those who hear the words of this prophecy, and keep those things which are written in it; for the time is near." – Revelation 1:3*

- *"Behold, I am coming quickly! Blessed is he who keeps the words of the prophecy of this book." – Revelation 22:7*

LASTLY, AS WE READ AND study the entire Bible, we continually see God's unfailing love for mankind, even to the end. In the book of Revelation, we learn that one of the greatest revivals in the history of the world will occur after the rapture, during the tribulation, when God shares His gospel throughout the earth. Countless numbers of those who rejected Jesus before the rapture will be saved after the rapture. Some will be martyred, some will die from disease, some will die from lack of food, water, and shelter, but all will suffer horribly in the process. We don't know all the ways and means God will save the lost during the tribulation, but we know He will use:

- 144,000 of the children of Israel (12,000 from each of the 12 tribes) – (**Rev. 7:4-8**);

- two witnesses who prophecy for 1,260 days and are then slain and resurrected – (**Rev. 11:3-13**);

- and an angel from heaven – (**Rev. 14:6-7**).

"Then I saw another angel flying in the midst of heaven, having the everlasting gospel to preach to those who dwell on the earth—to every nation, tribe, tongue, and people—saying with a loud voice, 'Fear God and give glory to Him, for the hour of His judgment has come; and worship Him who made heaven and earth, the sea and springs of water.'" – Revelation 14:6-7

Anyone who does not know Jesus as their personal Lord and Savior should wake up, open their eyes to the pure truth of God's word, and pray for faith from God to believe in Him. Jesus can rescue you, as He has rescued me and every other believer, living and dead, who comprise His church.

"Let us hear the conclusion of the whole matter: fear God and keep His commandments, for this is man's all. For God will bring every work into judgment, Including every secret thing, whether good or evil." – Ecclesiastes: 12:13-14

28

SPIRITUAL LESSONS

"Men are God's method. The church is looking for better methods; God is looking for better men… What the church needs today is not more machinery or better, not new organizations or more and novel methods, but men who the Holy Ghost can use—men of prayer, men mighty in prayer. The Holy Ghost does not come on machinery, but on men. He does not anoint plans but men—men of prayer…" – E. M. Bounds

In closing, let me share a few spiritual lessons I am learning—some for believers, some for unbelievers, and some for both. For believers, I would like to begin with the certainty that Satan—the devil, our archenemy, the ruler of the world—will always try to convince us that we have lost our salvation and can never again be right with God, because of something we have thought, said, or done. Never believe it.

Jesus paid the price for all of our sins: past, present, and future. If you are following Jesus, never be tempted by Satan to doubt your salvation. If you have confessed with your mouth that Jesus is Lord and believed in your heart that God raised Him from the dead, nothing can separate you from Him. If you are practicing sin continually without remorse and a repentant heart, such as engaging in an adulterous relationship, as opposed to slipping into sin from time to time by being deceitful, losing your temper, etc., you may have not received Jesus as your personal Lord and Savior in the first place. If

so, you need to repent and do so now. God never turns away a repentant sinner.

"Who shall separate us from the love of Christ? Shall tribulation, or distress, or persecution, or famine, or nakedness, or peril, or sword? As it is written: 'For Your sake we are killed all day long; we are accounted as sheep for the slaughter.' Yet in all these things we are more than conquerors through Him who loved us. For I am persuaded that neither death nor life, nor angels nor principalities nor powers, nor things present nor things to come, nor height nor depth, nor any other created thing, shall be able to separate us from the love of God which is in Christ Jesus our Lord."
– Romans 8:35-39

Sometimes God leads us to a place from which we feel there is no escape. We feel trapped. We feel that there is no way out. We are beside ourselves and we can become so self-obsessed that we are constantly looking inward rather than upward. We begin to indulge to a greater and greater degree in the worst sin a believer can commit: the sin of unbelief, the rejection of Jesus. We are depending upon ourselves for the strength we don't have, rather than depending upon God for the strength only He can provide.

"I can do all things through Christ who strengthens me." – *Philippians 4:13*

Even the Israelites, after God had performed all the miracles in Egypt prior to the exodus, cried out to God at the shore of the Red Sea in disbelief. They were trapped. They were hemmed in by mountains to the north, mountains to the south, Pharaoh's army to the west, and the Red Sea to the east. In their eyes, there was no escape. However, God had led them to this place and God delivered them from it. God is leading you and He will deliver you.

We don't need to spend a certain number of hours per day in prayer, read a precise number of books of the Bible each day, or attend an explicit number of church services or fellowship meetings to draw close to God. God doesn't want sacrifice. He wants our hearts. God is not measuring our devotion or setting any minimum thresholds. He just wants to be our Dad, and like any dad, He loves it when we draw close to Him and feels saddened when we turn away.

If we have children, how would we feel if they never wanted to talk to us or listen to what we have to say? William Law, a famous Christian scholar and writer of the 18th century, said:

"God is like us in this also, that He takes it worse to be slighted, to be neglected, to be left out, than to be actually injured. Our inconsideration, our not thinking of God in our actions, offends Him more than our sins."

God's ways are not our ways. His ways are always much better than anything we can ask, think, or imagine. It may not seem like it at the time, but God always answers our prayers perfectly. It may not be what we were expecting, it may take a long time, or it may be the answer to an arrow prayer.

Corrie ten Boom, a prolific Christian writer during the 20th century, helped many Jews escape the German holocaust in Holland during World War II, before she was caught and sent to a Nazi concentration camp. She was released by the Nazis shortly before the end of the war because of a clerical error. A week later, all the women in her age group were sent to the gas chambers. She shared about prayer:

"Any concern too small to be turned into a prayer is too small to be made into a burden."

Corrie ten Boom [1]

Sometimes no answer is the best answer, or it may take years. I prayed for a friend to come to the Lord for many years. One day, as I was sitting in church before the service started, a fellow sitting behind me tapped me on the shoulder, introduced himself, and said he was a friend of my friend. He had heard I was praying for our mutual friend. He shared how God had led him to guide our friend to Jesus during a business trip to North Carolina. Answered prayer!

HERE'S A CHARACTER TRAIT THAT for most people like myself is a lifelong challenge: humility. I've been privileged to know a handful of people with humility ingrained in their character. It's as natural to them as opening their eyes. My wife is a perfect example, so were her mother and father.

I sometimes believe God measures out humility like he measures out faith: we either possess an extra measure of it or we don't. We can't manufacture humility, but the Holy Spirit who dwells within us can help us to grow in humility. As we draw closer to God, He will teach us to know and understand His word. He will fill us with His love, and we will grow in modesty as we grow in selflessness.

The best test of humility is the amount of time we devote to thinking about ourselves versus loving, blessing, and praying for others. For most of us it is an everlasting prayer, "Lord, empower me to grow in humility." However, it is a prayer with a promise:

"...God resists the proud, but gives grace to the humble..." – 1 Peter 5:5

Charles Spurgeon shared the following poem, bracketed by his comments:

"How often do we find out our weakness when God answers our prayer!"

"I asked the Lord that I might grow in faith, and love, and every grace; might more of his salvation know and seek more earnestly his face.

"I hoped that in some favor'd hour at once he'd answer my request, and by his loves' constraining power subdue my sins, and give me rest.

"Instead of this he made me feel the hidden evils of my heart, and let the angry power of hell assault my soul in every part.

'Lord why is this?' I trembling cried, 'Wilt thou pursue thy worm to death.'

'Tis in this way,' the Lord replied, 'I answer prayer for grace and faith.'"

"That is, the Lord helps us to grow downward when we are actually thinking about growing upward."

FOLLOWING JESUS IS NOT A free pass to a life of joy and peace on earth. The closer we follow Him, the greater a target we are to the one who seeks to destroy us: Satan. Until we have moved to heaven, praying, reading His word, and regularly joining other believers in fellowship will always remain vital in order to rest in Him and obey His call on our lives. There will never be a moment on earth that we don't need to draw close to Him.

"Be sober, be vigilant; because your adversary the devil walks about like a roaring lion, seeking whom he may devour." – 1 Peter 5:8

The Bible promises that those who follow Jesus will experience trials, tribulations, and persecutions, but the Bible also promises that He who is in us is greater than he who is in the world. We can trust that whether we are rejoicing or suffering, He is working out His perfect plan in our lives.

"Yes, and all who desire to live godly in Christ Jesus will suffer persecution." – 2 Timothy 3:12

George Muller, who faithfully founded schools and orphanages in Bristol, England, testified:

"God delights to increase the faith of His children. Our faith, which is feeble at first, is developed and strengthened more and more by us. We ought, instead of wanting no trials before victory, no exercise for patience, to be willing to take them from God's hand as a means I say—and say it deliberately—trials, obstacles, difficulties, and sometimes defeats, are the very food of faith."

Billy Graham, who recently went home to heaven, was used by God to share His word with over two hundred million people in over 180 countries and territories. The magnitude of his outreach might have been diminished but for a two-word telegram, "Puff Graham," sent by newspaper magnate, William Randolph Hearst, to all his editors in 1949, when Graham was conducting a crusade in Los Angeles.

What "Puff Graham" meant to his editors was that they were to promote Graham and the crusade. As a result, Graham gained national and international coverage, the crusade extended five weeks longer than planned, and Graham became known around the world.

What Hearst didn't know, was that the crusade was being prayed over by more than 1,000 prayer groups organized in and around the city of Los Angeles. They were not specifically asking God for Hearst to promote Graham, but that God would bless the crusade and enlarge His kingdom.

In response to their prayers, God prompted Hearst to compose and send his telegram. This is a perfect example of how God's ways are not our ways, and how He answers prayer and orchestrates the patterns of our lives beyond anything we can ask, think, or imagine. Hearst and Graham never met.

Charles Spurgeon, speaking about faith, tells the story of a poor countryman in England who said to him:

"The old enemy has been troubling me very much lately; but I told him that he must not say anything to me about my sins. He must go to my Master, for I had transferred the whole concern to Him, bad debts and all."

In Spurgeon's words:

"That is believing. Believing is giving up all we have to Christ and taking all Christ has to ourselves. It is changing houses with Christ, changing clothes with Christ, changing our unrighteousness for His righteousness, changing our sins for His merits."

We also need to remember that we are living in the last days. Now, it's true, every generation of believers imagine they are living in the last days and they are. That's a good thing, because that's how we should always live. But the fact of the matter is, at this point in history, we are living in an age when the opportunities to fulfill the lust of the flesh, the lust of the eyes, and the pride of life are tempting many Christians to abuse their Christian liberty. Simply consider the plagues of divorce and pornography that have infected the church. Light and darkness cannot be mixed in the eyes of God.

We need to spend as much time prayerfully considering how we are investing our lives spiritually as we are planning our retirement. Even though it's hard to turn on the radio or the television without hearing an advertisement about planning for retirement, the words retire and retirement are not mentioned in the Bible.

There's nothing more exciting and fulfilling than experiencing and obeying God's call on your life. I believe God called me to write this book. He has a calling on your life, and as you spend time with Him in prayer, in His word, and in fellowship with other believers, He will speak His calling into your heart. He will then give you the passion, spiritual gifts, and means to fulfill it. He is not only the source of our salvation; He is the power of every aspect of the lives we live in Him.

"... 'not by might nor by power, but by My Spirit,' says the Lord of hosts.'" – Zechariah 4:6

Our spiritual vision becomes clouded when we immerse ourselves in worldly things. We begin to lose sight of the eternal, and that's when Satan can slip in and deeply hurt us and those we love. God is always viewing us from an eternal perspective, outside of time and space, and He is always guiding us in an eternal way. We often respond in frustration or despair when we consider our temporal situations and can't figure out why God lets something happen or not happen, that doesn't fit into our limited perception of circumstances, but God always has a perfect plan!

"The secret things belong to the Lord our God, but those things which are revealed belong to us and to our children forever, that we may do all the words of this law." – Deuteronomy 29:29

The history of man has been dark and bleak. Yes, we can point back to certain historical periods like The Renaissance or The Enlightenment, but these are simply words that some historians crafted to elevate the genius of man. The truth of the matter is that man has always lived in darkness—a darkness characterized by sorrow, pain, suffering, anguish, and tragedy. Man, under Satan's thumb, has brought these outcomes upon himself through his wars, greed, atrocities, and exploitation of the weak and poor. The church shines forth as the morning and declares to the world that there is a new day dawning. This has always been the message of the church to the world. If you don't know Jesus, a new day can unfold in your life as it has in mine. The darkness which has held your life captive, as mine was, can transform into a new day. God's work is always about a new beginning.

In the introductory section of this book, "His Story", I presented a perspective of man in relation to the earth, the sun, and the universe. I also shared that the light of the moon is the reflected light of the sun, and in a similar way, the church is the reflected light of Jesus, the Son of God. Like the moon, which God created to be the lesser light to rule the night, the church, despite its imperfections, continues to reflect the light of Jesus to a dark world.

"For it is the God who commanded light to shine out of darkness, who has shone in our hearts to give the light of the knowledge of the glory of God in the face of Jesus Christ." – 2 Corinthians 4:6

As the moon goes through phases of brightness, from a sliver to a full moon, so the church, an imperfect body of believers, goes through phases of reflecting the light of Jesus, at times clearly and brightly, but often hidden and clouded by human imperfection. Every follower of Jesus is a flawed being on a journey to perfection. Each of us is unique and each of us is being conformed into the image of Jesus in a unique way.

"Those who are well have no need of a physician, but those who are sick. I did not come to call the righteous, but sinners, to repentance." – Mark 2:17

We will all be perfectly healed and made holy, as Jesus is holy, when He takes us home. Until then, our work is to rest in Him and pray His will be done. Even as the light of the moon declares that the sun still shines, so the church affirms that the Son of God still shines through those who believe in Him. In 1986, I saw the reflected light of the Son through my sister's church.

Phases of the Moon [2]

WE KNOW FROM THE SCRIPTURES that there was one man who possessed everything anyone might desire in this world. His name was Solomon and he became the King of Israel when his father David passed away. During his life there was nothing he wanted that God withheld from him. At the end of his life, in the book of Ecclesiastes, he reflected on everything he had experienced:

"Whatever my eyes desired I did not keep from them. I did not withhold my heart from any pleasure, for my heart rejoiced in all my labor; and this was my reward from all my labor. Then I looked on all the works that my hands had done and on the labor in which I had toiled; and indeed all was vanity and grasping for the wind. There was no profit under the sun." – Ecclesiastes 2:10-11

King Solomon despaired over the emptiness of self-absorption. He was not the first, nor the last, to do so. In every generation there are some who grasp for power, wealth, fame, or some other worldly idol, only to despair when they attain it and experience an emptiness that leaves them hopeless. Our generation is no exception; there are numerous people who have achieved their ambitions only to realize, as Solomon did, that they have grasped the wind. Perhaps you know someone like that; I do, his name is Joey Buran (see Chapter 25).

In 1984, at the end of the Off Shore Pipeline Masters surfing championship, Joey stood on the presentation platform flanked by fellow professional surfers Mark Occhilupo and Tom Carroll. When it was announced Joey had won, he was shocked. A few minutes later, after he had proudly lifted the trophy over his head to the cheers of the crowd, a torrential rainstorm opened up and everyone ran for cover. Then, standing alone on the beach, trophy in hand, Joey experienced an overwhelming feeling of emptiness and despair over all he had worked so hard to achieve.

Joey Buran winning the 1984 Off Shore Pipeline Masters [3]

Several months later Joey hit bottom, found Jesus, and entered a life of ministry to others. After ten years of pastoral ministry, he returned to surfing in 1998 and won the ASP World Masters Championship in Puerto Escondido, Mexico. He was inducted into the Surfing Hall of Fame in 2009. Throughout 2018, Joey served as the coach of the U.S. Olympic Surfing Program. In 2005 he founded the Worship Generation church in Fountain Valley, California, where he currently serves as Senior Pastor. He is a loving husband, father of four, and doting grandfather.

"Do you not know that those who run in a race all run, but one receives the prize? Run in such a way that you may obtain it. And everyone who competes for the prize is temperate in all things. Now they do it to obtain a perishable crown, but we for an imperishable crown." – 1 Corinthians 9:24-25

Like each of us, J. Paul Getty, King Solomon, and Joey Buran were created by God, loved by God, and free to believe in God or free to reject Him. The bridge to God is the Word of God, Jesus. We can't cross that bridge by being good, helping others, or making charitable donations. We can't cross that bridge by attending a church, synagogue, temple, or mosque; obeying certain rules and regulations; or practicing certain manmade religious rituals and traditions.

The only way we can cross that bridge is by believing that Jesus died for our sins and that His victory over death is God's free gift to mankind—to receive or reject. Everybody lives forever! Receiving God's free gift of salvation imparts eternal love, joy, and peace in His kingdom now and forever. Rejecting His free gift leads to self-absorption and—upon death—eternal suffering in the horror of hell. Although there is no profit under the sun, there is eternal life in the Son!

"And we know that the Son of God has come and has given us an understanding, that we may know Him who is true; and we are in Him who is true, in His Son Jesus Christ. This is the true God and eternal life." – 1 John 5:20

MENTORS

A mentor is an experienced and trusted advisor. I have been privileged to have had numerous mentors over my lifetime. Each has played an integral role in forming the person I am today. Two who profoundly impacted my life are Desmond Bittinger and Bob Theetge. There were many others I have never met in person but look forward to meeting and visiting with in heaven. These are my brothers and sisters in Jesus whom God introduced me to through the books, sermons, and Bible commentaries He empowered them to share over the centuries. They include the following in alphabetical order:

E.M. Bounds (1835-1913)

John Calvin (1509-1564)

Arno Gaebelein (1861-1945)

Matthew Henry (1662-1714)

Wetherell Johnson (1907-1984)

Martin Luther (1483-1546)

John MacArthur (1939 -)

Alexander Maclaren (1826-1910)

Vernon McGee (1904-1988)

D.L. Moody (1837-1899)

G. Campbell Morgan (1863-1945)

John Newton (1725-1807)

Alan Redpath (1907-1989)

Chuck Smith (1927-2013)

Charles Spurgeon (1834-1892)

J. Hudson Taylor (1832-1905)

Corrie ten Boom (1892-1983)

Alexander Whyte (1836-1921)

George Whitefield (1714-1770)

David Wilkerson (1931-2011)

BIBLIOGRAPHY

Gaebelein, Arno C., *The Annotated Bible*. 1917. Reprint. Neptune, New Jersey: Loizeaux Brothers, 1971.

Henry, Matthew, *Matthew Henry's Commentary on the Whole Bible, New Modern Edition*, 1714. Reprint. Hendrickson Publishers, Inc., Complete and Unabridged in Six Volumes, 1998.

MacArthur, John, *The MacArthur Study Bible, New King James Version*, Word Publishing, a division of Thomas Nelson, Inc., 1997.

McGee, J. Vernon, *Thru the Bible in Five Volumes*, Thomas Nelson, Inc., 1981.

Smith, Chuck, *Through the Bible, C2000 Series Bible Studies, Audio, Genesis Through Revelation*, 1979-1986.

Spurgeon, Charles Haddon, *Spurgeon's Sermons*, 1883. Reprint. Baker Books, Grand Rapids, Michigan, Five-volume edition, 1996.

Spurgeon, Charles Haddon, *The Treasury of David, An Original Exposition of the Book of Psalms*, 1886. Reprint. Hendrickson Publishers, In Three Volumes, 1988.

ACKNOWLEDGEMENTS

The genesis of this book was an instructional narrative I wrote about bodysurfing without fins, which I felt led to write because I didn't know anybody else that had focused on this aspect of surfing. I shared it with a few people, and as I did, found myself "talking story" with a surf buddy, George Alexander. Now George is not someone I've known for a long time, but we both share a passion for the ocean and we both like to share surf stories. As George listened, I began to think and pray about memorializing some of mine.

I had written one other book before this, *Words of Wisdom*, but that was a case of using my organizational skills to assemble memorable quotations from anointed men and women of God, that I thought worthy of sharing with others—then actually writing something myself. Although I had never written a book before, I felt called to write this one. Being called by God to do something is simply an indescribable sense of being drawn to do something that begins with taking a step of faith, not knowing what's next.

As I began to memorialize my stories, I also began to pray and ask God to direct my steps. He led me to people whom I felt comfortable sharing this calling with. One of the first was Eric Geerdes, one of the most humble and gifted people I know. He is also a gentle giant, both physically and personally. Eric read my first draft, several years ago, and provided the encouragement I needed to take the next step. Eric also brought me over the finish line by contributing his IT skills to launch *Connected – Above & Below* on Amazon.

With Eric's reassurance and encouragement, I began to pray harder and dig deeper. As I did, I began sharing subsequent drafts with others who were equally encouraging and provided the support I needed to continue. Scott Clark, a talented surfer and fellow Walking on Water board member, listened to one of my first drafts on tape. He then shared with me that he wanted to buy several copies of *Connected – Above and Below* to keep in the trunk of his car to hand out at the beach. Scott also encouraged me not to hold back on including Scripture.

Another person whom God used to help me along the way was Natalie Harp. Natalie is the daughter of a home-school family we became close to when we were homeschooling Allison. She is an amazing lady and one of the most gifted young people I know. She is also a very talented writer. Natalie introduced me to an editor she knows, Quynh Nhu Nguyen. Quynh was a Godsend. She is a talented editor with a special flair to guide and direct.

As this book began to take shape, I was concerned I might have shared something that was not in alignment with the word of God. Fortunately, I have a wonderful pastor and friend, Mark Foreman, Lead Pastor, North Coast Calvary Chapel, Carlsbad, California. Mark was not only kind enough to read successive drafts, he was also caring enough to encourage me to publish. He reassured me that what he had read was Scripturally sound and shared several insightful editing suggestions. Anyone who knows Mark, or has heard him preach, knows Mark ranks right at the top as a master storyteller.

During the final phase of completing the first edition, God directed me to others whom He used to refine what He was leading me to share. My nephew, Jonathan Van Ryn, encouraged me, as did my brother-in-law, Gary De Graff, who read through an early draft with a fine-toothed comb, providing several perceptive edits and an extra measure of inspiration.

All along the way, and before I began this book, I have been blessed by my association with two brothers, Adam and Todd McWethy, and Scott Hancock, who together, lead an amazing brand development company, BLVR, located in San Diego, California. These men, and the incredible staff God has led them to assemble, have not only been a great encouragement and help to me in ministry, they have also been faithful to come alongside many others in using their creative talents to grow God's kingdom. Special thanks to BLVR's intern, Sabrina Baker, for the creative design and layout of the book and cover, and to Joe Mitchell and Katie Murphy for their diligence in correcting numerous edits.

I also want to acknowledge my wife, Judy. Although Judy asked me to minimize what I shared about her in this book, she provided a critical eye to this project and helped me to shape it. After fifty years of marriage, including some rocky roads before my salvation, Judy knows me almost as well as God and she can sharpen my life, and my work, like no one but God. In her special way, Judy helped me to share my story as only she could, because the essence of my story is our story.

Thank You, Jesus, for blessing me with the opportunity to write this book and for the many people, mentioned and unmentioned, who made it possible. You have made it perfectly clear that this was a collaborative effort and I am eternally thankful to You for the opportunity to be involved.

PHOTO AND IMAGE CREDITS

ESSENTIALS:

1. Personal photo collection

HIS STORY:

1. "In the beginning God created the heavens and the earth." Genesis 1:1 – NASA archive – image created by Reto Stockli, Nazmi El Saleous, and Marit Jentoft-Nilsen – This file is in the Public Domain in the United States because it was solely created by NASA.

2. "Comparison of Betelgeuse to our Sun" – Author: Ankit Das – Quora platform

3. "Dwight L. Moody, 1837-1899" – Image from page 255 of "The Life and work of Dwight L. Moody" – Flickr – No known copyright restrictions

4. "Arno C. Gaebelein – 1861-1945" – Wikimedia Commons (commons.wikimedia.org) – This work is in the Public Domain in the United States because) it was published (or registered with the U.S. Copyright Office) before January 1, 1924.

PART ONE – THE BEGINNING:

CHAPTER 1:

1. Personal photo collection

2. Personal image collection

3. Personal photo collection

4. "Faneuil Hall – Boston, Massachusetts – early 1900s" – Unknown photographer – This media file is in the public domain in the United States – Wikimedia Commons (commons.wikimedia.org

5. Personal photo collection

6. Personal photo collection

7. Personal photo collection

8. Personal photo collection

9. Personal photo collection

10. "Pan American World Airways (PAA) Boeing Stratocruiser (early 1950s) San Francisco Bay Bridge (background)" – Flickr – No known copyright restrictions

11. "TWA Connie at London Airport (since renamed Heathrow Airport) – Author: Unknown – 1954" – Creative Commons Attribution – CC BY 3.0 – Created 11 September 1954 – Wikipedia

12. Personal image collection

13. Personal photo collection

14. "St. George Hotel – Beirut, Lebanon" – Author: Unknown – Source: Unknown (this photograph was linked to a website: danger-man.co.uk/locations.asp on TinEye)

15. "Old Beirut café and souk – circa 1950s" – Author: Unknown – Source: Arabic Post

16. Personal image collection

CHAPTER 2:

1. "Hanging bat in cave" – Author: All-stock-photos – Source: shutterstock – Royalty-free stock photo ID: 343642814

2. "Seafront Hotel Casino Uaddan (center-left) – Tripoli, Libya – circa 1960s" – {{PD-US-no notice}} – Public Domain

3. "Roman ruins – Leptis Magna, Al-Khums, Libya" – Author: Plamen Galabov – Source: shutterstock – Royalty-free stock – Photo ID: 1137357083

4. "Poster for 'Around the World in 80 Days", 1968 – Author: Natan Hughes Hamilton – Creative Commons Attribution 2.0 Generic (CC BY 2.0) – Wikimedia Commons (commons.wikimedia.org)

CHAPTER 3:

1. "Rio 2016. Polo aquatico. A33 06" – Author: Jonas de Carvalho from Rio de Janeiro, Brasil – Creative Commons Attribution-Share Alike 2.0 Generic license. Wikimedia Commons (commons.wikimedia.org)

2. "Front of the Kurhaus Casino and Restaurant – Wiesbaden, Germany" – Pixabay License – Free for commercial use. No attribution required.

3. "Kurhaus Park (back of Casino and Restaurant) – Wiesbaden, Germany" Author: Pedelecs – This file is licensed under the Creative Commons Attribution 3.0 license – Wikimedia Commons (commons.wikimedia.org)

4. "U.S. Army Rhineblick Golf Course, Wiesbaden, Germany" – U.S. Army MWR: Rhineblick Golf Course – wiesbadenarmymdr.com – Wikimedia Commons (commons.wikimedia.org)

5. Personal photo collection

6. "King Farouk's Abdeen Palace, Cairo, Egypt" – Author: Leonid Andronov – Source: shutterstock – Royalty-free stock photo – ID: 247008895

7. Personal photo collection

CHAPTER 4:

1. Personal photo collection

2. Personal photo collection

3. "Wallace Hall – Monmouth College" – Author: Jason Lonsberry – Source: Wickimedia Commons – Public Domain

4. "National Gallery of Art, West Building" – Author: Kunar Klack – Creative Commons Attribution-ShareAlike 2.0 Generic (CC BY-SA 2.0) – flickr

5. "Dr. Martin Luther King, Jr. – 1964" – Wikimedia Commons (commons. wikimedia.org) – {{PD-US-no notice}} – Author: Nobel Foundation – This Swedish photograph is in the public domain in Sweden.

6. Personal photo collection

7. "Soldiers set up a machine gun emplacement on the steps of the U.S. Capitol" – Creative Commons Attribution-ShareAlike 2.0 Generic (CC BY-SA 2.0) – Flickr

8. "Soldiers standing guard on the corner of 7th & N Street NW in Washington D.C." – Wikimedia Commons (commons.wikimedia.org) – Author: Warren K. Leffler / Library of Congress – This work is from the U.S. News & World Report collection at the Library of Congress. According to the Library of Congress, there are no known restrictions on the use of this work.

9. Personal photo collection

10. Personal photo collection

11. Personal photo collection

12. "Maasai Warriors" – Author: S. Skulina – Source: Pegas Studio, Nairobi – Postcard dated 1969 – East African Types – Masai Warriors – Pinterest

CHAPTER 5:

1. "Dragonara Casino, St. Julian's, Malta" – Author: Tony Hisgett from Birmingham, UK – This file is licensed under the Creative Commons Attribution 2.0 Generic license. – Wikimedia Commons (commons.wikimedia.org)

2. Siege of Malta – World War II" – Wikimedia Commons (commons.wikimedia.org) – Public Domain – Author: Russell, J E (Lt) – Royal Navy official photographer

3. Personal photo collection

4. Personal photo collection

5. Personal photo collection

6. "Messerschmitt Bf 109" – Author: Ben – <u>Creative Commons</u> Attribution- NoDerivs 2.0 Generic (CC BY-ND 2.0) – Wikimedia Commons (commons. wikimedia.org)

7. "Roman Catholic celebration and procession – Sliema, Malta" – <u>Public Domain</u> pxhere

8. Personal photo collection

CHAPTER 6:

1. "Congressman Alexander Pirnie (R-NY) drawing the first capsule for the Selective Service Draft Lottery – December 1, 1969" – Wikimedia Commons (commons.wikimedia.org) – 2004-03-23 17:51 Wile E. Heresiarch – <u>Public Domain</u>

2. Personal image collection

3. "R.M.S. Queen Elizabeth" – Author: Roland Godefroy – This file is licensed under the <u>Creative Commons</u> Attribution 3.0 Unported license. – Wikimedia Commons (commons.wikimedia.org)

4. "R.M.S. Queen Elizabeth" – The Main Lounge featuring a painting of Queen Elizabeth – Author: ssMaritime, Reuben Goossens – Photo: Unknown

5. "Chapman College, World Campus Afloat, SS Universe Campus" – Author: Unknown – Source: Orient Overseas Lines (possibly <u>Public Domain</u> – if not, please advise – this image was included as a postcard on the ssmaritime.com web site)

6. Personal photo collection

7. "Wilkinson Hall, Chapman University" – Author: Tracie Hall – <u>Creative Commons</u> Attribution-ShareAlike 2.0 Generic (CC BY-SA 2.0) – Flickr

8. Personal image collection

9. Personal photo collection

CHAPTER 7:

1. "Downtown Port Moresby, New Guinea" – Author: MSchlauch – Source: Good Free Photos – CC0/<u>Public Domain</u>

2. "Australian patrol officers (kiaps) working with indigenous tribesmen – Papua New Guinea" – Author: unknown – Source: Keith Jackson & Friends: PNG Attitude, September 2, 2019

3. "Traditional thatched-roof hut – Papua New Guinea" – Author: sunsinger – Source: shutterstock – Royalty-free stock photo ID: 147924059

CHAPTER 8:

1. Personal photo collection

2. "Charging Black Rhino" – Author: Joel Alves – Source: shutterstock – Royalty-free stock photo ID: 774324220

3. "Elephants charging" – Author: JMx Images – Source: shutterstock – Royalty-free stock photo: 1142783780

4. "Daily life in Freetown, Sierra Leone, West Africa" – Author: UNMEER – Creative Commons Attribution-NoDerivs 2.0 Generic (CC BY-ND 2.0)

5. Personal photo collection

CHAPTER 9:

1. Personal photo collection

2. "Seawise University burning in Hong Kong Harbor – January 9, 1972" – Author: Unknown – Orient Overseas Lines (possibly Public Domain – if not, please advise – this image was included as a postcard on the ssmaritime.com web site)

3. Personal photo collection

4. "1960 Chrysler Imperial Crown Convertible" – Author: Unknown – Source: RemarkableCars.com

5. An Indian soldier from the international peace keeping force (IPKF) instructs young Sri Lankan recruits in shooting, part of the training given to the citizen's volunteer force in the North-Eastern Sri Lankan city of Batticaloa, September 28, 1989." (Photo by Barbara Walton/AP Photo) – avax.news

6. "Mississippi River drawbridge" – Author: Unknown – (possibly Public Domain – if not, please advise.)

PART TWO – CONNECTING THE DOTS:

CHAPTER 10:

1. Personal photo collection

2. Personal photo collection

3. Personal photo collection

4. Personal photo collection

5. "Pilot boarding a ship at sea prior to entering harbor" – Author: Danny Cornelissen – dcornelissen@chello.nl – Used with Mr. Cornelissen's permission.

6. Personal photo collection – photo by Vince Streano

CHAPTER 11:

1. "Main Beach, Laguna Beach" – Photo: SunflowerMomma – Source: shutterstock – Royalty-free stock photo ID: 726541621

2. "Hurricane Linda – September 1997" – Main image credit: NASA/NOAA Inset image credit: NRL/NCEP – This file is in the Public Domain in the United States because it was solely created by NASA Jet Propulsion Laboratory, California Institute of Technology, and the Naval Research Laboratory's Marine Meteorology Division.

3. "Barreling Wave"– peterjamesanthony – Pixabay License – Free for commercial use. No attribution required

4. "NGC 2775 – A spiral galaxy located 67 million light-years away in the constellation of Cancer" – Image: ESA/Hubble & NASA, J. Lee and the PHANGS-HST Team; Acknowledgment: Judy Schmidt (Geckzilla)

5. Personal photo collection

6. "Aaron Gold – Guinness World Record paddle-in 63-foot wave January 15, 2016 – Jaws, Peahi, Maui, Hawaii" – Photographer: Erik Aeder, Erik Aeder Photography – Permission granted by Erik Aeder to use this photo.

7. "The Story of Eric Liddell" – inspiration for the film "Chariots of Fire" – Author: Unknown – Source: Noah's Dove

CHAPTER 12:

1. Personal photo collection

2. Personal photo collection

3. Personal photo collection

4. "Red Sea coral and marine life" – Author: Vlad61 – Source: shutterstock – Royalty-free stock photo ID: 491087482

5. "Tiger Shark" – Photo by N. Hammerschlag, courtesy of Oregon State University – Creative Commons Attribution-ShareAlike 2.0 Generic (CC BY-SA 2.0) – flickr

6. "Underside of a Manta Ray" – pug50 – Creative Commons Attribution 2.0 Generic (CC BY 2.0) – flickr

7. "The Californian – San Diego Harbor" – Author: Dale Frost – Creative Commons Attribution 2.0 Generic (CC BY 2.0) – flickr

8. "Brass Cannon" – Author: Unknown – Source: Yahoo! Store, Teamuniform.com, Frank Bee Enterprises, Inc.

9. "Steve McQueen – 1930-1980" – Author: Kate Gabrielle – Creative Commons Attribution 2.0 Generic (CC BY 2.0) – flickr

10. "The Rendering of Jeddah Tower" – thetowerinfo.com

CHAPTER 13:

1. "Early morning – La Jolla Cove, La Jolla, California" – Author: Jeff Shewan <u>Creative Commons</u> Attribution 2.0 Generic (CC BY 2.0) – flickr

2. "California sea lion pup" – Author: Andrea Izzotti – Source: shutterstock – Royalty-free stock photo ID: 228323578

3. Personal photo collection

4. "Abalone Point" – Image provided courtesy of www.CrystalCove.com – Dean Ledger, Real Estate Broker

5. Personal photo collection

CHAPTER 14:

1. "Monuments surf break – Cabo San Lucas, Baja California Sur, Mexico" – Author: Joe Tyson, JoeTysonPhotography.com – Permission to use received from Joe Tyson.

2. "Skeleton Coast, Namibia" – Source: MyWaveFinder – Photographer: Teddy Jones

3. "Shallow reef bottom with no room for forgiveness" – Author: Vladimir Kudinov – Free to use. No attribution required. – Pexels

4. Personal photo collection

5. "Mikala Jones (1979-2023) – 5' barreling wave (Hawaiian) – Bali, Indonesia" – Photo: Mikala Jones [5]

CHAPTER 15:

1. "Dawn patrol" – Author: C Levers – Source: shutterstock – Royalty-free stock photo ID: 1154473782

2. "Peeling left" – pxhere – CC0 Public Domain – Free for personal and commercial use. No attribution required.

3. "La Jolla's Marine Room Restaurant" – Author: Unknown – Source: La Jolla Light – marineroom.com (Courtesy)

4. "Baja Malibu – A-Frame – Northern Baja, Mexico" – Author: Unknown – Source: found this image on Surfline, Baja Malibu – Travel Guide, travel@ surfline.com, BajaMalibu_Userimage.jpg, surfdata/report_breakfastdata.cfm

5. "Spitting Tube" – Billabong Pipeline Masters – December 21, 2015 – Author: TF – Source: Santa Cruz Waves

6. "Entrance to Baja Malibu private residential community" – Author: Unknown – found this photo at Srfer.com, Archives #2 – srfer.com is hosted by Derek Dobbs and sponsored by wave tribe

7. "Warped bicycle rim after a crash" – Author: Unknown – Source: Cycling Weekly, Richard Windsor

CHAPTER 16:

1. Personal image collection

2. Personal photo collection

3. Personal photo collection

4. Personal photo collection

5. Personal photo collection

6. Personal image collection

7. Personal image collection

8. Personal photo collection

9. "Scorpion Bay, Baja California, Mexico" – Source: MyWaveFinder – Photographer: Fillipo Maffei

10. Personal photo collection

11. Personal photo collection

12. Personal photo collection

13. Personal photo collection

14. Monarch Butterfly Chrysalis – Source: shutterstock – www.learnabout nature.com. –   Royalty-free stock photo

15. Monarch Butterfly Adult Metamorphosis – Pixabay License – <u>Free for commercial use. No attribution required</u>.

PART THREE – CONNECTED:

CHAPTER 17:

1. Personal photo collection

CHAPTER 18:

1. Personal photo collection

2. *Victory at Sea* conditions – Pixabay License – <u>Free for commercial use. No attribution required</u>.

3. Personal photo collection

4. "Surfer duckdiving a wave Wikimedia Commons" – Pixabay License – <u>Free for commercial use. No attribution required</u>.

5. "A pod of pelicans gliding through the air foil created by an incoming wave" – Author: Bill Abbott – <u>Creative Commons</u> Attribution-ShareAlike 2.0 Generic (CC BY-SA 2.0) – flickr

CHAPTER 19:

1. "Bryan Jennings, Ex-Pro Surfer and Founder, Walking on Water" – Author: Tim McCaig – Source: Bryan Jennings – permission to use received from Tim McCaig

2. "Windansea, La Jolla" – Author: peasap – Creative Commons Attribution 2.0 Generic (CC BY 2.0) – flickr

3. "Changes – Video jacket – 1998" – Source: Walking on Water – Courtesy: Ed Feuer archives – Photo on jacket: Mike Balzer

4. "Chris O'Rourke" – Source: Above the Roar – Encyclopedia of Surfing – Photo: Warren Bolster

5. Personal photo collection

CHAPTER 20:

1. "A California spiny lobster (bug) tucked inside a reef crevice on the ocean floor" – Photographer: Kirk Wester – Source: shutterstock – Royalty-free stock photo ID: 719071141

2. Personal photo collection

3. Personal photo collection

CHAPTER 21:

1. Personal photo collection

2. Personal photo collection

3. "Black Marlin (Makaira indica) leaping out of the sea off Australia" – Author: Georgette Douwma – Science Photo Library – Model release not required. Property release not required.

4. Personal photo collection

5. Personal photo collection

6. Personal photo collection

7. "Great White Shark" – Author: Elias Levy – Creative Commons Attribution 2.0 Generic (CC BY 2.0) – flickr

8. "California sea lion at rest – La Jolla, California" – Author: fon thachakul – Source: shutterstock – Royalty-free stock photo ID: 483553597

9. "Unknown bodysurfer at the Wedge" – Newport Beach, California – Author: Snoty Pimpin – Creative Commons Attribution-ShareAlike 2.0 Generic (CC BY-SA 2.0) – flickr

10. "J. Hudson Taylor – 1832-1905, British missionary and Founder, China Inland Mission" – Image from page 9 of "Hudson Taylor and the China Inland Mission: the growth of a work of God" (1918) – No known copyright restrictions – flickr

11. "Single bunch of Shiraz grapes on a vine" – Photo: Andrew Hagen – Source: shutterstock – Royalty-free stock photo ID: 253302160

PART FOUR – THE END OF THE BEGINNING:

CHAPTER 22:

1. Personal photo collection

2. "Bethany Hamilton – September 8, 2016" – Author: Troy Williams – Creative Commons Attribution-ShareAlike 2.0 Generic (CC BY-SA 2.0) – flickr

3. "Wicked Witch's Hat from the "Wizard of Oz" – Author: Unknown – Source: Unknown

4. "Charles H. Spurgeon, 'Prince of Preachers"" – Author: Unknown – Source: Unknown

CHAPTER 23:

1. Poster designed by Joe Hall – Visions Unlimited

2. "Two champions following Jesus: Tom Curren (left), three-time World Champion and Joey Buran, Pipeline Masters Champion – Hollister Ranch, Santa Barbara County, California – 1997" – Author: Unknown – Source: Unknown

3. Personal photo collection

4. Personal photo collection

CHAPTER 24:

1. "Entrance to Lava River Cave near Bend, Oregon" – Author: Ryan Harvey – Creative Commons Attribution-ShareAlike 2.0 Generic (CC BY-SA 2.0) – flickr

CHAPTER 25:

1. Personal photo collection

2. "Is this how God sees the earth today?" – image created by the Centers for Disease Control and Prevention (CDC) – Image Library – PHIL ID #2331 – Public Domain Images.

3. "Molech, the ancient pagan god of child sacrifice." – Author: Unknown – Source: Unknown

4. "Child on a smartphone" – Pixabay License – Free for commercial use. No attribution required

5. "Rainbow over rippling sea in nature" – Author: Ben Mack – free to use

CHAPTER 26:

1. "Rev. Billy Graham preaches at his crusade June 25, 2005 in Flushing, New York" – Author: Anthony Correia – Source: Shutterstock.com – Royalty-free stock photo ID: 13713805

2. "Pastor John MacArthur – Shepherd's Conference – Grace Community Church – Sun Valley, California" – Source: The Christian Post – Photo: Grace Community Church

CHAPTER 27:

1. "Timeline depicting the 70 weeks of Daniel" – Author: Ilyas Mughal – Source: YouTube – August 30, 2017

CHAPTER 28:

1. "Corrie ten Boom" – Author: Sandra Hopkins – Inspirational Christians – inspirationalchristians.org

2. "Phases of the Moon" – Wikimedia Commons (commons.wikimedia.org) – Pixabay License – <u>Free for commercial use. No attribution required</u>.

3. "Joey Buran winning the 1984 Off Shore Pipeline Masters" – Author: The Editors – Source: Carlsbadistan, March 31, 2009 – "Joey Buran Inducted into Surfing Hall of Fame"

"Most assuredly, I say to you,

he who hears My word and believes in Him who sent Me

has everlasting life, and shall not come into judgment,

but has passed from death into life."

John 5:24

Leith and Judy Swanson – Jackson Hole, Wyoming – October 2015

Made in the USA
Columbia, SC
01 November 2023